Intellectual Property in Industry

Intellectual Property in Industry

Trevor Black LLB, LLM (Cantab), Dip I PL
Solicitor

Butterworths
London and Edinburgh
1989

United Kingdom	Butterworth & Co (Publishers) Ltd, 88 Kingsway, LONDON WC2B 6AB and 4 Hill Street, EDINBURGH EH2 3JZ
Australia	Butterworths Pty Ltd, SYDNEY, MELBOURNE, BRISBANE, ADELAIDE, PERTH, CANBERRA and HOBART
Canada	Butterworths Canada Ltd, TORONTO and VANCOUVER
Ireland	Butterworth (Ireland) Ltd, DUBLIN
Malaysia	Malayan Law Journal Sdn Bhd, KUALA LUMPUR
New Zealand	Butterworths of New Zealand Ltd, WELLINGTON and AUCKLAND
Puerto Rico	Equity de Puerto Rico, Inc., HATO REY
Singapore	Malayan Law Journal Pte, SINGAPORE
USA	Butterworths Legal Publishers, ST PAUL, Minnesota, SEATTLE, Washington, BOSTON, Massachusetts, AUSTIN, Texas and D & S Publishers, CLEARWATER, Florida

A CIP Catalogue record for this book is available from the British Library.

ISBN 0 406 10140 X

Typeset by Phoenix Photosetting, Chatham
Printed and bound in Great Britain by Mackays of Chatham PLC, Chatham, Kent

Preface

It is hoped that this book will prove useful in extending an understanding of intellectual property rights by raising the level of awareness of their nature among those who create them and those who have to advise on or deal with their protection in their various activities as lawyers or business men. I hope it will stimulate further speculation about the ability of the intellectual property system to respond adequately to the needs of the nation's innovators and the protection of its industrial innovative assets.

It is designed to act as a practical guide to intellectual property, a subject which is increasingly receiving attention but about which little is generally known outside specialist legal circles. It is intended to alert the reader to the UK intellectual property system by dealing systematically with the main topics comprising this system, namely, patents, copyright, trade marks and confidential information.

The law is stated as at April 1989 and includes where appropriate the relevant provisions of the recently enacted Copyright, Designs and Patents Act 1988. Part I of this Act repeals the 1956 Copyright Act and provides a restatement of the law on a 'more logical and consistent basis'. Part II provides remedies for performers and is outside the scope of this book. Part III creates a new unregistered design right. Part IV amends the 1949 Registered Designs Act. Part V relates to the regulation and activities of patent and trade mark agents. Part VI provides for the granting of special jurisdictions for county courts in patent matters. Part VII deals with miscellaneous and general provisions.

The industrial setting of intellectual property law

I set the discussion of intellectual property in an industrial context because today it is within the innovative enterprise that there is the greatest need for more awareness of, and advice in, intellectual property. In doing so, the commercial, as well as the legal qualities of the legal principles, become apparent, making clearer the nature of intellectual property rights as they operate in the broader industrial context, how they arise and interact with one another.

The structure of the book

PART I

In the first part of the book I describe the substantive law relating to intellectual property: patents, copyright and trade marks, the nature of each individual right, why it exists, its rationale within the political and economic structure, and its commercial significance. Each chapter begins with an account of how such a right is created, and, where appropriate, describes the procedures involved and the problems surrounding its creation and subsistence.

The second part of each chapter deals with these rights, when they are used and exploited by the owner or others permitted to do so under a licence agreement. I describe the licensing context and appraise the advantages and disadvantages of licensing in that particular context. I have thus dealt with the licensing of each right separately in order to draw out its special features in the light of what preceded it. The protective clauses in each licence reflect the nature of the right already discussed highlighting both its distinctiveness and its vulnerability. Although there are clauses in each licensing situation common to all three – patents, copyright and trade marks – there are also those which are only germane to the protection of that particular property right.

There is a need to consider licensing as a commercial activity which falls within the general marketing policy of the innovative enterprise. Therefore I set out the legal and commercial considerations pertinent to establishing a proper policy for each right. Only if a concern operates a proper licensing policy, not at variance with its marketing strategy, can these rights be exploited to their maximum. They need to be counted as assets meeting the needs and requirements of its sales and marketing departments.

The third part of each chapter prescribes further means of protecting these often vulnerable rights which, if neglected, can be diluted, negated, devalued or lost entirely. By applying some fairly straightforward precautions as advised, their value can be maintained and in some cases enhanced.

PART 2

In this part of the book I concentrate on the law of copyright and the reforms now effected by the Copyright, Designs and Patents Act 1988.

In my discussion of these reforms I hope to illustrate the multi-faceted nature of copyright, its flexibility and its adaptability in responding to the needs of innovative industries. I show how it operates in traditional industries and how it is capable of being developed and extended to the requirements of new industries. This versatility is under challenge by developments in the field of information technology. In discussing developments in these diverse fields I try to bring out not only the strengths of copyright but also its weaknesses. In some instances the law of copyright has been impotent to protect the rights of copyright owners in the light of these developments. The traditional balances which once existed between equipment manufacturers, the creators of copyright works and the consumer have gone, shifting from the copyright owner to favour the producers of new technologies and the consumer. I argue that this shift could operate as a major disincentive towards the innovation so badly needed by UK industry and that the law must play a central role in maintaining this balance. The Act has done this in dealing with reprographic rights but has failed in the writer's view in redressing the problems of the copyright owner in the field of audio reproduction. In other instances the law of copyright is used to establish a regime where a new technology is not yet in place, as in the proposed copyright regime provided under the new Act for the new independent satellite communications industries.

In questioning the strengths and weaknesses of copyright the nature and function of this highly adaptable legal concept is demonstrated and the many ways in which it can function to protect innovation are made clear.

Finally, I look at some possible future challenges to copyright as a result of developments in technology, this time in the fields of artificial intelligence and expert systems. I explore whether copyright will be able to adjust, adapt, develop and respond to the needs of the innovators of the potential products of these important future industries and whether the latest provisions contained in the Act are of any assistance.

Legislative reforms have now taken place. In order to understand these I examine some of the main arguments for them as advanced over the past decade and conclude with an appraisal of the main proposals of the government's 1986 White Paper and the reforms themselves provided by the new Act. This explores the issues which have led up to the present Act so that the reader is in a position to assess its provisions and decide whether these remedy the defects apparent in the system of intellectual property rights or not.

PART 3

The ability of the patent system to protect the inventions of the small to medium size enterprise has been in doubt and the subject of criticism for some years. For this reason in the third part of the book I assess the patent system's ability to respond to the requirements of the innovative entrepreneurial enterprise. I also look at the main proposals of the White Paper to reform this system, initially sweeping in their effect, but now in the light of the Act, disappointingly modest.

Developments in the field of trade marks have already been incorporated in Part 1 of the book. The passing of the Trade Marks (Amendment) Act 1984 now extends importantly to the provision of services. The Act provides for a new offence, that of the fraudulent application or use of a trade mark and this will be mentioned briefly.

Finally, my grateful thanks go to the following who have read and criticised portions of the book but who are in no way responsible for its contents nor necessarily endorse my views; Michael Brunner, Gill Jennings and Every, London and Cambridge Science Park, Iain Baillie, Ladas and Parry, London, JM Myall, Assistant Registrar, The Trade Marks Registry, London, Gillian Davies, Associate Director-General and Chief Legal Adviser of the International Federation of Phonogram and Videogram Producers, London, Michael Flint, Denton Hall Burgin and Warrens, London, CP Hadley and C Clarke of the Copyright Licensing Agency Ltd, London, Fiona J Nalder, Linklaters and Paines, London, Simon Chalton, Dibb Lupton, Leeds, Dr Yoko Mitsui, GST Technical Services, Cambridge Science Park, Benedict Heal, Faculty of Mathematics, Open University. My special thanks go to Dr SJ Wilsmore, senior lecturer in philosophy, the Polytechnic, Hatfield.

Trevor Black,
Cambridge,
April 1989

Contents

Table of statutes

References in this Table to *Statutes* are to Halsbury's Statutes of England (Fourth Edition) showing the volume and page at which the annotated text of the Act will be found.

List of cases

Part 1
The creation, exploitation and protection of intellectual property

CHAPTER 1

Patent creation

Introduction

1.1 It is to the patent system that the innovative concern will turn for the protection of its investment in its innovations and this chapter attempts to set out the main features of the system, the legal criteria to be satisfied in obtaining a patent, the procedures involved, and the protection granted on a successful application.

Why a patents system at all?

1.2 The underlying economic, commercial, and political justification for the patent system is that it acts as a stimulus to investment in industrial innovation. Innovative technology leads to the maintenance of, and increase in, the nation's stock of valuable, tradable, industrial assets. The currency of the nation's industrial assets is thereby increased.

How does it operate to achieve innovation?

1.3 In consideration of an inventor disclosing an innovative technical idea or information he is granted an exclusive right to prevent others from using that idea or information. This exclusive right or monopoly is granted upon the condition that the patent is actually exploited by the owner in some way and that it is not in any way suppressed. If not used, or insufficiently used, the exclusive right can be revoked or removed. The intention is that the inventor is rewarded with a monopoly right to commercially exploit his patented invention by being allowed to prevent others from doing so, and that the technical information disclosed is used for the benefit of industry. Obviously the aim of the patent system is not to suppress new technical ideas but to encourage their disclosure and use.

1.4 The legislation governing patents is the Patents Act 1977, and the Patents Rules 1982. A system for the practical regulation of patents is operated by the Patent Office. This office deals with applications, grants and dealings in patents and maintains a public register to record these matters. It assesses claims to alleged inventions and grants a patent if the substantive and procedural requirements set out in the Act and Rules are satisfied by the applicant. A Certificate of Grant issued by the Office is a formal legal document stating in effect that, so far as the Office is aware in the light of its investigations, the technical information embodied in and disclosed by the patent is novel, inventive, and capable of industrial application.[1] The right it grants to a patent holder is a legal monopoly to prevent others from commercially exploiting the ideas disclosed for a period of 20 years from the date of application, providing renewal fees, payable annually for the first year onward, are received.[2]

Three qualifications to this are:

—first: that the Patent Office gives no guarantee of the validity of the patent (the conditions of it having been granted may not have been satisfied, in ways I will shortly describe);

—second: the right will not remain justified, as I have said, if the patented invention is not actually used;[3]

—third: no guarantee is given that there is no prior, senior patent, that is, a patent which precedes the present patent and upon which the new patent is based. For example, if the new patent is an improvement on an already existing patented invention then the owner of the new patent will only be able to work his patented invention provided that he obtains the consent of the proprietor of the senior patent.

1 Patents Act 1977, s 24(1).
2 Patents Act 1977, s 25.
3 Patents Act 1977, s 48(1).

1.5 A patent is personal property. It may be assigned, mortgaged, passed by operation of law, and most importantly for the purposes of this book, it may be licensed and sub-licensed.[1] The patent is a creation of statute, not of common law. The creation of, and dealings in, patent rights and interests are regulated by a formal registration system. As it operates as a reward for technical innovation through the grant of monopoly rights for the disclosure of the invention, the patent on the one hand, and the disclosure on the other, can be thought of as two sides of a 'bargain' which the inventor makes with the state through the Patent Office.

However, there is no reward or 'bargain' available for someone who independently may have invented exactly the same thing. Protective rights are granted to the first to file for patent protection.

1 Patents Act 1977, s 30.

How do patentable inventions normally come about?

1.6 Innovative technical information is usually generated by the concentration of effort in a particular scientific or technological field. To be innovative it must break new ground in, or advance or improve, a particular technology in some way. That is, inventiveness is defined in terms of either resolving existing problems in a technology in a non-obvious way or breaking entirely new ground within such a technology. In the main, inventions are the result of problems overcome, and the inventive step is a measure of the degree to which the new solution is more advantageous than that which has existed previously.

After having expended considerable amounts of time, energy, expertise and financial investments in achieving this new state of affairs the inventor naturally considers that he should benefit the most from the exploitation of his invention. Obviously he would not want to see the fruits of his labour taken and exploited by someone else. As he needs the comfort of a maximum degree of protection for his invention if he is to be encouraged to invest in it and if investment is to be encouraged in innovation as a whole, the object of the patent system is to ensure that this protection is available to him.

Clearly such monopoly protection can be very valuable and any innovative concern must consider patenting as being one of the most important methods of protecting their investments.

However there are substantive legal and procedural requirements to be satisfied before a patent for an invention will be granted. Before we look at the effectiveness of such protection we must be clear about these requirements, what they omit and enjoin. So what is required to obtain a patent?

The substantive legal requirements

1.7 Not all new technical information is patentable, ie of protectable quality, under the provisions of the Act. Indeed section 1(2) of the Act declares the following to be unpatentable:

(*a*) a discovery, scientific theory or mathematical method,
(*b*) a literary, dramatic, musical or artistic work or other aesthetic creation whatsoever,
(*c*) a scheme rule or method for performing a mental act, playing a game or doing business, or a program for a computer, and
(*d*) the presentation of information.

1.8 Further, section 3 goes on to provide that patents shall not be granted for the following:

(1) an invention which might encourage offensive, immoral or anti-social behaviour;[1]
(2) any variety of animal or plant or any essentially biological process for the production of animals or plants, not being a micro-biological process or the production of such a process.[2]

1 Patents Act 1977, s 3(1)(a).
2 Ibid, s 3(1)(b).

1.9 Having now seen what cannot be patented, let us now look at the substantive legal requirements which have to be satisfied in respect of the sort of inventive subject matter, including processes, which may be afforded protection.

Section 1(1) of the Act provides that a patent may be granted for an invention if all the following conditions are met:

(1) the invention is new,
(2) it involves an inventive step,
(3) it is capable of industrial application.

Let us consider now each of these qualities which the invention must have:

(1) THE INVENTION MUST BE NEW[1]

1.10 The person who has disclosed new technical information for the first time is granted a monopoly right by the Patent Office to use the invention embodying that new information. However, if such information has already been disclosed then clearly it cannot satisfy condition (1) of being new. The party disclosing the information clearly has nothing to bargain with and nothing to claim protection for—that is, the claim that the information is new cannot be sustained when it is already a part of the 'state of the art'.

Obviously, it is important to understand what is meant then by this phrase, 'state of the art'.

Section 2(2) defines 'state of the art' very widely as:

> '. . . in the case of an invention [this] shall be taken to comprise all matter (whether a product, a process, information about either or anything else) which has at any time before the priority date of that invention been made available to the public (whether in the United Kingdom or elsewhere) by written or oral description, by use or in any other way.'

Thus 'state of the art' refers to more than information about the invention disclosed by the inventor himself or by someone who has access to it. We shall see later how important this is. It refers widely to any information existing anywhere, in written or oral form, or even through use, which has been made available to the public and which is technically relevant in that it may describe the invention. If there is a document in existence which describes the invention and this is exposed in some way to the public or some part of the public, for example in a bookshop or a library, this could be deemed to be sufficient disclosure fatal to the application.[2] Even if it is in a foreign language it could be deemed to be published and thus disclosed.[3] Even oral disclosure of an invention is possibly sufficient to invalidate an application for a patent.[4]

If the invention has already been placed in the hands of the public for example, by way of sale, and it is possible to see how it has been made, this too could be deemed sufficient for it to have been disclosed and any subsequent application for patent protection will fail accordingly.[5] Any such information could therefore negate the claim that the invention is new. For this reason, as I explain more fully later, the Patent Office cannot give absolute guarantees as to the validity of patents granted by it. In its examining claims to new inventions it is impossible for the Patent Office to discover all actual, possible or potential disclosures of the invention worldwide. For example, articles written in foreign scientific journals or periodicals may yet disclose or point to technical information embodied in an invention which is being claimed to be new. Such disclosures would make that information public and thus a part of the state of the art under section 2(2) of the Act. Obviously if this were known to the Patent Office when assessing the claim, and the information, as disclosed, was relevant, then the application would fail for want of novelty. If it only appeared relevant it would then be a matter for the applicant to decide whether he wished to press his application and call for more substantive proof as to relevance. It is best to clarify the situation at this stage because if the Patent Office grants a patent to the inventor in ignorance of prior published information the validity of that patent could be challenged by someone who, after grant, at a later date discovers this information;[6] that is, whether discovered before or after application, such relevant information means the information in the application has been 'anticipated'.

A popular example of an invention having been anticipated was where the party applying for a patent claimed for a new type of mechanical hay rake incorporating a novel feature. Objection to the grant of a patent came from the fact that there had already appeared in a magazine a photograph showing a mechanical hay rake with the claimed novel feature incorporated. Thus in the eyes of the Office the invention had already been revealed and it failed for want of novelty.[7] There is very little that an inventor can do to guard against such anticipation from world-wide sources. However, what he can and must do is to implement stringent precautionary measures to minimise the risk of disclosing any technical information about the invention, either by himself or third parties who may have legitimate access to it before applying for a patent. We shall look later at the sort of precautionary measures which the innovator should be advised to take in assuring the initial protection of his invention.

Thus novelty is of first importance in the patent system, as a pre-requisite for the grant of a valid patent. This substantive legal requirement is of commercial significance as exposure at any stage in the creation and development of an invention may render inapplicable or irrelevant the protection of the very legal mechanism designed to protect it.

1 Patents Act 1977, s 1(1)(a).
2 *Lang v Gisborne* (1862) 31 Beav 133.
3 *Harris v Rothwell* (1887) 35 Ch D 416, CA.
4 *Humpherson v Syer* (1887) 4 RPC 407, CA.
5 *Re Bristol-Myers Co (Johnson's) Application* [1975] RPC 127, HL.
6 Patents Act 1977, s 74.
7 *Van der Lely v Bamford's Ltd* [1963] RPC 61, HL.

(2) IT INVOLVES AN INVENTIVE STEP[1]

1.11 Before deciding whether the invention satisfies the second quality, that of being inventive, the examiners at the Patent Office examine the prior art at their disposal doing their best to see whether the technical information embodied in the invention has been previously disclosed or anticipated. The test applied to satisfy the next requirement, that of inventive step, is set out in section 3 of the Act as follows:

> 'An invention shall be taken to involve an inventive step if it is not obvious to a person skilled in the art, having regard to any matter which forms part of the state of the art . . .'

In other words, when the inventor applies to the Patent Office, his application is deemed to be to a person who is skilled in the art of the relevant technology, who will decide whether his claims to have invented something are well grounded or not. The requirement to establish the quality of inventiveness or non-obviousness is a legal one but clearly the ascertainment of whether this is satisfied will depend upon an essentially scientific comparison of the invention claimed against the existing state of the art in that technology. The ascertainment of that quality of inventiveness is clearly expressed as a practical question to be decided upon by someone who is skilled in the art of a particular technology.

The courts have been asked to adjudicate on both the question of what is obvious and who is skilled in the art. Have they been able to give sufficient guidance here?

The courts have had difficulty in applying patent rules and principles about what is to constitute inventiveness because of their application to fields requiring such scientific and technical expertise. An input of practical as well as legal knowledge is needed. The question of what counts as being inventive can only be answered within the framework of the relevant specific scientific field or technology itself. The notional person skilled in the art will be someone who is familiar with the particular technology within which the claims to inventiveness have to be made. If referring to an expert in an old technology such as weaving, the expression 'someone skilled in the art' will have quite a different meaning from that same expression used in reference to an expert in the complexity of laboratory techniques relating to the genetic engineering of recombinant DNA. In these different cases the courts would be dealing with different technologies, trying to ascertain from the evidence of expert witnesses before them, whether the technical information claimed is obvious or innovative in the light of the evidence.

1 Patents Act 1977, s 3.

Who is the person 'skilled in the art'?

1.12 Despite these difficulties of application, some important guidelines as to what is meant by 'someone skilled in the art' have been produced by the courts. The person to whom the new technical information is addressed is the competent skilled worker who understands all relevant technical literature in the technology but who, on the other hand, would not have the capacity to create or invent new technical information.[1] Where the particular art is highly technical, involving perhaps convergent technologies for example, the notional addressee of the patent may be considered to be a team of people with different technical backgrounds, rather than an individual.[2]

1 *Technograph Printed Circuits Ltd v Mills and Rockley* [1972] RPC 346, HL, followed in *General Tire and Rubber Cor and Firestone Tyre and Rubber Co Ltd* [1972] RPC 457.
2 *Osram-Robertson Lamp Works Ltd v Pope's Electric Lamp Co* (1917) 34 RPC 369, HL.

What is meant by 'inventive step'?

1.13 Someone who is engaged in the creation of new scientific information will want to know at the end of the day how the Patent Office, or possibly the courts, will view his claim to have made an invention of some kind. He should, of course, take the advice of a patent agent who will be expertly qualified to give him some initial idea as to whether what he has produced will find favour and be deemed to be an invention. Let us however look at the requirement of the Act and see whether there is any initial guidance to be had from the decisions of the courts on the interpretation of the expression 'inventive step'.

It will be helpful if we look at the technical context in which most inventions will occur, because the decision as to whether something is inventive or not will, as we have seen, depend largely upon the comparison of the claim to invention with the developments within a particular technology.

Most inventions will not of course occur *in vacuo*, but will rather be the result of efforts to achieve a particular objective. This may be within a technology which has advanced in a particular direction as far as it can and is unable to proceed further because of certain problems which need to be overcome. The stages of invention may typically take the following form:

(1) there is a specific problem or a difficulty to be overcome within a particular technology;
(2) there are a number of scientific or technical principles which could be applied in seeking a resolution of the above;
(3) there are different practical methods or means which can be employed to deal with the problem.

It is helpful to look at the process of invention in this way because the Patent Office and the courts tend to view each or all of these stages as having potential 'subject matter' which may be patentable. Thus any innovative concern should consider the stages of development of its products in the light of the above as it may well be that there is sufficient merit at various stages of its activities to warrant the grant of a patent on the basis of the satisfaction of the requirement that there has indeed been an inventive step achieved.

Some general principles have been developed of use to the potential applicant. However it is important to note that there are no general rules laid down. Although there is of course a considerable number of decided cases on the question of how inventiveness is to be evaluated, in terms of there being protectable subject matter, the decisions are limited to the particular case in point and should therefore be treated as useful rather than as giving a definitive statement as to what inventiveness is to be applied in all cases.[1] Each matter will depend upon the facts of the case and on the technical evidence adduced in support of the application in the light of the particular technology.

1 *Allmanna Svenska Elektriska A/B v Burntisland Shipbuilding Co Ltd* (1952) 69 RPC 63, CA.

Some guidelines to inventive step

1.14 What can be gleaned from the cases which might be of assistance to the innovator in reaching a decision as to whether he should seek patent protection?

(1) The courts measure inventive step qualitatively rather than quantitatively; that is, an inventive step need not necessarily be a major advance but might be a minor improvement in a process. In general, the more highly developed and intensively worked a particular field is, the lower is the height of the inventive step required to qualify as a patentable invention. It could be a simple solution to a complex problem, ie, a 'scintilla' of invention will suffice[1] and the result may be more significant than the means or methods used to achieve it. There must however be 'sufficient' patentable subject matter.

(2) An invention need not be the result of years of painstaking research, but could be the result of pure accident or indeed luck, but there will be no inventiveness where there is mere discovery.[2]

(3) Does the applicant have to demonstrate that his invention has made a technological advance in the sense that it breaks new

ground entirely? It has been held that this is not necessary but certainly this factor may assist where such progress results in the solution of a problem which has existed for a number of years.[3]

(4) Many innovative concerns will operate in the fields of convergent technologies. Is it possible to claim inventiveness for something which is an amalgam or a 'collocation' of different technologies? The courts have held that the putting together of two well known things will not be considered inventive. Thus the putting together of a cutting machine and a filling machine for the production of sausages was held not to be inventive.[4] Nor was it in the case where a pill was a compound of two separate therapeutic substances which had no interactive or heightened effect.[5] But where the collocation produces an improved result by the working relationship between the two which is brought out by the collocation, then this may well be considered inventive.[6]

(5) What is the position where the inventor is not claiming inventiveness in a product of some kind but rather in the new way in which he is employing that product? In one case it was held that the mere use of an old thing in a new way would not be sufficient for inventiveness. Thus the use of the thermos flask for domestic purposes where the invention had been used in industry for some time was held not to be inventive.[7] But it may be inventive if an analogous use involved some ingenuity in the overcoming of some fresh problems or difficulties.[8] In cases of doubt or in disputed cases it will be for the courts to decide upon the scientific and technical evidence of expert witnesses whether this has occurred or not.

1 *Killick v Pye Ltd* [1958] RPC 366.
2 *Lane Fox v Kensington and Knightsbridge Electric Lighting Co* [1892] 3 Ch 424, CA.
3 *S Parker & Co Ltd v Cocker Bros Ltd* (1929) 46 RPC 241, CA.
4 *Williams v Nye* (1890) 7 RPC 62, CA.
5 *Beecham Groups Ltd (Amoxycillin) Application* [1980] RPC 261.
6 *British Celanese Ltd v Courtaulds Ltd* (1935) 52 RPC 171, HL.
7 *Thermos Ltd v Isola Ltd* (1910) 27 RPC 388.
8 *Gadd and Mason v Manchester Corpn* (1892) 9 RPC 516, CA.

1.15 The Act requires that patentable technical information be both new and inventive as we have seen. Novelty alone is insufficient. There is a reason for this. If it were sufficient, then in theory scientists might produce unlimited compound variations from the materials at their disposal and claim that each new compound was patentable. As I have said, any claim to patentable technical information is measured against the state of the art and is granted protection only if it is of some relevance in the context of its technology. It is thus only relevant or material technical information which enjoys the quality of being patentable technical information to which protection will be afforded. This concept or notion of the 'inventive step' is reinforced by the next requirement of the Act: that the invention must be capable of industrial application.

(3) IT IS CAPABLE OF INDUSTRIAL APPLICATION[1]

1.16 This requirement of the patent system demonstrates that patents are about the practical application of inventions. Not only must the technical information be novel (not form a part of the state of the art) and inventive (not obvious to someone skilled in the art) but it must also be capable of industrial application. The system does not protect all new or inventive technical information. Thus ideas, concepts or notions are not patentable *per se*. Technical information incorporating ideas, notions, or intellectual concepts only becomes patentable to the extent that it is embodied in some practical, technical and industrial application, as well as satisfying the previous criteria of being new and inventive. Generally speaking, if such an invention satisfies the previous conditions and relates to a product or a process capable of industrial application because it can be made or used in industry, including agriculture, then it will be patentable.

1 Patents Act 1977, s 4.

1.17 In research-oriented organisations, many ideas are explored, whether in the field of pure research or when applied in the creation of a specific product. Many ideas, theories, etc, produce, as by-products, valuable scientific data or knowledge. As such, these ideas are not protectable under the patent system. Some could become embodied later in an invention and assume patentable quality, others may not. The reasoning behind not protecting the latter by patent is this: though it is true that the according of patent protection to ideas as such could have the advantage of a possible recouping of expenditure on their creation and generation, weighted against this is the likelihood that giving such protection would prevent access by others altogether from certain areas of research. This would operate as a restraint rather than a stimulus to research, investigation and the creation of ultimately useful, practical and valuable innovation. Further, there would be considerable difficulty in attempting to identify the precise boundaries of an idea. In any case, the actual data or knowledge which is not patentable can be protected by its owner, by ensuring that it is kept secret. This can often be effective, only of course if it is practical for there to be limited access to it. If this is practical then legal protection of some kind could be provided by making those allowed access contractually bound under an obligation of confidentiality to keep such information secret and not to disclose it. I shall discuss trade secrets and confidentiality later (para 3.1) and give fuller details of what is implied here.

1.18 The provisions as to capability of industrial application have some unusual features.

Certain categories of activity are specifically excluded by the Act as not being capable of industrial application. The Act reads as follows:

> '4(1) Subject to subsection (2) below, an invention shall be taken to be capable of industrial application if it can be made or used in any kind of industry, including agriculture.'

However,

> '4(2) An invention of a method of treatment of the human or animal body by surgery or therapy or of diagnosis practised on the human or animal body shall not be taken to be capable of industrial application.'

In this case, though there is no stated reason why this should be so, we might suppose a principle which runs as follows is implied: it would be unethical and unwarranted to allow a monopoly of new methods of treatment for the curing of illness. We might consider that this principle prevents greater stimulus to innovation in this area which might be achieved through allowing patenting to take place, with the safeguard that licences would be automatically granted upon payment of a reasonable royalty.

The prohibition relates only to the method of treatment and section 4(3) of the Act provides specifically that this does not operate to prevent any substance or composition used in the method being considered as capable of industrial application and thus patentable. For example, if a new pharmaceutical is used in any method of treatment of the human or animal body, the method by which it is applied or administered will not be patentable, although the actual pharmaceutical itself may be. Further, it is possible that any apparatus or instruments used in the method of treatment, such as new types of dressings or splints, could be capable of industrial application and therefore patentable.

The procedural requirements

1.19 Provided that the inventor is reasonably confident that he is able to satisfy the substantive legal requirements set out above, he may decide to proceed to the next stage, that of prosecuting the patent.

The patent system is based upon a formal structure of rules and procedures which have to be met before the grant of patent rights in inventions. We have looked (para 1.7) at the substantive legal requirements which define the substance or quality of the technical information, or subject matter, which may lead to a patent (novelty, inventive step and industrial application). Let us now look at the structure of the patent system to see how claims to new technical information embodied in inventions are made and processed by the Patent Office.

The patent system is designed to facilitate the grant of valid patents for inventions. It is a bureaucratic system headed by the Patent Office which is a part of the Department of Trade and Industry and is directed by the Comptroller of Patents. The Office employs examiners with scientific backgrounds, who are versed in most fields of technology and whose function it is to examine and assess the quality of the technical information contained in applications submitted to the Office for patentability. They are skilled and experienced in the technology pertaining to the substantive claims made. The system of examination of the new technical information is rigorous in its application and all the quality tests discussed above (para 1.9) must be satisfied before a patent will be granted. If an applicant is not satisfied with a decision of the Office he can have the decision reviewed by the Patent Court, which is a part of the Chancery Division of the High Court of Justice.

1.20 Anyone can apply for a patent. Those unfamiliar with patent law and procedure should seek expert advice. It is advisable to engage a patent agent to assess the technical information embodied in the invention. He is trained in assessing the claim to novelty and inventiveness in that particular technology and is able to prepare the technical documents (the 'specification' including the 'claims') for submission to the Patent Office. He is able to deal with objections or points of clarification raised or required by the examiner assigned to the assessment. Patent agents have technical as well as legal qualifications and are experts in the drafting and prosecution procedures. Early employment of these skilled people helps minimise the risk inherent in making an application. Their help enhances considerably the chances of obtaining a good, strong patent at the end of the day. The initial patent specification is a technical document embodying a claim to new technical information. If it satisfies the quality tests as to patentability it will emerge as a legal document, the patent itself, granting valuable monopoly rights in the use of that information.

After assessing the claim to invention, if the chances of obtaining a patent do not appear to be good, the inventor may decide not to proceed. All is not lost. He may well be able to keep the substance of his invention secret.

The application

1.21 Section 14 of the Act provides that every application to the Patent Office must contain the following:

(1) a request for the grant of a patent;
(2) a specification;
(3) an abstract.

The requisite fees must be paid and a statement of the identity of the applicant or applicants must accompany the application.

The most important of the above is the specification. This contains (a) a description of the invention, and (b) the claims to inventiveness which set out the monopoly rights sought by the applicant. The specification must ensure that the invention is disclosed in a manner which is clear enough and complete enough for it to make sense to, and be performed by, a person skilled in the relevant art. It normally sets out the subject matter to which the invention relates, the old state of the art which exists in that field and how the invention is an improvement in that existing art.

The specification ends with what are called the 'claims' which delimit the monopoly to be granted by the patent. The section further requires that these claims:

(1) define the matter for which the applicant seeks protection;
(2) be clear and concise;
(3) be supported by the description; that is, the description of the invention must not be inconsistent with the claims.

The abstract gives technical information and operates for the purpose of enabling the examiner to search the relevant technical field to which the subject matter belongs.

Thus we see that the application for a patent must be set out in such a way as to ensure that the notional addressee of the patent, the person skilled in the art in the technology, is provided with sufficient information to be able to apply the substantive legal tests of whether what is claimed is a new invention, whether it involves an inventive step, and whether it is capable of industrial application.

The preliminary examination and search

1.22 The system is such that the Office will do nothing in respect of the application unless it is requested to do so, and the applicant should be made aware of the time frame within which certain things must be done or requested by him.

Within 12 months of the filing of the application the applicant must make a request for (*a*) a preliminary examination and (*b*) a search.

(*a*) The preliminary examination is to determine whether the application complies with the formal procedural requirements of the Act.

(*b*) The search involves the examiner of the application searching all relevant material at his disposal. What the examiner is doing is bringing to the attention of the applicant all the prior art he considers relevant, so that the applicant can assess the value of the invention as measured against the prior art. This is not a complete search by the examiner, his brief being to 'make such investigation as in his opinion is reasonably practicable and necessary for him to identify the documents which he thinks will be needed for him to decide, on a substantive examination [that is, a fuller examination] . . . whether the invention for which a patent is sought is new and involves an inventive step.'[1] If the applicant does not request this examination and search, then the Office will consider the application is withdrawn.

1 Patents Act 1977, s 17(4).

Publication

1.23 The next part of the procedure involves publication of the materials submitted to it, by the Patent Office in the Patent Journal.

At or shortly after 18 months from the priority date (that is the date that the application was lodged), the Office will publish the specification as filed, any amendments, and any new claims submitted to it. Up to this point the information submitted is secret between the inventor and the Patent Office. Though publication in the Patents Journal does not yet make it public information in the sense that it may be used by anyone with impunity, the whole substance and detail of the invention is now disclosed. It is disclosed not only to potential financial backers and licensees, but also to trade rivals, competitors, and more importantly to predators and potential infringers.

The substantive examination

1.24 In order that the application may proceed further, the next step requires the applicant to request a substantive examination of the application. This may be made at the time of requesting the preliminary examination or within six months of the date of publication. At this stage the Comptroller refers the application to an appropriate examiner in order that a substantive examination be carried out. This examination is to decide whether the applicant has shown that the invention as claimed is novel, that there is an inventive step involved, and that it is capable of industrial application.

The examiner will then report to the applicant on his findings, and if he raises any objections, then the applicant is given an opportunity either to refute the examiner's findings or to amend his application accordingly. For example, if what he is claiming is not justified in its scope, given the information which the examiner has at his disposal of the prior art in the particular field of technology, the applicant may wish to modify his claim. Provided that the examiner is satisfied that all the procedural and the substantive legal requirements of the Act have been satisfied, a Certificate of Grant will be issued to the applicant and his name will be placed on the Register as owner.

There are no formal opposition procedures available to third parties who may wish to object during the prosecution of the patent application. However, it is possible for someone who wishes to do so to make a written observation on the application after publication, but before grant, to the effect that he considers the invention unpatentable, eg that he has evidence that the technical information is not new, or is obvious, etc.

Some legal and commercial considerations of patenting

1.25

(1) Although anyone may apply for a patent, the Patent Office will want a statement to the effect that the applicant is the inventor

and thus the owner of the patent, or, if he is not the inventor, that he is entitled to the invention.[1] Therefore the applicant ought to make stringent investigations into claims to title to the invention before proceeding to apply. The story is often complex because the technical information embodied in the invention could be the result of joint concerted effort, for example the product of a research team. We shall see later (para 3.9) the commercial ramifications, importance, and consequences of establishing legal title to ownership to the invention. The Act provides that the inventor or joint inventors of an invention have the right to be mentioned as such in any patent granted for the invention.[2]

(2) The interests in an invention might already have been established beforehand by consent or by contract. This will almost certainly be the case where the invention is the result of specifically targeted public or private sector funding by such institutions as the British Technology Group or the Department of Trade which supports innovation schemes for innovation-based companies, or other financial institutional funding.

(3) It is important to note that patent protection in the UK is granted to the party who is the first to file an application whether or not the full potential of the invention has been worked out or not. What are the legal and commercial ramifications of this?

We have seen that it is not possible to patent ideas as such. However, the system operates in such a way as to encourage an early filing of inventions when these may be little more than an idea. They may not have been fully worked out by the inventor himself and be in inchoate form. Though new, the precise details of what the invention is capable of might yet have to be established or ascertained. At this stage the inventor might be wise to merely file what is called a 'basic' or 'provisional' specification, that is, a document containing only a description of the invention. At a later date he could file his claim or claims defining the matter for which he seeks protection. The inventor is then given a 12-month period in which to develop the full potential of his invention at the end of which time he should be able to file his claims defining the extent of the monopoly sought. Are there any advantages to early filing? One is that the inventor gains priority, in that the invention operates as prior art against any subsequent application for the same, or substantially the same, invention.[3] Thus if there is an application made by another party for substantially the same invention, the earlier application will be said to have already disclosed the invention, and the second application will fail for want of novelty.

Weighed against the above advantages of gaining priority for an inchoate invention is the need to satisfy the requirement that the inventor achieve certain objectives within a limited timescale. Within 12 months of the application date he must lodge a full specification showing not only the invention, but his claim defining the boundaries of the monopoly he seeks.

1 Patents Act 1977, s 7.
2 Ibid, s 13(1).
3 Ibid, s 5.

1.26 We have looked briefly at the patenting process in the UK. What if the patent owner intends the invention to be either sold or used in a foreign territory and requires patent protection in those territories? In this case he must either file for patent protection in each jurisdiction in which he needs protection, or he may take advantage of some international conventions to which the UK is a signatory. Briefly, these are as follows:

The European Patent Convention (EPC) provides that someone requiring protection for an invention may file a single application for a patent at the European Patent Office. The application must specify in which states he requires protection. The application is examined for patentability by the office and if satisfied a European patent may be granted. This patent takes effect as a bundle of national patents and will operate in those convention states designated by the applicant.

The Patent Co-operation Treaty (PCT) provides that an applicant may file a single application for a patent, which is known as an 'international application'. A single international search is then carried out by the Office and, if the applicant wishes, a single international preliminary examination. The application is then filed with those national patent offices which the applicant has specified in his application.

Finally, having seen what is required in terms of the substantive law and procedure in the patenting process, let us see what the advantages of patenting are.

The advantages of patenting

1.27

(1) If a patent is obtained, this gives a monopoly right to prevent anyone else using or working the invention for a period of 20 years from the date of application and may form a part of worldwide protection for that invention.

(2) The inventor is seen to be asserting his legal rights to what he considers to be a legitimate protectable monopoly in a particular area of technology. This may have the effect of warning off rivals in the same technology who have been pursuing the same path of research. They may discontinue their research in this direction in the light of the disclosure of the invention, because further development along the same lines could result in them infringing the eventual patent granted—the protection dating from the date of priority. The effective elimination of competition allows the inventor greater opportunities to exploit his invention leading to the recoupment of research and development (R&D) expenditure and the generation and maximising of profits.

(3) The inventor signals the creation of a piece of potentially significant innovative technology perhaps serving to generate external funding for further development and eventual exploitation.

(4) The patent operates as an advertisement to interested parties who may wish to use that technology, either by taking an assignment of it or by obtaining a licence. The invention becomes a more valuable tradable asset than if it were not protected by a patent.

(5) Perhaps most importantly, the inventor will be seen to be adopting a high protective profile for his commercially valuable intellectual property rights.

CHAPTER 2

Patent exploitation

Introduction

2.1 Before looking at the methods or mechanics of exploitation (and in particular industrial licensing) it will be helpful to look at the whole concept of licensing in its commercial context. Most industrial licensing which takes place in the UK is carried out by large industrial concerns. They normally operate a policy where they license out the products of their R&D, and, where it is needed, they license-in new technology. Most large companies such as the pharmaceutical giants have integrated the licensing concept into their business and it plays a strategic part in their overall sales and marketing strategy. They are able to identify markets, fund R&D projects extensively for new and existing markets, and, at the same time, engage in pure and applied research. They also have the necessary expertise, experience and resources capable of exploiting and protecting the products of their research and are able to maximise profitably potential licensing opportunities. Especially if multi-nationals, they have world-wide links or industrial contacts giving access to already established distribution and marketing outlets for their products. They are well geared to create, exploit and protect the fruits of their technology, and they often occupy and maintain market strength through this. Often they have at their disposal in-house legal and licensing experts who have a deep understanding of the range of their particular products and who are thus able to obtain the maximum protection and exploitation of those products.

2.2 In direct contrast to the above, more often than not, licensing is not incorporated into the marketing strategy of the small to medium-sized enterprise. This is largely because of a lack of development of skills or expertise in the field of licensing. Such concerns may have great difficulty in identifying, exploiting and protecting the products generated by their R&D programmes. If licensing does take place it is often unplanned, unco-ordinated and often on an *ad hoc* or haphazard basis. They seldom have in-house legal representation or other skilled licensing personnel to advise on exploitation and protection. Therefore these are the concerns which will have the greatest need for an awareness and understanding of the methods and mechanisms of exploitation and protection of the investment in their vital and valuable, tradable assets.

What is industrial licensing?

2.3 Industrial licensing is not about the sale of goods, although this may form a part of the licence package. It is about the limited transfer of technology, ie, only limited rights in the intellectual property are actually transferred. These property rights may be protected by a patent as has already been explained, or alternatively, they may subsist in such a form that they are unpatented. The technology transferred may consist of valuable secret information or know-how, known only to the licensor. It may subsist in this form either because it is unpatentable, or because the owner has decided against patenting, preferring to keep the technology secret. If know-how is to be licensed, this may take the form of a licence of technical documents, drawings or formulae and may include the transfer over of the services of some skilled personnel capable of showing the correct use of the invention. A patent licence may incorporate such know-how where the patented invention has remained silent on the best method of employing or using the invention. There may also be incorporated copyright, registered design and trade mark licences.

2.4 What sort of licensing policy or marketing strategy a concern has will depend largely upon the nature of that concern's composition, its position within a fairly clearly defined commercial and technology context, its range of products and processes, and of course, as I have already said, its capacity to protect and exploit these either through itself or others. We have seen that a concern may wish to patent its new technology. In doing so it gains the protection of monopoly rights granted under the Act. The patenting of inventions has the advantage of creating a readily identifiable piece of personal property which can be licensed. The patent itself can operate as an advertisement to potential licensees who may need that technology. Further, with the development of a portfolio of patents the stock of the concern's valuable and tradable assets is increased and its overall market value enhanced.

Having seen the advantages accruing to patents, a concern may wish to develop a licensing programme as a part of its business strategy for the following reasons:

(1) In doing so it will be able to retain overall control of the intangible property rights in the technology in that the licensee only gains limited rights to use the invention. Outright sale or assignment of the patent rights would mean relinquishing control over the rights.
(2) By licensing others to exploit the patent, it can penetrate new markets through the marketing and distribution channels of others either here or abroad and produce considerable revenues through the generation of a royalty stream.
(3) It recoups on its R&D in that technology, and, at the end of the day, it makes a profit sufficient for it to invest in further product development.
(4) The patent licence, as I have said, can be valuably combined with a mixture of copyright, registered designs, trade mark and know-how licences.

What sorts of licences are available?

2.5 Licences come in many shapes and forms, and there is rarely a standard type of licence. The licence will reflect the agreed terms negotiated between the parties. There are, however, certain fairly well defined categories or types of licence which have been developed over the years to reflect fairly standard commercial requirements. There are also certain licence categories peculiar to the patent system.

Let us look at some of these licences (a fuller exposition of the usual terms to be found in a patent licence will follow in a later section).

(A) THE EXCLUSIVE LICENCE

This is granted to the licensee alone and precludes exploitation and use of the patent even by the licensor. Total exclusivity to work the patent may be justified in one or all of the following circumstances:

(1) Where the licensee himself is required to expend sums of money on, for example, further development of the product embodying the patented invention or in the setting up of plant or production facilities. He may also incur costs in organising the marketing and distribution of the product. The licensee clearly

requires the security and comfort of the fact that he alone is entitled to work the patent, and thus be in a strong position to profit from it and recoup his element of investment in its exploitation.

(2) Where the licensee requires a lead-time, for example in a new geographic market. This could justify exclusivity for a short period to prevent undue competition and to give him sufficient time to establish himself in the market.

The degree of exclusivity may thereafter be adjusted and may be reduced in due course to a licence granting a less than exclusive right, thus allowing some competition through the owner of the patent granting licences to others to exploit the patent.

(3) Where the licensee has the capacity to satisfy the market demand. If the market is large then the licensor may feel that a single licensee would be able to satisfy that demand. If not he may prefer to grant a number of non-exclusive licences.

(B) SOLE LICENCE

This is a licence granted to a licensee to work the invention to the exclusion of all others, except the licensor. This is appropriate where he has an already developed market which he wishes to continue to serve, together with the assistance of one further licensee. The licensor is then unrestricted in his own exploitation of the patent, but he cannot grant licences to others.

(C) NON-EXCLUSIVE LICENCE

As the name implies, this confers no degree of exclusivity on the licensee. The licensor is free to work the patent himself and to grant licences to others. This is obviously the licence which will be granted where there is no justification for any degree of exclusivity.

2.6 We have so far been dealing with voluntary licences. These are licences where the terms for use of the technology, and the methods and means of working the invention, are freely negotiated between the parties by agreement, at arm's length, in a commercial context. In these circumstances the licensor of the technology will effectively control the terms upon which the invention is used.

Special forms of licence under the Patents Act 1977

2.7 Let us now look at some special licensing mechanisms provided for under the Patents Act.

(A) COMPULSORY LICENCES

The patent system operates on a bargain theory. In consideration of the disclosure to the public of information about new technology, an exclusive right is granted to the discloser to use and work that new technology. There is an underlying reason for this. Through the grant of the protective right of a monopoly, inventors are encouraged to invest in innovation. This grant is made in order to stimulate innovation for the benefit of British industry. For this benefit too the monopoly right is subject to the proviso that the invention is in fact sufficiently worked. The nation's stock of industrial assets will not be increased if the technology embodied in the invention is suppressed. Therefore the Act has built in certain safeguards to try to ensure that the industrial and economic justification for the grant of monopoly rights is not negated by the suppression of the new technological information disclosed by that invention. Suppression is considered an abuse of that monopoly. This is the reason why section 48 of the Act provides that at any time after the expiration of three years, from the date of the grant of the patent, any person may apply to the Comptroller of Patents for a compulsory licence to be granted to him on one or more of the following grounds:

(1) the invention is not being worked to the fullest extent;
(2) the owner or proprietor of the patent is refusing to grant a licence on reasonable terms;
(3) demand for the product is being met by importation and the invention is not being worked commercially in the UK;
(4) in refusing to license on reasonable terms, the owner or proprietor of the patent is unfairly prejudicing an export market in the product;
(5) because of the conditions imposed on a licence granted, these have an adverse effect on the manufacture and disposal of materials not protected by the patent.

Any of 1–5 would amount to an abuse of the monopoly right granted.

If on application to him, the Comptroller is satisfied that the monopoly has been abused he may do any of the following:

(*a*) make an order that a licence be granted to the applicant on terms as he thinks fit;
(*b*) make an entry in the register that licences may be granted to anyone making an application.

Further, any licence granted pursuant to an order under these provisions may either deprive the proprietor of the patent of any right to work the patented invention or to grant any licences under it or revoke all existing licences granted under the patent.[1] Of course the proprietor of the patent can object to or oppose such an application on the grounds that his acts were justifiable and legitimate and appeal against any order made.

The principle behind the above rules is that within three years of the grant of the patent, the patentee should have had sufficient time, either to exploit the patent himself, or to have made arrangements for others to do so. The benefit to industry of the patent should be current or apparent after this time. These provisions should clearly be borne in mind in the formulation of any individual or corporate policy involving the exploitation of the patent through the licensing medium or mechanism.

The patent owner must also consider the following:

(1) In the selection of licensees, regard must be had as to whether the licensee has justified the grant of an exclusive licence to work his invention. If an exclusive licensee lacks the capacity to satisfy the market demand for the actual or potential invention, it could be unwise to make such a grant to him. If this is done, not only will the licensor not be able to work the patent himself or grant licences to others, but he may expose himself to the possibility of being forced, unwillingly, to grant compulsory licences under the terms set by the Comptroller under ground.[1] This could be to possibly undesirable licensees, such as competitors or rivals whom the patent owner had no intention of licensing. He will have effectively lost control of his intellectual property rights. He must consider his licensing policy very carefully indeed and then leave his options open so far as the grant of any degree of exclusivity is concerned. We shall see later how, in the licence document, this potential problem can be overcome through the use of the minimum royalty clause whereby insufficient working of the patent by the licensee will result in a termination of the licence, or at least the degree of exclusivity granted.

(2) There are inherent dangers in formulating a licensing policy which is based upon the grant of licences only on very stringent conditions, or where the policy is to refuse the grant of licences in certain circumstances or only to certain parties. These may be considered unreasonable and may lead to the terms of a compulsory licence being set by the Comptroller and to the grant of licences to the very parties whom it was hoped to exclude.

However, it should be borne in mind that it is the applicant who must prove his case to the Comptroller, and the patent owner may well have good justification and legitimate reasons for refusal to license, if, for example, the proposed licensee has a reputation for abusing other people's intellectual property rights.

(B) LICENCES OF RIGHT

We have seen that the patent system exists to stimulate the dissemination and application of new technical information to the benefit of British industry. This may be effected through the medium or mechanism of the voluntary licence. In addition to seeking to reduce the suppression of technical information by invoking powers granted to the Comptroller under the compulsory licensing provisions, the Act seeks to actively encourage licensing as a method of technology transfer. This can be effected by the owner of the patent making use of a statutory mechanism known as the licence of right.

The Act provides that at any time after the grant of a patent the owner of that patent may apply to the Comptroller for an entry to be made in the register to the effect that licences may be applied for by any interested party as of right.[2] In the event that there is such an endorsement notified on the register the following provisions will apply:

(1) Any person is entitled, as of right, to a licence, to use the patent or work the invention, either on reaching agreement with the patent owner or, if not, upon terms settled by the Comptroller.
(2) A party who has already been granted a voluntary licence—that is, one freely negotiated with the patent owner, before the endorsement—may apply to the Comptroller to exchange such an existing licence for a new licence as of right on no less favourable terms.
(3) The endorsement may be cancelled by the owner only if no licences have been granted under it, or if any existing licensees of right agree to its cancellation.

As can be seen, considerable care must be taken in the formulation of a policy which seeks to incorporate the statutory concept of the licence of right either as a general policy or to introduce it into an existing licensing policy, as this may severely limit the options open to the patent owner in terms of the control of the exploitation of his patent.

The following points relating to the grant of licences of right should be borne in mind:

(1) It is only possible for the patent owner to obtain an endorsement on the register to grant licences as of right if no exclusive licence has been granted. Such a grant of an exclusive licence precludes the granting of any other sort of licence whether voluntary or as of right, or otherwise. Similarly, if licences of right are granted, then no voluntary licences can be granted.

(2) If the patent owner and the licensee cannot agree terms these will be fixed by the Comptroller. This is a severe limitation on the ability to freely negotiate the terms of the patent rights.

(3) If a licence of right is granted giving more favourable terms than those under an existing voluntary licence, the voluntary licensee can exchange his licence for a new licence of right under the terms already agreed. These may be more favourable and result in a reduction of the licensor's royalty revenue in the long term.

(4) The endorsement on the register can only be cancelled if no licences have been granted or the existing licensees of right consent to its removal.

The licence of right, while having the advantage of increasing the availability of licensees, severely limits licensing policy and strategy. If the patent owner already has a voluntary policy in operation he will have difficulty in controlling this as his licensees may opt for entirely new licences under the provisions of the Act. He also restricts his ability to change his policy or adopt a new policy for the future without the consent of his licensees.

The benefits to be derived from increasing awareness of the availability of licences for his invention are at the expense of the patent owner's freedom to control the terms of such licences and thus the use of his intellectual property.

1 Patents Act 1977, s 49.
2 Ibid, s 46.

Pre-licensing matters and licensing policy

2.8 Let us now look at patent rights, not in their passive mode, as mere registered rights, but as they are being actively engaged in the process of being exploited by someone to whom the owner has granted a licence. It is probably at this stage that these rights are most vulnerable because, to some extent, the invention is now leaving the safety of the controlled environment of the proprietor.

Any licensing policy should be aimed at maximising the value and return from the original investment in the patented invention. This can only be done by analysing the exact scope of the claims in the patent, and the number of different uses to which the patented invention may be put. As we shall see later with copyright, the rights inherent in any original work are divisible, and thus it is possible to split them into different rights and to license them separately. The same is true of patents. The licensor, in order to exploit his intellectual property rights to the full, wants to maximise the available number of licensing opportunities. At the same time he wishes to retain maximum control of these rights, and keep his options open for further potential profitable licensing. Therefore he must look to the short, medium and long term when considering his licensing strategy.

Clearly the patent owner's industrial strategy has a considerable bearing on the type of licences which he is able and willing to grant, especially where any degree of exclusivity is purportedly required by the licensee. In order that he may maximise profits at the licensing stage it is important that specific safeguards and measures are taken to ensure that the owner of the invention retains as much control as possible of his intellectual property rights. What he is proposing to do in the licence—and this is true of the licensing of all intellectual property—is to allow someone the right or permission to do something with his property which would otherwise be unlawful. In a sense he is entrusting the licensee with possession of his invention, with the right to operate or use it in a particular manner. Ought he to allow the user of those rights to proceed purely on a basis of trust? Not if he wants to retain his rights. Any use of intellectual property rights by anyone other than the owner must be subject to the most stringent of legal contractual controls on pain of losing them. It is important that any concern which relies heavily on revenues from its royalty stream establishes a sound licensing policy which takes due regard of the necessity of legally and contractually protecting and safeguarding its intellectual property rights. At all times the owner needs to be seen to be aware of the value of his rights, and actively engaged in their protection. Therefore he needs to implement a rigorous licensing policy to ensure the following:

(1) that he is satisfied with the qualifications of his proposed licensee;
(2) that the documentation which he is using is adequate;
(3) that the agreed terms and provisions of the licence agreement are strictly adhered to during its currency and in the working of the invention.

Many organisations rely heavily on their revenues from the royalties received through the licensing of their rights, especially in the field of patents. If the rights of use are not controlled strictly their value could be negated. If they are, this could lead to a subsequent loss of royalties. The stemming of the revenue stream might result in the eventual demise of the intellectual property right.

An examination of a typical licensing situation helps to show how intellectual property rights become vulnerable and how, through taking precautions, some of these problems are overcome.

2.9 As we shall see when I discuss confidentiality, it is clear that in any licensing situation it is essential that a potential licensee who is allowed access to the invention must be required to enter into a confidentiality agreement binding him in express terms to keep secret and not to use any secret information which may be disclosed to him in the course of negotiating the terms of the licence. This pre-licensing negotiation measure should always be adhered to as a matter of good practice.

The licensee

2.10 The pre-licensing stage of any negotiations with a potential licensee should always include a thorough investigation of his status (both commercial and legal), background, track record, his capacity to exploit the invention to the full, and most importantly, his history of dealings with other commercial concerns. It should be borne in mind that if a licence is successfully concluded, the intellectual property now passes into the possession of the licensee. Some comfort will be gained from the knowledge that the licensee has established his commercial bona fides—ie that he is acting in good faith in seeking access to, and use of, the intellectual property. Of course there must be some basis of mutual trust between the parties if they are to be associated for some time, as they will be if the licence is for any length of time. Initial caution should however be seen to be a pre-condition for the proper protection of valuable intellectual property rights.

The licence

2.11 Let us now move from the pre-licensing stage to the terms of the licence itself generally, and in particular the sort of clauses and conditions which should be expressly included to maximise protection of these valuable rights being licensed.

(1) RECITALS

Most licences will commence with the recitals. As the name suggests these recite who the parties are and why they wish to enter into an agreement. This is helpful later if the licence has to be interpreted, perhaps by an arbitrator or a court in the case of an eventual dispute. It is also helpful for a fuller understanding of the purpose of the agreement when and if someone has to deal with it at a later date who was not a member of the original negotiating team. More fundamentally, from a legal point of view, it establishes the parties to the agreement. At English law it is only those parties to the agreement who are bound by and can enforce the terms of that agreement against the other party. It is therefore vital to ascertain who is to be bound and to make sure, especially when dealing with an entity from another legal jurisdiction, that that party is capable of being legally bound by the terms of the agreement.

At this stage, where the intentions of the parties are being spelt out, it is useful to clearly express that the licensor is the proprietor of the intellectual property rights to be licensed. If numerous, these should be scheduled at the back of the document and include such identifying data as the patent application number, date of grant, etc.

(2) DEFINITIONS

Often the parties to a negotiation will have different ways or methods of describing materials, processes, usage, etc. The grant of the licence will be for the use of the licensor's intellectual property rights and is usually fairly narrowly defined. It may be limited to a particular function. In order to make it perfectly clear to the licensee that this is so, and so that the licensee does not mistakenly consider that he has additional rights over and above those intended to be granted to him by the licensor, the parties must have a common and not a unilateral understanding of the nature of the licensable matter. Much confusion and misunderstanding could be avoided now by an early agreement between them as to the precise manner in which certain common terms are to be used where possible. It means that when a term or word is used it should be used with only one possible meaning. Obviously this reduces the possibility of future contention giving greater certainty and definition to the agreement between the parties.

(3) THE LICENSED PRODUCT/PROCESS

Having achieved a common vocabulary of terms for use in the licence it is usual, and in the licensor's interests, to have a clause isolating and identifying the licensed product/process etc. This should be the precise definition relating to the intellectual property to be licensed, and must be clear and unambiguous. Further, the precise use to which that invention may be put must be agreed upon, and thus the scope of the licence ascertained. The parties come to the negotiating table in an expectation that they will achieve something to their mutual benefit. The licensee wants a transfer of the licensor's technology for a number of reasons. He usually has some clear required use in mind, possibly to the exclusion of any of the other uses to which the invention may be put.

(4) EXCLUSIVITY

In general terms we have already discussed the sort of commercial situations where the licensor is prepared to grant, and the licensee requires, an exclusive licence, and what this means in legal terms. The main motives are financial, and the licensor must be satisfied in granting an exclusive licence that the licensee has the practical, commercial and technical capacity to manufacture the product, embodying his patented invention, in order to exploit it to the full. The grant of any degree of exclusivity is a fetter on the licensor's own abilities to exploit his invention, and is naturally and rightly considered with initial reserve. There are no hard and fast rules relating to licensing, but the legal consequences of allowing another party exclusive use of the intellectual property rights must be traced through. At one and the same time the commercial limitations must be carefully weighed. The most effective form of exploitation could be through the grant of a number of licences and not just the one.

(5) FIELD OF USE

We need now to consider what are known as 'field of use' restrictions. The licensor may decide to limit the use or uses to which a patented product or process may be put. He may allow one licensee to use the process or method in one type of commercial exploitation, while allowing its use in a different form of commercial exploitation by a different licensee. For example, the licensor may limit the production or use of a patented invention to one licensee for veterinary use, and to another for human use. Or, if it is a patented method or process, its use may be restricted to only one area of technology, or one specific stage in a manufacturing process. In this way the proprietor structures his licensing policy so that he is able to (*a*) place strict controls upon the use of his intellectual property, and (*b*) keep his licensing policy options open, not committing himself to one licensee.

(6) TERRITORY

Just as it is possible for the licensor to divide up the uses to which his invention may be put, so he can create further divisions by restricting the territories in which any licensee may operate. These rights in turn can be divided into manufacturing and selling rights in each of these territories. We can see that there could be an infinite variety of permutations available to the licensor in respect of the exploitation of his invention. In dividing up his licensing rights he tries to ensure that the licences which he grants enable him to exercise a degree of flexibility to respond readily to any changes in the market for those patented goods. However, it must be borne in mind that under EEC legislation the licensor may grant exclusive licences either to manufacture or to sell in a particular Community territory, but that he cannot prevent any importer from importing goods which have been manufactured in another part of the EEC under one of his licences. This is known in EEC competition law as the doctrine of the 'exhaustion of rights'.[1] Briefly, his position is that he can carve up his markets in the European Community and guarantee his licensees' exclusive manufacturing territories, but only give very limited guarantees of exclusivity in respect of the selling rights.

The protection given by a patent only extends to those countries where a patent is actually granted. A patent granted in France, for example, does not protect a product of the patent owner in Germany, unless it is either specifically granted there or advantage is taken of the EPC or PCT, already mentioned (see para 1.26), when a patent may be granted to cover a number of jurisdictions, as we have already seen. If the patented invention is to be licensed either for sale or use in a foreign jurisdiction, the licensor needs to protect his rights in that jurisdiction by patent registration. The assistance of a patent agent should be sought early on in the development of a licensing programme of an international dimension. He is able to advise on the extent of protection available in any jurisdiction and to advise on the prosecution of the patent application abroad. In considering international licensing, the cost of protecting the asset needs careful consideration as international patenting is not cheap.

Such decisions will require to be made in the light of the resources of the organisation, the extent of the proposed exploitation, and ultimately the extent to which the intellectual property is valued.

(7) DURATION

The duration of the licence of the intellectual property rights in the invention cannot extend beyond the duration of the patent. Obviously there will be no protectable rights left when the patent expires. It is possible to extend the agreement beyond this period where the package of intellectual property rights granted includes matters such as know-how, trade marks or copyright, but then the licensor cannot claim for payment of royalties on the unexpired patent rights.

The duration of the licence reflects the requirements of the parties. In some cases the licensor and the licensee may be looking forward to a long association in the mutual exploitation of the patent. Of course, the longer the licence term granted by the licensor the more constant will be the royalty stream in the long term.

Another factor influencing duration, but which is outside the control of the parties, is the possibility of rapid obsolescence of the invention in a field such as electronics where developments are very rapid indeed. This factor influences not only the *de facto* length of the licence agreement, but also its value.

(8) SUB-LICENSING

The licensor's interests are in maximising exploitation of the patent, while maintaining strict control of its use by the licensee. Even so it could be that the licensor wishes to make use of the full range of the licensee's production, distribution and retailing capacity, in which case he might be prepared to allow the licensee to sub-license the rights granted under the licence to others. The idea of increasing the number of licensees is often an attractive one to the licensor. This could result in an increase in the flow of his royalties. However, he must ensure that the careful control of his rights which he has protected under the original licence is not lost through lack of attention in this matter of sub-licensing. The position is that under the terms of the original licence the licensee is contractually bound to the licensor. If the licensee is in breach of the terms of the agreement he is legally liable to the licensor. What degree of control can the licensor exercise over the use of his intellectual property rights when used by a sub-licensee? He has at least three options:

First, where the licensee wishes to sub-license one of his subsidiary companies. The licensor can license the rights to the main licensee together with the right of that licensee to grant further licences on the same or similar terms as the main licence save for the right to sub-license. In this case the licensor wisely ensures that the main licensee is in a position to exercise sufficient control over the sub-licensee's actions. He secures this by allowing sub-licensing only to a full subsidiary company. This subsidiary enters into a licence with its parent company which has full powers to enforce the terms of that licence against it. Further, the licensee, in his licence with the licensor, must be made contractually liable for the actions of his subsidiaries. As there is no direct contract between the owner of the intellectual property rights and a sub-licensee, the contract is between the owner of the rights and the parent company.

To recap: It is necessary in this licensing situation for the licensor to ensure that (*a*) the parent company is able to enforce its contract against its subsidiary, and (*b*) that the parent company is contractually liable to the licensor for the actions of its subsidiaries.

Second, again where the licensee intends licensing a subsidiary company the owner of the rights could insist that any subsidiaries of the licensee enter into a licence direct with the owner, thus ensuring a direct contractual link, enforceable by the owner. This might be rather cumbersome and the owner may prefer the first arrangement, provided the safeguards outlined are implemented.

Third, where the licensee is permitted to sub-license others who are not its subsidiaries. In this case the licensee must be required to obtain the written consent of the licensor before granting any licences, and the sub-licensee should be required to enter into a licence with the licensee on the same terms as the original granted to the original licensee, save again for the right to sub-license. Again the licensee should be made responsible for any breach of the sub-licence by the sub-licensee. However, the licensor may prefer to enter into a licence directly with the proposed party to ensure a direct contractual link on a principal to principal basis. Provided that proper precautions are taken, the whole sub-licensing mechanism can be valuable for the licensor.

(9) PAYMENT

Intellectual property rights are rights to an exclusive use of something. The return to the owner in terms of income depends upon the amount of use which is made of that exclusive right. Any organisation which relies heavily upon revenues from the exploitation of its intellectual property rights needs to ensure that its pricing mechanism operates to produce the maximum return on investment. Obviously, questions of valuation of the licence are made easier where the licensing of the intellectual property rights takes place within the framework of a fairly well defined technology. There are no hard and fast rules relating to the evaluation of a licence, and it is largely through the process of precedent, experience, commercial usage and negotiation that a reasonable price is reached.

As we have seen, the licensor will want to realise the fruits of his innovation in order to recoup his R&D costs and his investment generally, in order to make sufficient profits for him to plough back into his business and to invest in further product lines or R&D.

What he can do in terms of maximising his profits is determined by such things as the importance and possible duration of the technology in the market, competition in that technology, the maximum amount which any particular market will bear, together with particular factors, such as the requirement of the licensee to expend his own capital in the exploitation of the invention.

The usual methods of payment for use of the owner's intellectual property rights are as follows:

(a) *Lump sum*

The licensor is looking for some degree of certainty of return on his investment. Clearly it is in his interests that he recoup his costs sooner rather than later. Thus he will be interested in obtaining an initial lump sum payment, if possible, from the licensee. In some cases this may be considered a negotiating fee payable by the licensee for the privilege of negotiating, and is often non-returnable. This is more usual where there is to be the grant of valuable exclusive rights.

(b) *Royalty payments*

Most licensing structures rely upon the tried and tested mechanism of the royalty, which by its very nature reflects the way in which intellectual property rights function. This is a fixed sum or percentage payable in direct relation to the intensity of the use of the intellectual property right. This use may be calculated by the number of times a product is either produced or sold embodying the intellectual property right, or if a method or process, the quantity of materials produced through its use.

Given this basis for payment, if the invention is worked by the licensee then he must pay to the patent owner either a sum based upon the intensity of use of the invention, or a proportion or percentage of the eventual selling price of the product embodying the invention, less any costs incurred, eg other than royalties. Normally costs which may be deducted are the costs of production, packaging etc, negotiable by the parties.

(c) *Minimum royalties*

Seeking to achieve the maximum return on his investment, the licensor will want assurances that the licensee works the invention to the full and, if he does not, or is unable to do so, that he, the owner, will not suffer as a result. There is no implied contractual obligation on the part of the licensee to work the invention at all, and it is thus usual in a patent licence to provide that the licensee shall pay a set amount of royalties to the licensor, whether he has worked the patent or not. An alternative measure would be to oblige the licensee to use his best endeavours to achieve a certain level of production and use. The licensor, once he has licensed his invention, does not want to see it lying dormant, and the minimum royalty mechanism goes some considerable way towards achieving vigorous exploitation of the invention. It is particularly appropriate in circumstances where the licensee has been granted an exclusive licence, otherwise the licensee would have exclusive rights to either use or not use the invention.

(d) Other payments

Often, what is being licensed is a package of intellectual property rights, the value of the licence being enhanced by the inclusion of know-how, copyright, registered design and trade mark licences, which for the sake of consistency should be negotiated at the same time.

(10) AUDIT

For the sake of security, the formula for payment having been agreed, there should now be included a clause giving the licensor the right to check that the terms of that formula are adhered to. Though the parties must proceed on a basis of mutual trust, because payment is perhaps the most significant part of the agreement, it is as well to ensure that control of the audit procedures is exercised. The licence should contain a clause obliging the licensee to give details of all relevant use or sales of the product. The patent owner should reserve the right to inspect, if necessary, the licensee's books of account, together with the right to enter the licensee's premises to be able to verify the licensee's statements.

We have dealt with the licence grant, the extent, scope and degree of exclusivity and any restrictions on that grant, the duration of the licence, and the way in which the licensor requires the licensed product to be exploited and paid for. These have been reasonably straightforward and we have seen that, with caution, the licensor is able to exert control over and thus protect the value of his intellectual property right. Now we must deal with matters contained in the licence which could have a bearing on the status of the very intellectual property right itself, and where the owner of the right must again tread warily.

(11) WARRANTIES AND INDEMNITIES

As I have made clear, it is in the nature of patent rights that they are essentially claims which are subject to 'defeasibility', that is, their validity may be challenged in a number of proceedings.[2] It is usual in actions for infringement that the defendant either claims that the patent is not valid or, that if it is valid, that it is not infringed. Validity frequently becomes the issue to be settled by the court. Is the licensor's legal position any stronger under a licence grant? He could be placed in an invidious position where he has entered into a licence with a licensee who subsequently claims that the patent owner's rights are invalid. The consequences of this would be that the licensee could refuse to pay the agreed royalties until such time as it is proven that the patent is valid and that the demand for royalties is therefore justified. If the licensor is forced to terminate the licence and the former licensee continues use of the invention he will be put to commencing legal proceedings against him to enforce his rights. This would be an expensive business, but if not done the licensor could find himself in the position of being unable to enforce these rights against any of his other licensees within his licensing portfolio who may refuse to pay. The result is that he could find himself unable to protect his intellectual property rights. These could have been effectively negated, and he could suffer considerable losses in revenue. The legal position is clear; the owner of patent rights cannot prevent a licensee from challenging the validity of the patent.[3] The principle is that it would be unfair not to allow the licensee the normal or usual rights of challenge which he would have had he not entered into the licence. Further, there could always come a time when the validity of the patent is genuinely in question. It would be inequitable in this case if the licensee could not challenge the patent, but was instead bound by strict terms of non-challenge. Given the above, is there any way in which the licensor can limit the potential damage to his position? Yes, if the owner of the intellectual property rights in the patented invention considers all, and carries out some, of the following measures:

(1) He resists any attempt of the licensee to get him to warrant the validity of the patent. The reason for this is clear: there is always the possibility that it could be found invalid by a court of law, either at the instance of the licensee, or by a third party. If the owner warrants the validity of the patent, the licensee might be able to terminate the licence and sue the licensor for any commercial damages which may flow from his inability to either use the patent because it is invalid, or, in the case where he has been granted an exclusive licence, for his loss of exclusivity.

(2) He includes a clause in the licence to the effect that if the licensee does challenge the validity of the patent, then the agreement will automatically terminate. This will deter a challenging licensee from working the patent pending the outcome of the issue of validity.

(3) He can deter the licensee from challenging the validity of the patent if the licence is not restricted to a licence of the patent rights, but is in effect one which contains a number of licences relating to other of the licensor's intellectual property rights. Such a deterrent package could include licences of know-how, copyright, registered designs and trade marks. Use of any of these other intellectual property rights, while challenging the validity of the patent, and where the agreement is designed to terminate on challenge, could then leave him exposed to legal action by the licensor.

(12) IMPROVEMENTS

The rate and pace at which technology advances often makes the licence for the patented invention obsolete and then neither party will be interested in the continuance of the agreement and it will die a natural death. On the other hand, as we have seen, the licensor, having made the often not inconsiderable investment in the R&D leading to the patented product, wishes to recoup on this. If so, he does not want his patent used as a springboard for the development of new inventions as a result of permitting use of his intellectual property rights, unless he is able to benefit in some way from these subsequent developments directly derived from his invention. Yet what is to prevent the licensee of the patent from amending and improving the technology licensed to him and exploiting the new and improved invention, in direct competition to, and to the detriment of, the licensor? It is probable that the most the licensor can claim is that the licensee be obliged to grant him a non-exclusive licence for any improvements which he may make to the invention. In all likelihood an attempt to obtain any further class of rights would be considered anti-competitive and thus prohibited under either UK or EEC law, and so should be discouraged.[4]

Therefore, the licensor should provide in the licence that the licensee grant the licensor a non-exclusive licence together with the right to use this, either for his own purposes, or for the granting of sub-licences. To secure these rights he should impose an obligation upon the licensee to inform the licensor of any improvements made by him. In this way any improvements operate for his own purposes and benefit if he is exploiting the patent himself, or he can pass these on to his other licensees. Thus any enhancements to his patent accrue to and operate in his favour, increasing the value of the patent as well as protecting it.

(13) RIGHTS OF ACTION

We have seen how the patent owner is able to protect his asset from being negated by the licensee, either through an attack on its validity or through its development or improvement by the licensee. What are the licensor's or the licensee's rights of action during the course of the licence, if the validity of the patent is attacked or it is infringed by a third party or if it is claimed that the patent infringes someone else's different patent? Obviously, from a commercial point of view the owner of the intellectual property rights in the patent must take action to protect his asset. As we have already seen, if he neglects to do so this could mean the end of his intellectual property rights. Therefore it must be spelled out in the licence who is responsible for taking the appropriate action. Normally the licensor wishes to retain control over whether or not he proceeds against an infringer or to defend or settle a matter. In effect a commercial decision must be made. The owner needs to consider such matters as the strength of his patent, its commercial value, the possibility of it being found invalid, and whether he has the resources, time, finances, etc for what could be a lengthy and costly legal fight. He must decide whether or not it would be unwise, because uneconomic, to sue.

The way in which the owner can keep his options open and control his intellectual property is to reserve to himself the right to sue an infringer of his patent or to defend or compromise any claim against the patent itself. It is unwise to enter into an express obligation to the licensee to take action as this could commit him contractually to protect that which he might consider commercially is not worth protecting. The point is that the licensor should at all times be able to respond to any change in the economic or commercial circumstances which may alter radically from the date of the licence to the date of the infringement. The actual intellectual property right could diminish in value during this period, and he will not want to have committed himself to the licensee to protect the right in any event.

(14) QUALITY CONTROL

Often the licensee takes a package of licences. For example, in the case of a pharmaceutical, such a package could include licences for the manufacture and sale of the product together with an authorised use of the licensor's trade marks. In order to ensure that the product bearing the licensor's name is up to his normal standards of quality, he should include a clause requiring the licensee to maintain certain production standards. There are two main reasons for this.

First, the licensor is concerned to maintain the value of his mark as this is associated with his quality goods in the market. If the licensee produces inferior goods these could be identified with the licensor, with the result that he may lose his brand loyalty in that market. He stands to lose market position built up on the reputation of his mark, with the attendant diminution of the value of the mark, both for the specific goods produced by the licensee and possibly for other and future goods bearing the same mark, associating his mark and name with the production of inferior goods.

Second, it is sometimes the owner of the mark who is liable for the effects of defective goods, and not his licensee, as is to be found in some jurisdictions, for example, in the USA. To protect the value of both his patent and his trade mark, the licensor should insist that the licensee satisfy the licensor's quality control standards, by inserting an appropriate clause in the licence obliging the licensee to do so. Furthermore, the licensor should oblige the licensee to submit samples of the product to him and should reserve the right to inspect the licensee's production plant. For, in the event of the goods not being up to standard, he must be in the position to terminate immediately both the production of the sub-standard goods and the use of any trade mark in order to minimise any damage which could flow from this. Indeed to ensure compliance with this production standard clause, the licensor should also seek to obtain an indemnity from the licensee against liability for defective goods.

(15) TYING-IN CLAUSE

In certain limited cases it is possible to oblige the licensee to purchase raw materials for the production of those goods embodying the patented invention from the licensor alone. This could be so where the standards of production could be maintained by use of raw materials produced only by the owner of the patent. Any other attempts to 'tie' the licensee will fall foul of both UK and EEC competition law.[5]

(16) TERMINATION

We have considered the main clauses relevant to protecting the value of the licensor's intellectual property rights. There are others which should be considered in any licensing transaction, such as the assignability of the licence, which in many cases the owner of the rights might wish to restrict and make personal to the licensee who is known to him; whether disputes should be submitted to arbitration—often there are arbitrators operating in specific technical fields who can adjudicate on such matters without the licensor having recourse to the courts, but their decisions are not binding; the sort of circumstances where there would be an automatic termination of the licence, for example, the bankruptcy of either party, non-payment of royalties, breach of production standard clauses etc and, what is of great importance to the owner of the intellectual property rights, the question of what happens to these rights upon termination for any reason. Any termination clause ought to deal not only with what might cause the licence to terminate, but also with the possible situation after the death of the agreement. The licensor should make sure that the cessation of the rights to use the invention is complete, that any trade mark licence granted terminates at the same time, and that there is a return of all products, documents, etc used or associated with the invention. Most important, he must make sure that the clauses relating to confidentiality of secret information belonging to the licensor remain operative and enforceable against the licensee upon the licence terminating for any reason.

1 Treaty of Rome Article 85(1) and *Centrafarm BV and Adriaan De Peijper v Sterling Drug Inc* 15/74 [1974] ECR 1147 at 1162.
2 Patents Act 1977, s 74(1)(a).
3 E Commission Regulation 2349/84.
4 Ibid.
5 Ibid.

2.12 From the above we can conclude that the licensing of intellectual property rights should not be undertaken lightly, and that great care must be exercised so that the rights maintain their value. Successful licensing can be profitable; indiscriminate, ill-advised licensing can be disastrous, sometimes resulting in damage to, or the total loss of, the intellectual property rights themselves. The maxim to follow in any licensing policy is to exert maximum control over the rights, before and during licensing, and upon termination of the licence. It is hoped that the above gives some indication of how to do this.

Monitoring the licence

2.13 The conclusion of a satisfactory licence agreement after a period of negotiation marks the commencement of a relationship between the licensor and his licensee constituted by the terms and conditions taking effect, each party being required to fulfil his part. The contractual terms agreed between the parties must now be performed. Each clause of the licence assumes significance. Now the licensor needs to satisfy himself that those clauses which he insisted upon in the licence which were designed to protect his intellectual property rights, if negative in form, are refrained from, and if positive, are carried out by the licensee. Therefore he must check, during the course of the duration of the licence, that the positive requirements are adhered to, eg, that quality control sampling is carried out, that payments are promptly made, and that he is kept informed of all matters pertinent to the use of the patent, such as the details of sub-licences granted by the licensee. There is little point in entering into a contractual document containing all the safeguards necessary for the protection of the licensor's intellectual property if he is not seen to be requiring strict adherence to the terms. Such neglect could operate against him at a later date if he were forced to sue the licensee for breach of contract. If the licensee were using the patent for an unauthorised purpose, and the licensor did not take the appropriate action to curtail this under the express terms of the contract at the material time, he might be said to have waived his rights through inactivity in not terminating the licence.

To sum up: the owner of intellectual property rights must protect his interests contractually, before, during and after licensing. By monitoring the licence he can ensure strict adherence to the terms of the licence, especially those provisions designed to protect the patent right. He demonstrates to the world at large that he is aware of his intellectual property rights and intends protecting them.

CHAPTER 3

Protection and maintenance of patents and technical information

Introduction

3.1 We have examined the nature of patents, the criteria to be satisfied in order to obtain a patent and the procedures involved. We have also looked at some of the measures which can be taken to protect the patent when it is being exploited under licence. In this chapter I seek to draw together the threads of the two earlier chapters by placing the legal problems of the innovator within the context of the industrial environment and to prescribe some further measures which he can take to protect and maintain his investment in his innovations. If implemented these can help to create the necessary controlled environment for the protection of his innovations and thus minimise the risks to them.

By highlighting some of these problems I hope to show a need to exercise care in the handling of the intellectual property rights which are generated by industrial concerns. The measures prescribed will apply to any industrial or innovative concerns engaged in the creation of intellectual property rights. I therefore intend using the word 'protection' in a wide sense, that is, to mean the implementation of measures or safeguards designed to prevent or minimise the risk of the loss of the value of the intellectual property rights. This chapter is about technical information generally as well as about patents and deals with such matters as secrecy, security and the regulation of such information.

3.2 As we have seen, part of the process of obtaining a patent grant involves the disclosure of information which satisfies certain rather arbitrary, statutory quality tests (novelty, inventive step, industrial application). These qualities elevate the status of such information to that of a legally, fully recognised and protectable property right. Patenting is the most widely recognised mechanism employed in the protection of inventions, or technical information. However, in any industry engaged in scientific or technical research, whether pure or applied and whether related to product or process, there is often produced a considerable volume of ideas, data, theories, etc. This information falls into two broad categories: that which is or may become patentable, and that which is not, and is thus considered inherently unpatentable. Such technical information, in either case, may be extremely valuable.

Clearly, if the information is patentable, it is likely to increase in value if a patent is obtained, as it will then become a legally protected right. If it is not patentable, for example because it is expressly excluded by the provisions of the Act, or it does not satisfy the requisite quality tests, it may still retain its value despite the lack of official legal protection.

3.3 A patent can give considerable protection, and its value in commercial terms should not be underestimated. However, there are some disadvantages associated with patenting in general. It depends largely upon the nature of the information produced as to whether the advantages of patenting outweigh its disadvantages. For example, if the technical information is in the form of a new process or method of production, it may well be more advantageous to suppress it rather than expose it during the prosecution of a patent. Exposure leaves the invention open to the gaze of licensees, rivals, competitors, and unscrupulous potential infringers alike. If the process can be kept secret then this may be a better protection than a patent. It may be known to very few people and could (subject to inadvertent or accidental disclosure) remain secret in perpetuity, unlike the limited period of protection accorded to the patent. In this form it enjoys a status akin to a personal property right and can be licensed under the condition that the licensee uses the process under the strict imposition of contractual obligations of confidentiality.

It must be said that a patent, while disclosing in some cases an advance in an existing technology, may not disclose sufficient for the invention to be used at its maximum efficiency. The best method of employing or working an invention may be known only to its owner. In this case a tradable package which could be offered to a licensee might be the consent to work the invention under the patent together with a licence to use such additional information as is necessary to use the invention more effectively. Thus new and valuable information created by an innovative concern can be exploited and protected, either through the formal medium of a patent or under the imposition of obligations of secrecy and confidentiality.

What is common to both situations is that, initially, in the first case of patentable material, and throughout in the second case of unpatentable material, if the information is to have any commercial exploitable value at all as new information, it must remain secret. If it is revealed, then it should only be under strict terms of confidentiality. For if revealed, say, by inadvertent publication by a member of the concern in a scientific paper, any subsequent attempt to patent the invention could fail for lack of novelty. Such disclosure almost certainly makes it a part of the state of the art. This cannot be overstressed for the small to medium-sized innovative concern. It is important to note however that the disclosure of any matter which may form the subject matter of a patent is to be disregarded if it is disclosed within six months of an application for the grant of a patent, and the matter disclosed was obtained unlawfully or in breach of an obligation of confidence. Again it will be disregarded if it was disclosed at an international exhibition, providing in this case that the applicant has notified the Patent Office of this in his application.[1]

All new technical information arising as a result of scientific and technical research and development should be treated with care. An awareness of the value of the potential of this information should be instilled in all those handling, or dealing in, or having access to it. In other words, all information should be treated as proprietorial and measures taken to ensure that it is safeguarded. Its creation, handling, and exploitation should take place within a strictly controlled environment.

1 Patents Act 1977, s 2(4).

3.4 We now need to investigate and isolate problems relating to new technical information. Let us look at the potential problems and the precautionary steps to be taken before and during its creation. This covers problems arising from security, title, employment contracts, employee rights of access, access by third parties, and of course confidentiality. Therefore it has to do with the security of the information within the industrial concern itself.

If properly implemented, the measures advocated should go some way towards alleviating the problems faced by those engaged in the creation of innovative technical information, whether this is to be formally patented or not. I hope that this will show the need to implement initial policies within innovative industrial concerns to ensure that the creation of such valuable assets takes place in as legally secure an environment as possible. For only by doing so will the benefits of the investment and the results of such innovation accrue to those who have made that investment.

The main problems

3.5 Two of the major problems faced by any innovative concern in respect of the generation of new technical information are posed by the following questions: First, if it is new, how can it be protected from exposure? Second, if it is proprietorial, to whom does it belong?

A brief look at a typical industrial scenario illustrates why these questions need to be asked.

The creation of new technical information may arise as the result of a solo performance of an individual self-employed inventor. It is he who might enjoy all rights to the invention and it is he who then ought to be in control of it. On the other hand, in an industrial scenario such technical information may well be the result of the efforts of an individual inventor who may be employed in such a position that an invention is likely to result from that employment. Or, it may be the result of the collective efforts of a team of people who have pooled their relative experiences towards its creation, and not necessarily the result of the efforts of only one individual. Thus scientists, researchers and technicians from many diverse scientific and technical backgrounds might have made contributions both in terms of quality and quantity of their skills and expertise. This is true where an amalgam of skills is acquired from a number of divergent technologies. Further, even the myriad skills or expertise and resources of the constituent elements comprising the concern might, in themselves, have been insufficient and thus have required the input of further temporary skills from outside sources such as specialist consultants or the commissioning of specific projects. Some elements of the new technical information may have been produced as a result of even wider ranging joint scientific and investigative effort with other commercial concerns or academic and research institutions. We see therefore that the ways in which new technical information may be created and exposed are practically limitless, as are the potential claims to ownership or other interests or rights in it.

Obviously substantial claims can occur as to the ownership and use of all or a part of such collectively created innovation. An individual contributor might reasonably consider that he enjoys a property right in what he has either created with, or disclosed to, the concern and that consequently he is in no way constrained as to its use either by himself or by others. The same considerations may be thought to apply to those subscribing from outside the organisation.

Unless there is a policy implemented which clearly identifies ownership and which regulates the flow and disclosure of that information in a strictly controlled way, the innovative concern may find that its inability to control the free dissemination and use of the information will render it virtually valueless.

Consequences of not regulating information

3.6 The consequences of not regulating information are as follows:

(1) Others may claim the free use, or even ownership, of all or part of it.
(2) The innovative concern itself may find that it is excluded from using either all or a part of it.
(3) Disclosure by anyone with access to, or use of, the information can make that information a part of the state of the art and thus render it incapable of being patented through lack of novelty. We saw earlier what was meant by novelty and state of the art, and its implications for the patenting process (see para 1.10).
(4) If the information is inherently unpatentable, disclosure or use by anyone will make it virtually useless as tradable know-how.

Problems of disclosure

(A) DISCLOSURE

3.7 First of all let us look at the issue of disclosure. Besides the purely technical and scientific information generated by an enterprise engaged in technical and scientific research, there is also other business information or data to consider, such as that resulting from business plans, marketing plans etc, much of which the concern might consider valuable and confidential, and so wish to keep secret. The concern may consider that its valuable interest in this accumulated data is of a proprietorial nature, ie that it enjoys some sort of property right in it. It may want to limit the number of people who have access to it and ensure that the information gained goes no further than those chosen recipients. Therefore it might seek to prevent that material from being deemed public and so usable by anyone by being disclosed outside the organisation itself. Thus at this stage we need to ask whether there are any measures available to check the dissemination of information, whether deliberately or inadvertently, whether technical or business.

I have already divided this technical information into two categories: the sort which is of such a quality that it satisfies the tests of patentability, and that which does not and is unpatentable. Over the years the latter forms of valuable information have acquired rights akin to property rights when certain criteria are satisfied. This latter protection of unpatentable material depends largely upon the development of the common law of confidentiality or trade secrets and is more difficult to grasp.

As we have seen under statute law, to be patentable the information must satisfy the tests of novelty, inventiveness and industrial applicability. How have the courts viewed this other category of information in deciding whether it should be accorded protection akin to a property right? In order to answer this question let us see how the claims to these rights arise and how the courts deal with them. For instance, such a claim is usually for the exclusive use of new technical information by the owner (as with patents) despite the fact that it has suffered varying degrees of exposure, sometimes to members of the concern itself or even to third parties outside. Are there yet circumstances where the information has been disclosed, but where it is still deemed to be novel and secret and in the sense of being private and not in the public domain? The answer is complex.

First of all we must note that there is no legislative or statutory recognition of an intellectual property right in such information and thus no absolute or exclusive monopoly to its use accorded to its creator. This leaves it in an exposed position, which may lead to its unfettered use by anyone. In order for it to be protected it must have a quality imposed upon it, which in some way renders it still private or secret, despite exposure.

(B) CONFIDENTIALITY

A body of rules, principles and doctrine have been developed under the common law, largely dating from the late nineteenth century, which assist in the recognition of rights in just such information.[1,2] They have recognised that rights exist in it akin to, if not the same as, property rights. This body of law is complex and its implications uncertain.

Generally, it provides that in certain circumstances where information is disclosed, it is implicit that its disclosure is imparted to any recipient under an obligation of confidence. The recipient impliedly undertakes not to use it himself except with the permission of the creator, nor to disclose it to any other party, again without permission. This means that it is still deemed to be secret, and its disclosure does not make it freely available or usable. These laws cover business[3] as well as technical information, the latter commonly referred to as know-how.[4]

It is important to see what constitutes confidentiality, the circumstances under which it operates, and the extent to which it can be relied upon by those claiming rights under it. In order to do so let us look at the sort of commercial scenarios where the law operates, the quality requirements of the information, that is, the status of the information, and the status of the recipient of such information, all of which are important considerations for the applicability of these laws. This will mean reviewing the main area in which the doctrine operates, in the relationship between employer and employee, before turning our attention to other areas of the laws relevant to the small to medium-sized enterprise.

(C) EMPLOYER/EMPLOYEE RELATIONSHIP

An employee equipped to apply his already developed skills to new problems in the course of his employment, may yet acquire further skills, techniques or information which may make him an even better technician, technologist, scientist or whatever. His natural expectations are that he will be able to offer those skills to others in the market thus enhancing his own marketability. He naturally considers that these new skills are essentially something to which he is personally entitled, due to his own responsible efforts in cultivating them. However, during the course of his own development in his employment he will have had access to, and absorbed, a considerable amount of information, data, etc, about his employer's business. The tension in such a situation is clear: how is it possible to rightly demarcate information which the employee is entitled to call his to do with as he wishes, and that information which the employer is entitled to deem secret in law as confidential, clearly proprietory, and not in any way usable by the employee outside the confines of the workplace during his employment or when such employment has ended?

Partially as a response to this recurring problem, the common law has developed precedents to guide different interests. It is clear from the cases, first, that confidentiality subsists automatically between employer and employee independent of any contract between the parties, and second, its extent depends largely upon the quality or character of the information itself. For the information to be so protected as confidential, it must satisfy the following conditions:

(1) It must be secret—ie not yet in the public domain[5] (this, of course, apart from the employee knowing it). This means that it must not have the quality of being public property and public

knowledge. Such technical information may be simple or even obvious. It will, however, still merit protection. Therefore the position appears to be that it is not possible to appropriate or protect information which is considered to be general knowledge in a particular industry or technology. This is obviously sensible.

Generally, information imparted in confidence remains secret between the parties even if the recipient later acquires that information by other means or channels. There are exceptions to this and the law is complex and by no means clear. However, it is clear that information given to an employee which is both regarded by the employer and recognised by the employee as confidential imposes a special duty upon the recipient to keep that information secret at all times.

(2) However, such information must be other than the general knowledge, skill or experience acquired at work for it is well established that it is against public policy to try to prevent someone using the general skill and knowledge which he has acquired at work, after he has left that employment.[6] The law makes a distinction between what are trade secrets and the employee who, in his capacity in his particular employment, acquires mental or manual skills: the former relates to knowledge which is 'as real and objective as the possession of material goods' and the latter concerns the subjective 'equipment of the workman which becomes a part of himself' and is to be used 'for his own maintenance and advancement'.[7]

Is it possible for an employer to rely upon this law of confidentiality as implied in the case of any employee? Here case law is uncertain, ambiguous and unreliable, and he would do better to insist that every employee enters into a written contract of employment which sets out categorically his job specification and what the employer regards as being in the realm of private or confidential information for the purposes of this job. In order to ensure that this takes effect, procedures at the workplace should be adopted which will specifically bring to the attention of the employee those matters which the employer regards as confidential and proprietorial. This goes some way towards ensuring that the employee is 'fixed' with recognising what his employer regards as secret, unusable (except within the confines of the workplace) and not to be divulged. Thus in any future disputes he has evidence of having taken substantial steps towards isolating and identifying what he considered to be secret, and further, that he brought this to his employee's attention.

(D) OTHERS

In situations where information of a secret nature is legitimately communicated to another party, other than in the employer/

employee situation, the communicator may again rely upon the common law of implied confidentiality. As before, the extent of the confidentiality protected by law is difficult to ascertain and reliance should instead be placed on express and specific terms in a confidentiality agreement.

Other than an employee who, if anyone, may have access to this information?

(*a*) In joint or collaborative ventures where there is a pooling of skills, be these business, technical or scientific, the individual contributors normally have access to sensitive information and materials. Can they be entitled to use it as they wish? Not necessarily. They can be contractually restrained from using any of that information either for their own use or for the use of others, which may be to the detriment of the party communicating that information to them. Thus the communication of a secret process to another party or the use of it by the recipient himself is actionable by the communicator under implied or express obligation of confidentiality. Any such agreement must be clear about what is secret and the way in which the recipient is to be fixed with it, either in oral or written form.

(*b*) In any negotiations with potential licensees, access to the secret information by way of the licensee appraising that technical information must be strictly regulated under the restraining terms of confidentiality. If not, the licensee, in possession of this information, may believe that he is entitled to use it without paying for it. Therefore the terms of disclosure should be expressed in a written document. This could be crucial in any claim of illicit use of this information in the future by the potential licensee should he decline to take a licence subsequent to the disclosure of the secret information to him.

1 *Tuck & Sons v Priester* (1887) 19 QB 629, CA.
2 *Lamb v Evans* [1893] 1 Ch 218 at 235, CA.
3 *Stephenson Jordan and Harrison Ltd v McDonald and Evans* (1951) 68 RPC 190.
4 The Law Commission, *Breach of Confidence* Cmnd 8388 (1981).
5 *Saltman Engineering Co Ltd v Campbell Engineering Co Ltd* (1948) 65 RPC 203, CA.
6 *Herbert Morris Ltd v Saxelby* [1916] 1 AC 688, HL.
7 *Provident Clothing and Supply Co Ltd v Mason* [1913] AC 724 at 740–741, HL.

3.8 These precautionary measures should be taken not once but each time there is exposure or disclosure of information as this will serve the function not only of preserving and protecting that information, as we have seen, but also of indicating that the concern is continually aware of its intellectual property rights, that it understands the nature of those rights and that it intends maintaining a high profile in terms of their protection. This assists it in building up a deterrent effect created by a heightened level of awareness of the value of the intellectual property rights, both within the concern and in its dealings with those outside.

Problems of ownership

3.9 There are yet further and more fundamental safeguards which can be implemented, again under the umbrella heading of protection, which relate to the initial entitlement to the new technical information generated by an innovative concern. All parties may well be aware that they are under an obligation of confidentiality to their employer as previously discussed. We have seen that this potentially difficult area can be alleviated by the use of a widely drawn confidentiality agreement. These fundamental safeguards must be implemented in order for the concern in question to be able to assert unequivocally that it is the proprietor of all innovation generated as a result of its investment. However, confidentiality is limited to the protection of secret information, and it usually only assists in the claim to proprietorship of that information. It is not usually conclusive of ownership, and of itself leaves many instances where disputes would arise as to proprietorship. Disaster could result for such an innovative concern if it neglects more fundamental safeguards, especially in the case of small to medium-sized enterprises which often place heavy reliance upon a single or limited range of developed products. If they cannot claim ownership of those rights, they cannot claim exclusive use. Disputes as to title may result in their being unable to obtain patents without threat of objection from others.[1] Even if they were to succeed in getting a patent its validity could be impugned later by others claiming to have rights in the invention.[2] Finally, they may be unable to exploit or engage in any exclusive dealings as they might be unable to give any guarantees as to their right to do so. Their product's value will be severely affected and what may have been a potentially valuable innovation, incurring considerable investment, could be unassured as to its ownership and thus virtually worthless.

1 Patents Act 1977, s 8.
2 Ibid, s 37.

3.10 We have seen that it may be the case that patentable or valuable inventions are the result of lengthy, extensive collaborative efforts of a number of people of widely differing backgrounds and disciplines, who have pooled their skills to produce an innovative product. The permutations are limitless, and it must be recognised that it is unlikely that any innovative concern will have the full range or gamut of personnel, skills, scientific and technological capacity or facilities to be able to operate without at some time or other seeking outside assistance.

Clearly, it is imperative that the concern does not expose itself to a claim by any of these outside parties to proprietorship in any of the intellectual property rights in inventions which arise as a result of such collaborative input, which it has paid for, or is responsible for, in developing any eventual product embodying the invention. If so exposed it could be prevented from maximising exploitation of its invention, from recouping on R&D expenditure, and in its ability to make profits and re-invest in its future product research and development plans or projects. Therefore, the concern must establish a policy to safeguard its entitlement to the invention, whether product or process, and no matter what the source.

(A) THE INDIVIDUAL EMPLOYEE

The present law is a codification of common law practice and principles. The common law implies that an employee who creates an invention does not enjoy any title to that invention but rather the invention belongs to his employer.[1] This is whether he was employed to produce an invention or not. Section 39 of the 1977 Act provides that:

> '. . . an invention made by an employee shall, as between him and his employer, be taken to belong to his employer for the purposes of this Act and all other purposes if—
>
> (*a*) it was made in the course of the normal duties of the employee or in the course of duties falling outside his normal duties, but specifically assigned to him, and the circumstances in either case were such that an invention might reasonably be expected to result from the carrying out of his duties; or
>
> (*b*) the invention was made in the course of the duties of the employee and, at the time of making the invention, because of the nature of his duties and the particular responsibilities arising from the nature of his duties, he had a special obligation to further the interests of the employer's undertaking.
>
> (2) Any other invention made by the employee shall, as between him and his employer, be taken for those purposes to belong to the employee.'

Any term which seeks to diminish any statutory rights of the employee will be unenforceable against the employee. Great care must be taken to ensure that all contracts with employees not only incorporate an obligation of confidentiality upon the employee, but also state as widely as possible the contractual duties of the employee in order to ensure that all that he invents belongs to the concern. This is to cover the position where there is any likelihood of an invention being created by the employee.

What rights does an employee have under the Act? The Act provides certain rights to employees, other than the right to claim an invention as their own if not in the pursuance of their clearly stated contractual duties. These too have commercial ramifications.

(1) If the employee has made an invention in the course of his clearly stated contractual duties, and this has resulted in the profitable commercial exploitation by his employer, he can make a claim for compensation based upon the benefit, provided that the patent granted to the employer has provided 'outstanding benefit'.[2] It should be noted that it is upon the patent and not the invention which has proved profitable that the employee may base his claim.

(2) If the employee has made an invention, not just in pursuance of the clearly stated contractual duties, he might obtain a patent for his invention which he then assigns to his employer. If that patent proves at a later date to be of considerable benefit to the employer, he is still able to claim. But he can only claim for compensation if the amount which he received on assignment bore little relationship to the eventual benefit to his employer. The claim in either case has to be made to either the Comptroller or the Patent Court.

This is designed to ensure that those who operate in a creative or innovative way, producing substantial benefits for their employers, are justly rewarded for their efforts over and above what is their due under the normal terms of their contract of employment. The rationale behind this is the hope of spurring on the individual inventor to greater innovation, within the organisation.

(B) RESEARCH GROUPS

(1) The creation of an invention might be the result of loose collaboration, rather than incorporation, between individuals who have pooled their respective resources, including know-how, skills, knowledge and possibly finances. It might be that at the outset they might not have established any legal framework as to their future ownership of any intellectual property which may evolve from their

pooling of talents and which may be embodied in an invention of some kind. An obvious but often disregarded danger in this sort of situation is that the composition of the original research team may alter considerably over a period of the time engaged in research and development. At the outset, if there was no agreement as to ownership of the intellectual property rights in their concerted input, at the end of the day it may be very difficult to decide who should be attributed with ownership of the invention. In the absence of agreement, joint invention means joint claims to ownership. Any joint entitlement to a patent or to a patentable invention means that each party entitled can work or operate the invention himself, but none of the parties can deal with the patent, eg assign or license it, without the consent of the other co-owners.[3] This is greatly to the disadvantage of each individual party who may wish to exploit the benefit of the patent, not merely by himself, but through a licensee, and he will be unable to do so without the express permission of his co-owners. This is clearly a legal status to be avoided as it may reduce the value of the invention to each and every one of them. On the other hand it prevents one of them getting more out of it than the others thus preventing a resultant loss to the others. It is something which must be borne in mind and preferably dealt with sooner rather than later.

(2) Another problem for research groups relates to the provisions of the Act which allow during and within two years of the grant of a patent an interested party to claim a substantial interest or claim to the benefit or entitlement to the patent.[4] This could occur where the party concerned has made a substantial input as an original member of the team, and has neither been named as one of the inventors nor indeed as one of the owners in the application.

Clearly, the issue of confidentiality is of importance in this sort of situation. Thus, an obligation of confidentiality could be established between the parties to prevent early disclosure by one or more of the team members. This operates to prevent them from divulging relevant information in respect of patentable material or know-how when they leave the team at any time, before or after a patent has been secured.

The issue of ownership should be kept clearly in mind at all times and early agreement established as to rights and interests in the invention.

There ought to be certainty in these matters, for otherwise delays and frustration thwart the potential to exploit what might be a valuable invention. This could mean the subsequent loss of commercial interest in the invention. Potential financial backers, licensees or assignees may go elsewhere if the delays are lengthy and the problems of title seemingly insoluble. Returns from what might have been a substantial investment in innovation are thus reduced sometimes to vanishing point.

(C) CONTRACTS FOR SERVICES

At some time or another any innovative industrial concern might need to augment its capabilities by contracting in those skills which it needs, if only for a limited purpose and duration. To ensure that it enjoys the intellectual property rights it needs, it should either obtain total rights to the input, or make certain that it has sufficient for its purposes.

Besides ensuring entitlement or sufficient interests, the concern must place any outside parties having access to confidential information under an obligation of confidentiality both during and after rendering its services. These measures go some way to ensuring that there is sufficient documentary evidence in the possession of the concern to render ineffective any claims to entitlement of all or part of the invention by any party other than itself.

(D) FINANCIAL BACKERS

Obtaining funding for R&D is difficult given the high risks involved in the successful commercialisation of innovative ideas and research. But there are a number of sources of finance, even the traditional ones like banks, which often have special divisions to deal with such matters. Funding can sometimes be obtained from government bodies such as the Department of Trade, the British Technology Group, and quasi-government bodies such as the Medical Research Council, the Science and Engineering Research Councils and the Agricultural Research Council, as well as a growing body of venture capitalists interested in the funding of investment in new industrial ideas. The terms of financial assistance differ in each case but rights and interests in intellectual property in any invention normally form a part of the lending institution's security. It may insist on the assignment of any future patent rights to it, or at least the notification of its interests on the register or a restriction on dealings with the patent. In these cases the innovator's hands are somewhat tied in the freedom he can exercise in respect of any patent rights which may flow from the funded research. But often the lender's restrictions only apply for a limited period during a recoupment of the advance after which time the lender may be prepared to relinquish its interests wholly or in part. It is important to note the conditions of advance carefully in each case.

1 *Sterling Engineering Co Ltd v Patchett* (1955) 72 RPC 50, HL.
2 Patents Act 1977, s 40.
3 Ibid, s 36.
4 Ibid, s 37.

3.11 We have now looked at specific policy relating to confidentiality and entitlement. The innovator or employer is going some way to secure the protection of his rights by ensuring the imposition of specific obligations of confidentiality upon all persons having the remotest access to the technical innovation, and by contractually ensuring that all intellectual property rights generated by, or emanating from, the commercial innovative concern vest in him. By doing so he is maintaining their value, and this will ensure that in due course he will be able to maximise his exploitation of them. In turn this helps him to recoup his investment in that innovation, and so generally act as a stimulus to further investment.

Noting the above should be part of any general policy of an innovative concern. It heightens the level of awareness of the nature of the sort of property interests which can subsist in its innovation. At each stage careful checks should be made in any R&D programme to ensure that the fundamental safeguards have been implemented.

Some practical measures to take

3.12 Besides the legal contractual element, elementary practical safeguards should be imposed as follows:

(1) For security purposes limited access only should be allowed to confidential or sensitive information.
(2) All confidential information including documentation, materials, designs, products, processes, etc should be physically secured and regular checks made on its safety.
(3) In institutions where considerable team and individual efforts are expended on research, an individual researcher often deliberately or inadvertently discloses information about the innovation in order to achieve academic esteem. This might be details of his own personal discovery which he discloses in a seminar or lecture to a learned society, or in a scientific journal. This could prove fatal to any subsequent patent application and is not to be encouraged except in cases where the

material has been closely scrutinised beforehand. It is true that the stimulus to new scientific developments often comes about as a result of the cross-fertilisation of ideas and discoveries of others. Even so, care must be taken that details of these discoveries are not disclosed in such a way as to prejudice the possibility of obtaining patent protection.

(4) Internal records should be kept of all matters relating to product R&D, such as who has access, the status of that person and the state and stage of development. This is not only for the sake of standard security procedures but in order to facilitate decisions as to whether to continue on a particular line of research and whether and when to file a patent application.

(5) Proper documentary records should be kept of contracts of employment, contracts for services used by the organisation, details of all confidentiality agreements, records of any patents, and of course any licensees permitted to work the patent.

(6) Patent renewal dates must be kept, as failure to renew may prevent restoration in the event of the patent lapsing due to inadvertence, mishap or otherwise. The life of the patent is 20 years from the date of filing the application but renewal fees must be paid to the Patent Office commencing on the fifth year of the patent and in each subsequent year, in order to keep the patent alive. The reason for this is to ensure that the patent is worked for the benefit of industry and that the monopoly granted to the patentee remains justified. If it is not worked it should enter the public domain. It is important to pay the renewal fees, as once the patent has lapsed, there is no automatic right to have it restored to the register.

(7) All standard documentation relating to the concern's intellectual property rights should be reviewed regularly and if necessary brought up to date to take account of any changes there may have been in the law since they were first drafted. Such changes might have rendered these agreements obsolete or indeed unenforceable.

By putting the above measures into effect the concern is exercising a degree of managerial control over information relating to its intellectual property rights.

3.13 To complete the corporate intellectual property housekeeping exercise let us briefly look at the obverse situation where an intellectual property right or technology is being licensed or transferred in and where loss can result from careless handling.

If the concern does not have the capacity or the technological resource to carry out a full research and development programme itself then the technology necessary may be purchased or assigned over, but increasingly the mechanism of licensing-in is being used to 'acquire' or transfer the technology necessary. This latter has advantages in that the rights transferred are clearly tailored to the user's needs, both in terms of specific use and duration. This results in a more cost-effective use of that technology. In licensing-in, the following should be considered that:

(*a*) all the necessary rights to work the invention have been transferred. If the concern has to go back for more rights it will most likely have to pay accordingly;
(*b*) the Register of Patents is checked to ensure that the state of the register is as the licensor claims, and that he is the unencumbered proprietor, entitled to deal in those rights;
(*c*) any necessary know-how is licensed in order that effective use may be made of the invention;
(*d*) any registrable rights which the concern may acquire in the patent are registered.

We have already dealt with the licensing of patents and the sort of clauses which it is essential should be incorporated in such documentation to protect the intellectual property (see para 2.11).

Infringement and remedies

INFRINGEMENT

3.14 Under 'Licensing' (para 2.1) I emphasised the need to protect intellectual property by activating the specifically protective clauses when necessary. As we saw, in a well drawn licence, the licensor has a substantial array of contractual remedies at his disposal to maintain the value of his asset against abuse by those to whom he has temporarily placed it in trust. However there could be occasions when the owner of the rights finds them under attack from an infringer. As we now know it is essentially a commercial decision as to whether he should take proceedings or not, based largely upon the value and strength of the patent and ultimately his chance of success in any subsequent litigation. Even so, I will deal with infringement briefly. Unfortunately if an invention is valuable it will sometimes be vulnerable to the determined infringer, despite all precautions.

Patent rights are infringed when an unauthorised person does any of the following in respect of a valid patent:

(1) where the invention is a product, he,
  (i) makes,
  (ii) disposes of,
  (iii) offers to dispose of,
  (iv) uses or
  (v) imports the product or
  (vi) keeps it whether for disposal or otherwise.[1]

The idea is of course to make sure that it is the owner of the patent who is able to control the use and commercial exploitation of his patented invention. Thus keeping patented products for eventual sale, for example, would be covered by the provision relating to disposal. Use of the patented invention is an infringement but it is important to note the exceptions to this provision. Use of a patented invention for private use or for experimental purposes would not infringe the patent; this is sensible and reasonable.[2]

(2) The Act states that it is an infringement of a process patent where someone uses the process or it is offered for use in the UK when that person knows, or it is obvious to a reasonable person in the circumstances, that its use there without the consent of the proprietor would be an infringement.[3]

(3) Further, where the invention is a process, the patent rights are infringed where someone disposes of, offers to dispose of, uses or imports any product obtained directly by means of that process or keeps any such product whether for disposal or otherwise.[4]

Additionally, where elements of the invention, for example, parts of a kit or the components of a machine, essential for putting the invention into effect, are supplied in the UK, this too is an infringement of the patent.[5] What is an essential element will depend upon the facts in each individual case but will not generally include 'staple commercial products', that is, the sort of products which are considered to be commercially commonplace.[6]

REMEDIES

Injunction

If someone is using the patented product or process or it seems likely that he will do so, the owner of the patent can apply for an interlocutory injunction. This is to stop the other party from infringing the patent. Injunctions are not granted lightly because an order for the cessation of the use of an invention could have serious commercial consequences for the alleged infringer. The court will wish to satisfy itself that the case is neither 'frivolous or vexatious' and that the plaintiff has at least an arguable case against the alleged infringer. It will take into account a number of factors before deciding whether to grant an injunction or not, such as the practical and commercial effects of the injunction, the relative market strengths of the parties, and whether damages after a full court hearing might not be a more appropriate remedy. The injunction is a very real threat to an infringer but it should be borne in mind that it is not an automatic right but a remedy available at the court's discretion.

Damages

If the matter goes to trial the owner of the patent can claim damages against the defendant or he may ask for an account of profits, that is, an account of the actual profits made by the infringer accruing to him and not to the owner. He can also ask for delivery up of any infringing articles or products. He can in addition obtain costs against the defendant.

It is now clear to us that one of the problems surrounding patent litigation is that the alleged infringer will counter-claim that either the patent is invalid or, if valid, that he did not infringe the plaintiff's patent. Thus in a successful infringement action, the patent owner usually requires the court to provide a statement to the effect that the patent is valid and infringed.

1 Patents Act 1977, s 60(1)(a).
2 Ibid, s 60(5)(a) and (b).
3 Ibid, s 60(1)(b).
4 Ibid, s 60(1)(c).
5 Ibid, s 60(2).
6 Ibid, s 60(3).

CHAPTER 4

Copyright creation

Introduction

4.1 Having discussed with patents one of the main systems of intellectual property law to which the industrial innovator should turn for the protection of his industrial assets, in this chapter I turn to the law of copyright. I describe the nature of copyright, show how its protection has been extended to the creation of artefacts in an industrial innovative context, and generally point to its increasing relevance in today's innovative industrial world. In subsequent chapters I deal with the licensing of copyright works, and prescribe measures which should be taken generally in the protection and maintenance of this the most nebulous of intellectual property rights. The law of copyright has undergone change with the passage of the Copyright, Designs and Patents Act 1988 ('the new Act'). The 1956 Copyright Act ('the old Act') has been repealed and replaced by a fresh statement of the law retaining much of the substantive contents of the old Act. In order to highlight the changes I have referred to the 1956 Act and incorporated the relevant provisions of the new Act.

4.2 Let us briefly consider the theoretical nature of copyright. This will assist us in identifying the sort of rights the law is trying to protect, and so enable us to grasp later their practical implications, which are our focus. The following provides a useful pointer to the nature of the rights which are protected by the law of copyright.

What is protected under the law of copyright is the labour, skill and judgement which someone, the author, artist or creator has expended in the creation of an original literary, artistic, musical or dramatic work. The notion of the ownership of property rights in such labour has its modern origins in the work of the seventeenth century philosopher John Locke.[1] He considered that a man has a property right in anything created by his own labour from the raw materials of existence. Labour gives title and adds value to everything. Translated into the modern day realm of intellectual property law, it is the original value of the labour expended in the production of an original work which is accorded protection as a property right, together with any subsequently accrued value which results from it, together with the value of the materials employed in its creation.

1 John Locke, *Two Treatises of Government*, Second Treatise, chapter 5, 'Of Property'.

4.3 Protection is in the form of a legal right of the owner of the property in an original work to prevent anyone else from reproducing the work in any way. If someone has laboured in the creation of an original literary work, such as a novel, the legal rights which pass to its purchaser are of the sort which anyone would expect to pass to him under the normal provisions for the sale of goods. Thus he can do what he likes with the physical object. He may sell it, hire it out, allow someone else the use of it, or destroy it if he so wishes. What he cannot do is reproduce or copy it without the express permission of the owner of the intellectual property right, in this case of the copyright, in the book. That is a right reserved to the owner of the work.[1] The new Act uses the word 'copy' rather than 'reproduce' and infringement of copyright by copying in relation to a literary, musical or artistic work means reproducing the work in any material form.[2] Legally copyright cannot pass without express provision for it to do so.[3]

1 Copyright Act 1956, s 1(1); Copyright, Designs and Patents Act 1988, s 16(1)(a).
2 Copyright, Designs and Patents Act 1988, s 17(2).
3 Copyright Act 1956, s 36(1); Copyright, Designs and Patents Act 1988, s 90(3).

What is protected?

4.4 Let us consider the labour, skill and judgement expended by an author in the creation of a literary work.

Often there is an original manuscript in which the work is written down. The finished article, a printed work, will be derived from this manuscript. Even if the original manuscript is destroyed, the intellectual property right or copyright in the work remains in every subsequently published copy of it, just as it did in the original manuscript in which the work was inscribed. To understand where this property right lies it is useful to look at the history of production of the work. It first resides in the results of the original creative labour which was expended in producing the work. Any reproduction of that work is considered to be a reproduction of the original, and obviously the same property right exists in each and every copy of the original. For each copy of the original is equally the same work. This illustrates what is often called the 'intangible' nature of the right, in that the property right in the work is deemed to exist in every reproduction of the original even though the manuscript may no longer be in existence. That written manuscript was no more the work than its copies—all have the same legal status as the work. Theoretically the same is true where the work is reproduced in a different medium. If the work is converted into binary electronic pulses and fixed on a magnetic disc capable of being read by a computer, this conversion from one medium to another is equally the work, as reproduced. Therefore, such a conversion is not permissible without the consent of the owner of the intellectual property right in the original work. Further, any reproduction of the contents of the magnetic disc upon which the work is fixed, will be a reproduction of the work. Thus the intellectual property right in the work can be seen to exist independently of the medium in which it was originally expressed and to reside equally in any subsequent medium in which it is reproduced.

4.5 Having looked at the theoretical basis of the property right, let us now turn to the actual legal right granted. The Copyright Act 1956, section 1, defines its legal nature as 'the exclusive right . . . to do and to authorise other persons to do, certain acts in relation to that work . . .'[1] Note that the Act does not say that the owner must do something with the work. The right granted here is in the nature of a negative right to prevent others from doing something with his work, namely, to reproduce it. The Act sets out the 'restricted acts' which only the owner may do in respect of the work. They are:

(*a*) reproducing the work in any material form;
(*b*) publishing the work;
(*c*) performing the work in public;
(*d*) broadcasting the work;
(*e*) causing the work to be transmitted to the subscribers of a diffusion system;
(*f*) making an adaptation of the work, to include translations, and the creation of versions of the work.[2]

The new Act provides that the owner of the copyright in a work has the exclusive right:

(*a*) to copy the work;
(*b*) to issue copies of the work to the public;

(*c*) to perform, show or play the work in public;
(*d*) to broadcast the work or include it in a cable programme service;
(*e*) to make an adaptation of the work or do any of the above in relation to an adaptation.

The above acts are referred to as the 'acts restricted by the copyright'.[3]

The underlying right is the same in each case. It is a right of the owner to prevent the reproduction of his work by others. In most cases this is an exclusive right to reproduce that work for a period of up to the life of the author plus 50 years from the end of the calendar year in which the author died.[4] This is retained in the new Act which additionally provides for a new 50 year period of copyright protection for computer-generated works from the date they are made.[5]

The new Act provides for the following additional rights under section 2(2) in relation to certain descriptions of copyright work. Thus new moral rights are conferred as follows in favour of the author, director or commissioner of a work, whether or not he is the owner of the copyright:

(*a*) the right to be identified as the author or director (s 73);
(*b*) the right to object to derogatory treatment of the work (s 80);
(*c*) the right to privacy of certain photographs or films (s 85).

Section 84 of the new Act retains the right under the old Act to object to a false attribution of authorship of a work.

1 Copyright Act 1956, s 1(1).
2 Ibid, s 2(5).
3 Copyright, Designs and Patents Act 1988, s 16(1).
4 Copyright Act 1956, s 2(3).
5 Copyright, Designs and Patents Act 1988, s 12(3).

Subsistence

4.6 The main rules governing the creation, subsistence and, to some extent, dealings in copyright, were contained in the Copyright Act 1956 as amended in subsequent legislation. It sets out clearly the type of works which could qualify for copyright protection, and the criteria to be satisfied before copyright is said to subsist.[1] Unlike most other forms of intellectual property there is no provision for the registration of copyright interests. In common parlance it is said to be 'on-line'. Provided that the work satisfies the substantive legal requirements of the Act, it is automatically protected whether the owner is aware of it or not. This offers considerable advantages to owners but it can also pose problems for them as we shall see shortly. The anomaly with other intellectual property rights which do require registration arises as a result of the UK's membership of the Berne Convention of 1887, an international convention which prohibits the requirement of any formal registration of such rights in any of the states which are signatories to it.

1 Copyright Act 1956, ss 2, 3, 12, 13 and 14; Copyright, Designs and Patents Act 1988, s 1(1)(a)(b) and (c).

4.7 Under the old Act copyright subsisted in the following:
literary works
dramatic works
musical works
artistic works.

These are categorised under that Act as Part I works, relating to what is known as "authors" copyright.[1] The Act further provides for copyright to subsist in other works. These are of the type in which an entrepreneur may be said to have an interest, and they are:
sound recordings
cinematograph films
television broadcasts
sound broadcasts
cable programmes
published editions of works.

These fall under Part II of that Act.[2]

The new Act removes the distinction between Part I and Part II copyrights and makes copyright a property right which subsists in the following descriptions of work:

(*a*) original literary, dramatic, musical or artistic works;
(*b*) sound recordings, films, broadcasts or cable programmes; and
(*c*) the typographical arrangement of published editions.[3]

Section 3 of the new Act defines literary, dramatic and musical works confirming specifically that protection extends to

(*a*) a table or compilation
(*b*) a computer program.

This confirms the subsistence of copyright in computer programs and probably databases although these are not referred to as such.

1 Copyright Act 1956, ss 2 and 3.
2 Ibid, ss 12, 13 and 14.
3 Copyright, Designs and Patents Act 1988, s 1(1)(a), (b) and (c).

4.8 One of the requirements of the Act is that the creator of the original work is a 'qualified person'. This only means that he is a British subject or is resident or domiciled in the UK, not that he is qualified in any artistic or literary sense to create the work.[1] The new Act creates broadly similar provisions.[2]

1 Copyright Act 1956, s 1(5)
2 Copyright, Designs and Patents Act 1988, ss 153–162.

4.9 It is important to remember that copyright does not protect ideas as such, but only the expression of those ideas. Therefore it is crucial to ensure that the original work is fixed in some way in order to be able to invoke the protection granted by the law of copyright.[1] Under the old Act the work had to be first reduced to writing or some other material form. As we are talking about such works as literary, dramatic or musical works, this normally means being fixed in writing in a traditional medium, although protection extends to material forms other than the conventional concept of writing, such as to the electro-magnetic medium of the computer.[2] With the new Act copyright does not subsist in a literary, dramatic or musical work unless and until it is recorded, in writing or otherwise.[3]

1 Copyright Act 1956, s 49(4).
2 Copyright (Computer Software) Amendment Act 1985, s 2.
3 Copyright, Designs and Patents Act 1988, s 3(2).

4.10 One of the fundamental requirements for copyright to subsist is that the work must be original. Unfortunately the meaning of 'original', although referred to as a pre-requisite for the subsistence of copyright, was not defined in the old Act (nor under the new Act) and it is left for us to seek guidance as to its meaning from decisions taken by the courts to establish the subsistence of copyright in any given work and also to ascertain the scope of protection.

What we find here is that the test as to whether the work is original or not, is not to be understood in the sense that the idea behind the work is an original idea, but only that the way in which the idea is expressed materially is 'original'.[1] That is, the idea or ideas behind the work may have their basis in antiquity or be hackneyed or standard, and in a first sense not original at all, but if sufficient labour, skill and judgement has gone into an original (ie a different) expression of the idea, then in all probability copyright will be said to subsist in that work as 'originally' expressed in a second sense. Thus with copyright it is the labour involved in the creation of the original mode of expression which is the element of the work given protection; ideas, as such, being unprotectable.

Why is this? In the case of copyright, if there are to be any criteria for its subsistence, they must be ones which operate uniformly, which can be covered by general legal rules, and apply to the many different types of work specified by the legislature. Therefore the courts are not charged with making decisions as to whether a work contains a new or original idea, what its value might be, or whether the work has literary, musical, dramatic or artistic quality. Such questions would engage the courts in making difficult judgments on the aesthetic merit of the work, and would negate the underlying principle of the legislation which, as we have seen, is to protect the result of the labour involved in the creation of the work.

Thus despite references in the Acts to 'literary', 'musical', 'dramatic' and 'artistic' 'works'—language which is redolent of notions of the 'artistic' or 'aesthetic'—clearly the UK courts have elected to deal only with those matters which relate to the result of the expenditure of effort in the work originating from the party or parties claiming copyright. The qualities or goods which are being protected have been described or construed variously as skill, knowledge, labour, judgement, research and development, capital, pains, or taste. Copyright protection has been extended successfully to the results of such qualities, to examination scripts,[2] horse-race betting forms, football fixture lists,[3] railway time-tables,[4] and many other kinds of work which have been described as 'small change',[5]—ie their literary merit is minimal and in many cases non-existent.

The judicial decision to protect such non-artistic creations accords with Locke's labour theory. It is labour which gives title to and adds value to everything, and it is accordingly the results of labour expended in the expression of some original work in some tangible form which is protected under the law of copyright. The classic statement of the case is set out in a judgment of the 1930s, as relevant today as it was then, giving a clear judicial statement on the basis of the law of copyright.

> '. . . it is the product of the labour, skill and capital of one man which must not be appropriated by another, not the elements, the raw materials, if we may use that expression, upon which the labour, skill and capital of the first has been expended. To secure copyright for the product it is necessary that labour, skill and capital should be expended sufficiently to impart to the product some quality or character which the

raw material did not possess but which differentiates the product from the raw material.'[6]

1 *University of London Press Ltd v University Tutorial Press Ltd* [1916] 2 Ch 601.
2 Ibid at 608.
3 *Football League Ltd v Littlewoods Pools Ltd* [1959] Ch 637.
4 *H Blacklock & Co Ltd v C Arthur Pearson Ltd* [1915] 2 Ch 376.
5 Adolf Dietz, *Copyright Law in the European Community* (1978).
6 *MacMillan & Co v Cooper* (1923) LR 51 Ind App 109, PC.

The relevance of copyright today

4.11 Today most copyright works do not normally emanate from the pens of isolated individual authors, but subsist in the context of processes for the creation and production of consumable products or artefacts generated by industrial or other entrepreneurial concerns. Such works are often valuable industrially. As we shall see later, the law of copyright is, and continues to be, an effective tool, not only to protect the intellectual property rights of diverse industries, but to actually underpin their very existence. This is obviously where time, money, skill, judgement, labour and capital investment have been expended on the creation of a purely commercial product for a purely commercial end. The commercial importance of copyright increases with the new information technology industries such as computer software, in providing a cornerstone for their protection. As we shall see later the law operates in the field of computer software by applying its rules analogously with the literary work, both mediums having as their end products linguistic entities or possibly graphical features. This illustrates the versatility, extent, scope and potential of copyright today, but, even so, it is limited in its effectiveness by some of the latest developments of the new technologies.

4.12 Given the range, diversity and importance of the protection of investment in an innovative industrial context offered by copyright, those engaged in the creation, manufacture and production of new and innovative products or artefacts should consider carefully how best to maximise opportunities for using its provisions; for instance, they may not realise the considerable variety of works generated within or by the concern which could qualify for automatic copyright protection on the basis of their being either literary or artistic works.

It is not always easy to ascertain the value of such rights. Such works may have immediate application, in which case their value is readily ascertainable, or they may feature at a later date in the industrial concern's plans, in which case, although their value is inchoate and not therefore immediately ascertainable, it should not be underestimated. This might be the case, for example, with the creation of complex and sophisticated engineering drawings which, although designed for immediate use, may have been shelved for a time for any number of reasons. Though they may never be used at all by the owner, they may yet be badly needed by others operating in the same or a similar field. So although the concern may have no use for the work itself it could recoup its expenditure in its creation, or profit further, by permitting use of it by others who need it, upon an appropriate payment being made. All copyright works created by an industrial organisation should be regularly reviewed for value or potential value in terms of the recoupment of the costs of the company's production and profit, either through the exclusive right to reproduce or use its works or through the potential licensing of those rights for others to use.

Industrial artefacts protected by copyright

4.13 The following list of items gives some idea of the variety of works emanating from an industrial context which are afforded copyright protection as either literary or artistic works which therefore cannot be reproduced without the permission of the owner; designs, sketches, prototype models, moulds, matrices, photographs, plates, layouts, models, drawings, computer aided designs, codes, flow charts, paintings, negatives, prints, etchings, engravings, photographic films, typographical layouts, lists, formulae, brochures, leaflets, charts, diagrams, maps, notices, labels, logos, promotional literature, advertising materials, graphics, directories, etc.

All these enjoy automatic protection either as literary or artistic works. In the case of designs the owner may prefer to take advantage of the Registered Design Act of 1949 which exists specifically for the protection of pure design rights of which we shall speak later.

Authorship and ownership

4.14 Before moving on to the process of exploitation of copyright, let us look at the issue of ownership which occupies a position of fundamental importance, because it is only the owner of the copyright work who is entitled to exploit it. It is therefore clear that in any innovative concern the issue of ownership must be put beyond doubt.

The relationship of authorship to ownership is not always a simple one. As we have seen, copyright protection is accorded to those literary or artistic works originated by an industrial concern, upon which there has been a sufficient amount of skill, judgement etc expended, regardless of any aesthetic merit in the finished work. The author of such works is their first owner entitled to prevent others from using the work and he alone is able to exploit it. How can the owner of an industrial concern, investing in the creation of new products, ensure that all rights to the intellectual property in any literary or artistic works generated by his concern vest either in himself or in his concern? He must avoid finding himself in a position where there could be claims to ownership in that intellectual property other than his own. His first task is to identify with certainty all his entitlement to such works in order to avoid the possibility of future contention. Contention is often the result of neglecting this first step.

Let us look at the current position on legal entitlement. Section 4(1) of the old Act provides that it is the author of a work (whether literary or artistic) who is entitled to any copyright subsisting in the work, with some important exceptions to that rule. This is still the case under the new Act where 'author', in relation to a work, means the person who created it.[1] He is also the first owner.[2] Problems could arise with some types of work such as those which are commissioned. These could be relevant to a concern which augments the skills of its personnel by commissioning specific works from those who have the necessary skills from outside. Care is also needed in considering claims to joint copyright, as I show later, by describing the sort of circumstances which mostly give rise to them. It is obviously crucial then that the owner of an innovative industrial concern is aware of the different types of copyright interests which can arise within his particular industrial sector. Though in most cases ownership of copyright in various literary and artistic works is not in doubt, there will be exceptions. Initial care will save money and time in avoiding contention later.

The most important exception to the rule that the author of the work is entitled to any copyright subsisting in the work relates to employment. This exception has been retained under the new Act which states that 'where a literary, dramatic, musical or artistic work is made in the course of his employment, his employer is the first owner of any copyright in the work subject to an agreement to the contrary.'[3]

It is here that all parties should tread with care. Let us look at these rules in order to pin-point possible pitfalls. The old and the new legislation provide that where a work is created in the course of employment, then the copyright in that work automatically belongs to the employer—not to the individual or individuals who created it personally.[4] It is important to note a distinction, in both law and fact, in the form or type of services available to an industrial concern, which is relevant to the law of copyright. In the case of an employee, the employee normally operates under a contract of employment of service. He provides services, such as his labour, to his employer on a regular basis, in exchange for a salary or wages, in such a way that he is considered to be integral to that business. By contrast, an independent contractor provides services to a concern and although his services are also for the business, they are not said to be integral to it. In the first situation, where there is an employer/employee relationship, the employer can rely upon the legal presumption that any works in which copyright subsists, or which are created by his employee in the course of his employment, belong to him. Even so, in the world of what are called 'intangible' interests, such as intellectual property, it is best to leave nothing to chance. The employer ought to secure his rights by spelling out in a contract his proprietorial interests in any such created works.

Where services are provided by an independent contractor, and thus there is no employer/employee status to take advantage of, the proprietor of the concern should insist in the commissioning contract that any intellectual property rights in the literary or artistic works etc are assigned to him as representative of the concern on completion of the work under the contract. If this is not possible and he might not enjoy ownership of the works, he should ensure that he at least enjoys full and unfettered rights to use the work, for example by ensuring that he has a free licence to use the work for whatever purposes he requires. If he fails to take such precautions, he may later face difficulties in dealing with the copyright, either with title to it still being vested in the party commissioned or with having inadequate rights to its use. The reason why such precautionary measures need to be taken is that legally it is the party who has been commissioned who will be the author and thus first owner of the copyright. The old Act provided exceptions to this rule when the party commissioned was not deemed to be the first owner. That was where the commissioned work was a photograph, or the painting or drawing of a portrait, or the making of an engraving. In such cases the commissioning contract did not have to provide for the assignment over of the copyright in the finished work to the commissioner.[5] The new Act rationalises the law making it consistent by excluding these exceptions, so that in future in all commissioned works, ownership of copyright will reside in the author of the work.

The commissioner should now always ensure that copyright in the commissioned work vests in him in his contract with the author.

The maxim is to exercise care in dealing both with direct employees and where the materials are commissioned from outside.

1 Copyright, Designs and Patents Act 1988, s 9(1).
2 Ibid, s 11(1).
3 Copyright Act 1956, s 4; Copyright, Designs and Patents Act 1988, s 11(1).
4 Copyright Act 1956, s 4(4); Copyright, Designs and Patents Act 1988, s 11(2).
5 Copyright Act 1956, s 4(3).

Joint authorship and ownership

4.15 Care should be taken in the following situations, where endless disputes as to ownership ensue because of initial failure to take precautions.

A feature of copyright law is that it is possible for joint authorship and ownership to subsist in a single work. It is also possible for parties to collaborate in the joint creation of a single work yet for the interests of the parties in the copyright in such a work to be separate and distinct, eg where one party creates preliminary drawings for a piece of engineering equipment, and another creates production drawings from these. Insufficient attention at the right time to the question of ownership of works which are generated by more than one contributor or author often leads to complex questions of ownership. It is clearly better to face this issue squarely early rather than later and to establish some degree of certainty of the future rights and interests of the parties over the ownership and use of the copyright work.

4.16 Let us look at joint authorship and ownership. Joint authorship is defined in the old Act as 'a work produced by the collaboration of two or more authors in which the contribution of each author is not separate from the contribution of the other author or authors'.[1] This is retained in the new Act save that the word 'distinct' is now used instead of the word 'separate'. At the outset of any collaborative or joint venture which could result in a work of joint authorship, the parties concerned should establish clearly their future legal rights. This should be done in the light of the legal certainty that the rights of the parties are indivisible and that no co-owner might grant a licence for the exploitation of the whole work without the consent of the other co-owner or owners.[2] This is because the exploitation by one co-owner is likely to substantially diminish its value in the hands of the others and this would be considered unfair and inequitable.

Each contributor might wish to enjoy the right to exploit commercially the completed work either jointly with the other party, or independently of the other party without having to obtain the consent of that other party to do so. Though the completed product or work may be of little value at the date of its creation, obviously it could acquire considerable exploitable commercial value later. If the parties have not already clarified their proprietorial interests in the work, contentious claims to ownership and the exercise of exclusive rights over the intellectual property rights in the work could arise in the future. The maxim is to establish initially by contract some degree of certainty as to the division or otherwise of any future copyright interests.

1 Copyright Act 1956, s 11(3); Copyright, Designs and Patents Act 1988, s 10(1).
2 *Powell v Head* (1879) 1 2 Ch D 686.

4.17 Just as likely to lead to contention is a situation where there has been collaborative effort in the creation of a single work but the skill and judgement of the parties has been expended in such a way as to produce two entirely separate copyrights. To refer back to the example of production drawings produced by one party which are based on the earlier drawings of another party, here there could be two copyrights in existence, one in respect of the preliminary drawings and one of the production drawings. In consequence there could be distinct and separate authors and owners. It would be prudent, to obviate any confusion or uncertainty as to the precise ownership of either copyright work based on the joint but separate inputs, to deal early with this issue.

In conclusion, to avoid the possibly litigious consequences of the above, the parties at the outset of any collaborative venture should establish the precise ownership of the individual input of each of the parties, determining if this is to remain a separate or individual identity, and whether at the end of the day, the copyright and any other intellectual property rights are to be held jointly.

CHAPTER 5

Copyright exploitation

Introduction

5.1 In the previous chapter it became clear that given the range of industrial assets protected by, and the value of copyright to, the modern industrial innovator, it is vital to establish at the outset title to the intellectual property rights in any copyright work. Now we will examine further why this is so. Only where a party enjoys unequivocal title to the rights can he exercise these by exploiting them commercially. Obviously any doubts as to his rights mean he cannot use them properly. The old Act and the new Act set out clearly negative and positive rights accruing to the owner of the copyright, as we have seen (para 4.5).[1] It is important to note that the right to prevent others from doing something in relation to the work, although couched in negative terms, clearly contemplates these as being active and not in any way dormant rights. These personal property rights in a work can enjoy a valuable and tradable commercial currency. The rules relating to the status and operation of these rights are contained in section 36 of the old Act and these are effectively retained under section 90 of the new Act. Section 36 of the old Act provides that the right created is:[2]

(1) personal or movable property;
(2) transmissible by assignment, testamentary disposition, or by operation of law.

The section further provides that in any assignment or transfer of the rights, the copyright owner may limit what he is transferring to the following:[3]

(*a*) one or more of all the classes of restricted acts eg reproduction in a material form, broadcasting etc;
(*b*) one or more countries where he enjoys an exclusive right;
(*c*) only a part of the term of the copyright period.

Copyright is thus divisible, in that several interests can subsist in the same work with the possibility of each interest being separately exploited, in any combination or computation of act, territory or period.

It is possible to provide by agreement for the vesting of future copyright, that is, copyright which will or may come into existence at a later date. Thus, where a work has been commissioned under such an agreement, when it is created it will automatically vest in the commissioner.[4]

1 Copyright Act 1956, s 1(1)(2); Copyright, Designs and Patents Act 1988, s 16(1).
2 Copyright Act 1956, s 36(1).
3 Copyright Act 1956, s 36(2); Copyright, Designs and Patents Act 1988, s 90.
4 Copyright Act 1956, s 37; Copyright, Designs and Patents Act 1988, s 91.

Commercial copyright licensing

5.2 It is not possible in a book of this nature to look at the full extent and variety of licensing which takes place in the diverse world of the copyright based industries, as each of these industries over the years has produced commercial usages peculiar to itself (such as the music and publishing industries). I am going to concentrate upon what is often termed 'industrial' or 'commercial' copyright licensing. These terms are used to describe the sort of licensing activities engaged in by commercial concerns negotiating at arm's length on a commercial market footing, for the exploitation and use of intellectual property rights in the fields of technology and manufacturing. Such licensing arrangements might be complex, and may often incorporate licences for the exploitation of other intellectual property rights such as patents, trade marks and know-how, as part of a general package deal.

Industrial or commercial licensing is often advantageous to the small to medium-sized enterprise. First, it enables it to license-in the technology, skills and know-how of others without having to go to the trouble of using its often limited resources in the creation and development of that technology itself. The licensee may be able to rely upon a degree of ongoing or continuing technical support from the licensor. It is the mutual aim of the licensor and the licensee in this case to achieve beneficial exploitation of the intellectual property right.

Second, it is often a financially attractive proposition for the company to license out its own industrial copyrights to others. Indeed commercial licensing of industrial copyright, such as designs, production drawings, computer software, etc, forms a considerable proportion of what is generally termed 'technology transfer', and it is largely in this context that I deal with the intellectual property rights in copyright exploitation.

5.3 In chapter 2 on patent exploitation we dealt with the sort of licences which could be employed in the exploitation of patents, and broadly similar types may be used in exploiting copyright works. There are no provisions for licences of right or for the compulsory licensing of copyright works. We shall look at the sort of clauses which should be considered for inclusion in a typical industrial copyright licence later (para 5.12).

Assignments

5.4 In some cases an assignment of the total intellectual property rights by the author of the work to another might be more appropriate than a licence grant. For example, if the other party is bearing the total risk of the commercial exploitation of the work, an assignment of the sum total of rights of the owner of the work might be advisably transferred to that party rather than limited or fragmentary rights. This is often the case in the publishing industry. The publisher bears most risk in the exploitation of the work. Therefore he normally requires an assignment of all the author's rights in the work if it is already completed, or all future rights if the work is yet to be written. The author of a work is not in a position to exploit the commercial potential of his work and so he relies upon the capital, capacity and commercial know-how of the publisher.

Advantages of licensing

5.5 The licensing mechanism, used extensively in the exploitation of patents and trade marks, is a device which has been adapted to satisfy the intellectual property and technology transfer requirements of the commercial and industrial world and this applies equally to industrial copyright.

The advantages of licensing are as follows:

(1) For the owner it has the advantage of allowing him to retain ownership of his rights, while exploiting them without losing control.
(2) He can maximise their value by dividing and delimiting their exploitation according to his commercial needs.
(3) The licensing arrangements can be as flexible and adaptable as commercial requirements allow and moulded to suit the

necessarily varied and often complex commercial requirements of the parties.

(4) If there is envisaged a long-term association between the parties, whereby mutual support is given to get a particular product incorporating the copyright work on to the market, the burden of any costs expended on research, development, production exploitation and eventual distribution can be shared. Because licensing transfers only limited rights to the licensee it does not follow that the arrangements are only temporary or fleeting.

(5) The owner can, by negotiating for an initial lump sum payment from a licensee who is in the privileged position of taking an exclusive licence, recoup on his R&D costs sooner rather than later.

(6) He can usefully license copyright materials for which he has no use himself but upon which R&D costs have been expended.

(7) The licensor and licensee gain access to each other's expertise and to possible other forms of intellectual property, thereby encouraging a cross-fertilization of technology transfer.

(8) Developments by either party based on the original intellectual property right licensed might pass in either direction, thus increasing the value of the asset for their mutual benefit. The licensor can make provision that he enjoys the advantage of any enhancements arising out of the licensee's permitted use of the property, the accumulation of which might profitably then be licensed on to his other licensees.

(9) In allowing the licensee use of his rights, the licensor gains access to the licensee's existing retail, export and distribution facilities and outlets. Thus the licensor's products penetrate into his licensee's marketing network and markets, preparing the way for future penetration of the market with additional products.

(10) Once penetration of new markets has taken place, the licensor is in a good position to develop goodwill and reputation there for his goods, helped on further when the licensee is permitted to use the licensor's trade marks on the goods.

(11) Where the owner of an industrial copyright is unable to satisfy the demand for goods incorporating a copyright work, by licensing others he can make use of their spare manufacturing capacity and in this way satisfy the market demand.

(12) Where innovative concerns are engaged in the same or similar fields of research, or in the production of the same or similar products, cross-licensing arrangements might be

useful, even with competitors in the same market, provided that this does not offend the principles of competition established through European Community legislation which we have dealt with briefly in chapter 2 on patent exploitation. After all, research and development in many industries is often substantial and the burden of this necessary expenditure can inhibit the proper development of new or innovative products. To reduce these costs the parties concerned could either license each other for the use of individual intellectual property rights, or alternatively, enter into a cross-licensing arrangement allowing each party access to, and use of, an agreed selection of intellectual property rights. The latter arrangement can reduce the problem of duplication in the pre-competitive stages of development, can reduce costs in research and development, and is convenient, in that it avoids the need for the parties to enter into new and individual licensing arrangements on each occasion when an industrial copyright is required. The arrangement can be as expansive, or as restrictive, as the parties require. All the usual benefits which accrue under individual licensing arrangements will apply.

5.6 If possible licensing should play an active part in any organisation's marketing strategy. Indeed in many industries the whole profit base lies in the ability to create and maintain revenue generated through the royalty stream derived from licensing. The advantages of the licensing in or out of industrial copyright apply equally to patents, know-how and trade marks. The rights are all different in form and substance, being designed to protect different types of interests, and the licensing arrangements will reflect this. Of course there are often areas of substantial similarity in the general licensing situation, and common terms and conditions contained in the licence agreement itself and many of the clauses already discussed in patent exploitation will apply equally to the licensing of industrial copyright. It is time to see what is involved in the exploitation of copyright and so review those clauses germane to the nature or quality of the particular intellectual property right of copyright, and which should therefore be specifically included in the licence agreement to protect it.

Licensing

5.7 Now let us examine the position of the copyright owner prepared to license out some of his technology, in the form of an industrial copyright licence. As with most intellectual property rights, at this stage they are probably at their most vulnerable because they effectively move out of the control of their owner into the hands of another party who is permitted or authorised to do certain acts in respect of that property. But for being authorised by the owner, such acts would constitute an infringement, actionable by the owner. Because of their more nebulous nature, copyright works are possibly more vulnerable than other intellectual property rights.

5.8 We saw in the licensing of patents that the subject matter of the licence together with ownership of the rights and any interests in the property could be clearly ascertained by the state of the Patent Office register. Both parties to the licensing arrangements could be fairly well appraised of the extent and limitations of the property right in which the interests were being granted. This is not so with copyright where the rights can subsist automatically and where there is no registration involved. The copyright owner enjoys the exclusive right to reproduce the work or to do any of the restricted acts already mentioned, but he is not enjoined to do any of these acts. Because the rights operate negatively he can prevent others from doing these acts. Further, copyright, as we have seen, is divisible. There may be one copyright work, such as a novel, but the owner of the intellectual property in that work can divide this up into as many rights as are granted to him under the provisions of the Act. Thus he might divide the interests up into, for example, film rights, broadcasting rights and so on, and he can also divide the use of these rights in terms of territory, and in terms of duration. He is also capable of granting various degrees of exclusivity of the use of each fragmented interest. There is thus a considerable range of permutations available to the copyright owner as to the manner in which he can exploit his interests. However, he must proceed with care in any licensing situation to ensure that what is granted is not the whole gamut of interests in the work but only that which is sufficient for the precise purposes of the licensee and no more. The copyright owner's interests are automatically protected by the law of copyright; therefore any unauthorised use of his work will be an infringement of his rights. He enters into licensing arrangements in order to set out with a degree of certainty the restrictions which he is imposing in respect of the use of those rights. Were he to allow a general use of the copyright work, then the licensee would be allowed to use the copyright material in any way he thought fit. With such a considerable variety of divisible rights available to him, the owner of these rights, if careful, can ensure that each division generates profitable royalties. In each of his licences he is basically saying that the grant is only for this or that specific purpose. Any of the other restricted acts constitute separate rights which must necessarily be the subject of separate negotiations and payment.

5.9 Therefore it is important, in order for him to maintain control of his intellectual property rights, that the copyright owner ensures in the licence grant that he spells out with clarity the precise limitations of the use to which the work may be put. Failure to do so could result in the licensee using the copyright work in a manner not envisaged or contemplated by the owner, resulting in use of the work without any corresponding royalty payment, and subsequent lowering of actual and potential revenues. This aspect of use which we shall look at shortly (para 5.12) is particularly important for those industries where there is considerable dependence on the royalty stream from the licensing of their products, as for example in the computer software industry.

5.10 Before proceeding to look at the risks inherent in the licensing of industrial copyright, it is important that similar pre-licensing precautions advocated in the chapter on patents should be implemented. The valuable copyright work will be passing from the hands of the owner into the hands of another party who will to a certain extent be entrusted with its use for a limited period of time. The same investigations as to the commercial viability, track record, ability to perform and general trustworthiness of the potential licensee need to be established. This is particularly so where there is to be the grant of an exclusive licence and where the licensee's commercial credentials and ability to perform the terms of the licence are crucial to the successful exploitation of the copyright work.

5.11 As with patent licensing, negotiations are often lengthy and protracted. In the case of industrial copyright licensing, the potential licensee is concerned to ensure that the copyright work which he requires is in fact adequate for his purpose. For example this could mean the inspection of the running of equipment based upon copyright engineering drawings or designs, in the verification of formulae or detailed instructions, or the demonstration of an item of computer software. In such cases, and in any event as a matter of course, the potential licensee should be required to enter into a contractually binding confidentiality agreement, obliging him not to disclose any of the information imparted to him during or at any time after the cessation of negotiations. As we have already seen, there is anyway an implied obligation of confidentiality imposed upon the recipient of secret information in circumstances such as these. It is better not to rely on rather vague assumptions of confidentiality in respect of the owner's trade secrets when the certainty of legal obligation can be imposed by a fairly standard contractual document. Confidentiality should be imposed upon the negotiating party, for as we have seen, he may acquire all the information he wants during the course of negotiations and demonstration, decline to take a licence, and use that information, some or all of which he may subsequently claim was, as far as he was concerned, not the subject of implied confidentiality.

The licence

5.12 Let us assume that the parties have now reached agreement and the owner of the copyright work is prepared to grant a licence limited to a specific use of the work to the licensee. Being a contractual document, the licence contains many of the standard contract licence clauses which we looked at under patent licensing (para 2.11). The commercial credibility of the licensee having been established, the licence should proceed in the usual way with clauses clearly setting out the parties to be contractually bound.

I intend looking at only those clauses which I consider to be germane to the protection and maintenance of the value of the copyright work.

(1) RECITALS

In the recitals to the licence the intentions of the parties should be clearly set out, along with a statement as to the proprietorship of the licensor of the copyright work. The works to be licensed should be appended to the agreement in a schedule and properly identified. If, for example, the work to be used is a piece of computer software which is to be restricted to use on a particular type of machine and no other, then this too should be identified in the schedule. It is crucial to ensure that the work is correctly identified to avoid confusion and possible future contention.

(2) EXCLUSIVITY

(a) Non-exclusive licence

We have already mentioned the non-exclusive licence. This is appropriate where the proprietor wishes to grant a licence permitting someone to do all or any of the restricted acts without allowing him any degree of exclusive use of the work. Such a licence may be oral or in writing.

The effects of the grant are as follows:

(1) the licensor might grant further licences of the same kind and exploit the interest himself, in which case there is no degree of exclusivity granted;
(2) the licensee is given no proprietory interest in the copyright work, in which case he could not sue for any infringement of copyright of the work.

(b) Sole licence

Here the licensor may decide that he should allow the licensee a limited degree of exclusivity of use of the copyright work. Under a sole licence agreement, only the licensor and the licensee may exploit the work.

(c) Exclusive licence

This type of licence must be in writing as the rights conferred by it are of a substantial nature, and are akin to a proprietorial interest in the work itself. For unlike a sole licence, where the licensor is not excluded from exercising his rights of exploitation of the copyright, an exclusive licence allows the licensee to do certain of the restricted acts to the exclusion of all others including the licensor.

Its effects are as follows:

(1) the licensee has unlimited rights of exclusivity in the use of the copyright against third parties and the licensor;
(2) he enjoys rights akin to the transfer or assignment for the duration of the licence;
(3) he can sue in his own name if there is an infringement of the copyright work without joining in the owner to the action and he can claim the same remedies.

The main legal and commercial reasons for the grant of any degree of exclusivity have already been explored in chapter 2 on patent exploitation, and they will be relevant in the licensing of industrial copyright works.

The clause on exclusivity might include provision for the sub-licensing of the licensee's subsidiaries, or possibly others, and the licensor should ensure that the licensee is made responsible for any breaches of the sub-licences granted. In the case of subsidiaries, the licensor should ensure so far as is possible that the licensee is in direct control of his subsidiaries. Alternatively, he could enter into direct contractual licences with them on a principal to principal basis. The licensor should ensure that he maintains as much control as possible over the use of his copyright and that any other parties using the work do so only under the authority of a licence.

(3) SCOPE OF THE LICENCE

Perhaps the most important clause in any industrial copyright licence, bar payment, relates to the right of use of the copyright work to be granted to the licensee. The grant made is the authorisation by the owner of the copyright in the work, to allow the licensee to use that work in such a way which would otherwise be illegal, but for the grant. We have seen that copyright is divisible, therefore it is normal that the owner will make a limited grant to the licensee to use the work in a specific way. By dividing the exploitation of his work, the owner can multiply the number of commercial opportunities available to him, and increase his licensing options. What type of licence is granted should be determined on largely commercial grounds based upon the type of copyright work, the market, the licensee's requirements and capacity to successfully exploit that market, and, at the end of the day, the return on investment which the licensor hopes to achieve through the generation and payment of royalties.

Therefore the licensor should take care in each licence grant to establish certainty as to the limit, extent and scope of the right granted, as only in this way will he be able to ensure an orderly division of his rights under his marketing policy. The rights granted normally relate to the use or reproduction of the work. A precise grant of rights reduces the possibility of there being any ambiguity in respect of those rights. The licensee must be made fully aware that use other than that contained in the grant is a breach of the terms of the licence leading to its immediate termination. He must be made aware that this leaves him open to an action for infringement of the copyright owner's rights based on unauthorised use.

(4) DELIVERABLE ITEMS

We referred to the copyright items to be scheduled (head (1) above). Provision could be made for the delivery of these into the possession of the licensee for his use. A requirement for the delivery of original drawings or designs should be resisted, as these are the vital proof of evidence of proprietorship; any use should be made of copies only.

(5) PAYMENTS

We have already looked at the legal principles and mechanisms involved in establishing the value of a licence, under patents. Now let us consider all the commercial factors which must be taken into account in the exploitation of industrial copyright works.

What commercial and other factors should be taken into account in the valuation of a licence? To answer this question we have to look at the valuation from both the licensor's and the licensee's point of view. Unless there is a history of a course of dealings between the parties or the licensor is in a position to dictate terms to the licensee, possibly because of his market dominance, the valuation of the licence will be the subject of negotiation between the parties.

Let us look at some of the considerations which will affect the value of the licence.

(1) The value of the licence revolves around the particular item of intellectual property owned by the licensor. His right as we have seen is to prevent others from using it, and although his right is termed an exclusive right, it operates negatively to prevent others from using it. The licensee is paying the licensor for the permission to use the intellectual property on the basis that to use it otherwise would be illegal and leave him open to legal action by its owner. He obtains the consent of the owner upon payment to do all or some of the restricted acts.

In the case of patents the exclusive right was to work or use an invention, whether this was a product or a process. In those cases the calculations for payment may be based on a number of factors, but they will revolve initially around the basic principle of use and intensity of use of the invention. Copyright gives a reproduction right, so again, although there is the possibility of different formulae to be applied for payment, this is normally calculated on the intensity of reproduction of the work.

(2) Why does the licensee wish to use the licensor's copyright? Normally it is because he is unable to produce or create an equivalent of that copyright work for himself. This may be because he does not have the skills, know-how, facilities or capabilities himself. By taking a licence from the licensor he obviates the need to go to the expense of creating that copyright work. But for the licensor's work, he might not be able to function or proceed further in his business. He has access to something which would otherwise be denied him and which might be of considerable value to him.

(3) Factors which will regulate the amount which the licensor

can charge the licensee for access and use of the copyright work will depend upon the market for that type of work. Clearly if there is only one of these works, then the licensor is in a strong position in terms of what he can charge a licensee, especially if there is to be any degree of exclusivity granted. If there are a variety of these works in a highly competitive market, such as a software package to do a particular type of job, what he can charge is considerably reduced by the presence of a strong field in which there are a number of functional equivalents which might do the job equally as well, and from which the licensee can choose. In this case the licensee will not be restricted in his choice of producer and he is able to choose from a wide range of equivalent software products.

(4) If the copyright work is of limited application and the licensee wishes to exercise some degree of exclusivity over its use then he will have to pay accordingly for the privilege and the licensor in this case is often in a position to charge fees for the negotiation of the rights of use. He may also negotiate for the payment of a non-returnable lump sum in order to recoup his costs early rather than wait for revenues generated by royalties.

(5) Having appraised and got some idea of the value of the licence in market terms, it is crucial to establish at the earliest possible time, first, the use to which the work is to be put and second, the intensity of that use.

(i) The use to which it is to be put

It must be established early on whether the specific use to which the work is to be put constitutes a reproduction of the work. It is upon this basis that the copyright owner bases his charge. Each time there is reproduction of the work in a material form then the legitimate right to charge for that reproduction arises. Reproduction of the work need not necessarily be in the same medium as the original, as the Act protects the work from unauthorised reproduction in any material form.

Further, any adaptation of the work, including a translation, is a restricted act and will constitute a reproduction of the work and must be paid for accordingly.[1]

Therefore if the licensor is to be able to fully exploit his copyright work he must establish: (i) what precisely is meant by reproduction of the work in a material form; (ii) the medium or mediums in which it is to be reproduced and used, and (iii) whether the licensee is to be allowed to adapt the work or not. The licensee must be made aware that any of the above activities triggers the provisions for the payment of royalties.

(ii) The intensity of use

The copyright work might be either reproduced per se, as with a text or graphic work, or it might be incorporated in a product of some kind, such as a design for an engine component.

As a general rule of thumb, the owner of the industrial copyright work, works to the established principle of charging a royalty of around 10% of the net selling price of the reproduced work or all articles incorporating the copyright work; that is, the licensee's gross selling price less his reasonable costs involved in the production of that article.

The other provisions as to the payment of lump sums or other payments, outlined in chapter 2 on patent exploitation (para 2.11), could also be relevant in establishing the value of the licence.

Other factors which may be taken into account in determining the value of a licence are as follows:

(1) the type of licence, ie exclusive etc, and whether it is in conjunction with a trade mark, patent, or know-how licence;
(2) what protection is available for the product;
(3) what precedents there are in the market for the licensing of this particular product;
(4) the market conditions as to size, demand, competition etc;
(5) third party competition with the licensee;
(6) the value to the product which the licensee brings with him to the table, such as further capital outlay, a distribution network, or a manufacturing capability;
(7) what the market will take in terms of the cost of the product, that is, whether too high a licence cost will depress the market for those goods, which will be in neither party's interests;
(8) any further burdens which may be assumed by the licensee, such as advertising and marketing the product;
(9) the actual cost of the licensor's development;
(10) any costs borne by the licensor in upgrading the product, such as software;
(11) any policing costs incurred in monitoring the licence;
(12) the traditional royalties paid in the business;
(13) the anticipated sales volumes;
(14) any problems in respect of possible or potential litigation;
(15) the possible obsolescence of that particular technology.

The above are just some of the areas which must be considered by the licensor and licensee in the attempted valuation of the licence.

It must be borne in mind that the owner of the copyright work cannot rely upon any implied terms of the licence that his licensee will exploit the work to the full. Therefore if he wants to protect his royalty and revenue stream, and indeed if it is an exclusive licence, he ought to contractually oblige the licensee to either use his best endeavours to exploit the work, or achieve a minimum royalty (secured by payment to the licensor in advance), otherwise the licence will terminate. Thus, in the case of an exclusive license, if the minimum royalty is not met in the licensee's exploitation of the copyright work, the licensor can terminate the contract and license elsewhere.

(6) AUDIT

Having ascertained a fair and reasonable valuation of the licence and the mechanism for the payment of royalties, the licensor now relies upon the licensee for their proper payment. He now finds himself in a rather passive role given that his intellectual property is being exploited by someone else who will be selling the product. It is the licensee who in effect interprets the payment provisions of the licence unilaterally, making payments to the licensor himself or most likely through someone who played no part in the original negotiations and who relies upon his interpretation of the licence. This could cause considerable misunderstanding and the licensor may find that he is not being paid what is due to him. For example, the payment clause may be interpreted by the licensee's accounts department, who may mistakenly interpret how to calculate what is to constitute gross or net sales of the product and thus the precise amount of royalty due. What can the licensor do about this?

An internal audit system should be set up to ensure that the statements received from the licensee correspond with the payment mechanism. Those responsible for payment and receipt of royalties should communicate on an ongoing basis so that if there is any change in, for example, the licensee's accounting system, it cannot in any way act to the licensor's detriment. Such monitoring of the payments procedure will assist in the elimination of errors, reduce the chance of misinterpretation, and in some cases counteract negligence, for example, in the case of the licensee placing unallowable expenses against royalties. The licensor may require the submission of detailed accounts where, for example, there are different territories, or where there are separate provisions for the deduction of expenses set against gross sales.

In the licence itself, there should be reserved the right to receive proper audited accounts of the sales of the licensee's products incorporating the copyright work, to order an independent inspection of the licensee's books, and to enter on to his premises.

These provisions protect the owner from unscrupulous parties who may be employing the work in a manner not permitted under the terms of the licence. At the very least it will go some way towards deterring the licensee from operating outside the agreed terms of his licence. The owner should reserve the right to terminate the licence forthwith in the event that there is discovery of discrepancies. It is desirable that there is a degree of mutual trust in any licensing situation but in order to protect his royalty stream and his business he ought to take all precautions in order to ensure that he is paid what is legitimately his due.

By taking the precautions of binding the licensee contractually to keep himself fully appraised of the exploitation of his intellectual property right, and in implementing an internal system of audit, the licensor goes some way towards achieving the following:

(i) he gains management information about the exploitation of his intellectual property;
(ii) he maximises his royalty income;
(iii) by maintaining a high protective profile he is seen to be aware of his valuable intellectual property, thus ensuring the maintenance of its value and reducing the risk of its being diminished or even negated.

(7) QUALITY CONTROL

Control of the quality of reproduction can be as important in industrial copyright licensing as it is in patents. Whether or not this is exercised depends very much upon the agreement between the parties and will depend upon the degree of involvement which the licensor must necessarily have in the activities of the licensee where, for example, the appearance of the finished product is important. If use of the owner's trade mark is to be made on the finished product, then the licensor will be concerned to ensure the maintenance of the standard of quality of that product. In this case the owner of the copyright and trade mark needs to protect his intellectual property rights by ensuring that the licensee meets his standard quality control requirements for the production of the goods. In such a case the licensee ought to be contractually obliged to regularly submit samples of the manufactured product incorporating the copyright work to him for inspection. If he fails to meet the licensor's set standards, the licensor must have the right to terminate the licence, not only for the production of the goods, but for use of any trade mark as well. This is because the production of inferior goods which are not up to the owner's standard, and which are then sold with the owner's trade mark or name on them, could seriously weaken and damage the owner's valuable reputation in those goods which he has built up in a particular market. We shall look at the commercial role, function and value of trade marks in the next chapter.

Swift action ought to be taken to protect intellectual property rights, and so limit any damage caused.

(8) TERMINATION

As with most commercial contractual agreements, provision should be made for the possibility of early termination of the agreement, and for the obligations and liabilities of the parties each to the other upon that event to be set out clearly. The licensor should insist that he has the right to terminate the agreement upon the happening of any events which might harm or prejudice his intellectual property rights. This includes such matters as the failure to pay royalties, failure to maintain quality or production standards, or use of the property in an unauthorised way. To reduce the possibility of any further damage being caused, he should require the licensee to immediately return all drawings, designs, etc and to undertake not to use them again without the authorisation of the owner. There should be similar provisions and undertakings inserted in the licence in respect of any trade mark used.

The prudent licensor should ensure that any obligations of confidentiality in respect of any trade secrets or know-how continue to operate and to bind the licensee, after the licence has terminated.

1 Copyright Act 1956, s 2(5) and (6); Copyright, Designs and Patents Act 1988, s 21.

Monitoring the licence

5.13 What was said about the importance and significance of monitoring and maintaining the licence in respect of patents is equally true of the licensing of industrial copyright. Given that there is no public register showing a definitive statement of the intellectual property rights of the owners of copyright, those parties are to some extent at a disadvantage in terms of their claims not only to the subsistence and ownership of those rights, but as to their exact extent. As pointed out, copyright is by its very nature nebulous and care must be taken in ensuring that the owner of the rights expressly asserts his claim to his rights, is seen to be aware of their value, and takes stringent precautions to protect them. This establishes the owner with a high protective profile in respect of his intellectual property rights which in turn can act as a deterrent to a would-be infringer.

CHAPTER 6

Copyright protection and maintenance

Introduction

6.1 We have looked at the fundamental nature of copyright, the legal requirements for its subsistence and ownership, and methods of commercial exploitation. A greater awareness and understanding of the nature of copyright will go some way towards encouraging the protection of those valuable creations which the innovative enterprise might never have considered being capable of protection. This chapter draws together the threads of the earlier chapters and prescribes some fairly straightforward measures a concern should take, which are designed not only to heighten awareness of the value of copyright, but at the same time to assist in the protection of works generated by it. The special characteristics of copyright mean that measures must be taken over and above those necessary in respect of intellectual property rights which can be registered, and a securer environment is required for its protection and maintenance. Our question now is, what are the risks, and how can they be minimised?

In order to understand how to minimise the risks we need to look at the general workings of the principles of the law of copyright within a general industrial, innovative and commercial context, because the substantial majority of works emanate from an industrial source. Indeed the law of copyright exists primarily for the protection of those who have invested in the exploitation of copyright works. Copyright is essentially an entrepreneurial right. It is not possible here to cover the full spectrum of copyright interests which have developed as esoteric embellishments on the general law of copyright; however the main principles of protection for all such cases can be gleaned from an examination of copyright in the industrial and commercial context, which is our main interest.

6.2 As we saw before, the language of the 1956 Act and the new Act seems, misleadingly, to indicate that the process of the production of copyright works is in the hands of an 'author' who produces a 'literary', 'artistic', 'dramatic' or 'musical' 'work', ie one having some sort of aesthetic appeal. Though appropriate in some cases, to discuss copyright within the context of aesthetics gives a misleading impression of its nature and function. It obscures the fact that most 'works' which are protectable under the law would not be considered to have any aesthetic appeal whatsoever. Copyright exists primarily to protect the labour and investment in commercial innovation even when it has little or no aesthetic appeal.

6.3 It is clear by now that problems might arise if there is a lack of certainty both in the subsistence and ownership of copyright in a work. This cannot be secured by a registration of rights because of the U K's adherence to the Berne Convention which, as we have seen, provides that copyright exists in any suitable work which is expressed in a material form, without any further requirement or formality. There is a form of registration available for designs provided by the Registered Designs Act 1949 which we shall need to examine later. But otherwise there is no such machinery available for copyright protection making it an intellectual property right very different from the other main intellectual and industrial property rights protected by statute under U K law, as we saw with patents, and which we will later see with trade marks. Rights in these are regulated under a strictly controlled registration system, operated by a government department which governs the creation, dealings and transmission of rights in inventions on the one hand, and the marks and names used in businesses and services on the other. This has distinct advantages. In both cases stringent, substantive legal and procedural criteria must be satisfied before the claimed rights in the invention or mark may be registered. There are opportunities available under the rules for third parties to object to claims. Thus with patents and trade marks there is a register of well-defined rights and interests which exists to reflect the true commercial state of play in so far as ownership, interests and dealings in those rights is concerned. Further, the registers are public and open to inspection by any party who may be interested in so doing, for whatever reason.

Therefore two main branches of intellectual property admit of registration systems where the owners of clearly identified rights may register these rights. Registration operates as a definitive statement of the subsistence, ownership and exclusivity of use of the rights as claimed. The owner of such rights is therefore granted a degree of certainty in respect of his intellectual property rights, and he has only to refer to the register for evidence of these in the face of any claim to the contrary.

6.4 In stark contrast to this seemingly neat and tidy system of ownership and dealings is the situation which prevails in respect of copyright interests and dealings. The advantages of copyright being 'on-line' is that normally, as it subsists automatically in a very wide range of works without the adducing of proof or evidence, and without having to satisfy any set of formal substantive legal or procedural rules, there are no registration costs involved. But the disadvantages are precisely the obverse of the advantages of those rights which can subsist under a registration system. There is no public authoritative statement of the subsistence of, or ownership of any rights in, any given literary or artistic work. There is no overt indication or statement as to proprietorial or other interests in a copyright work which might serve to distinguish it from any other form of work which may exist in the public domain and which may be freely usable. Therefore copyright works suffer from the fact that they do not have a distinctive protective profile. There is often inherent uncertainty as to whether a work is protected or whether it is in the public domain. It often takes a court case, or at least the threat of legal proceedings, to settle questions such as whether there is subsistence and/or ownership of copyright. Any innovative business which is concerned with the generation of valuable copyright works must ask itself whether it is sufficient for it to rely upon legislative provisions, given the inherent problems outlined above, or whether it can take measures to assert its claims to rights of ownership in the work to avoid doubt as to either subsistence or ownership.

Furthermore, a commercial advantage of the ability to register patents and trade marks is the deterrent effect which this might have on potential infringers. The rights owner often has only to point to the fact that he has an exclusive right registered for a would-be infringer to cease his infringing activities. The owner of the rights can point to a clear and definite claim to ownership of a particular monopoly right as evidenced by the state of the register. This is his protection. Unfortunately, as the high profile claim to a legitimate publically recognised right is lacking in the field of copyright, the owner may find himself hard-pressed to prove subsistence and ownership of the right in the work against a persistent and determined infringer.

Are there any measures which the copyright owner can take to minimise these risks?

6.5 We have seen that an innovative commercial organisation will be capable of generating a substantial portfolio of copyright works, usually in the form of 'artistic' 'works' such as drawings (including diagrams, maps, charts and plans) or designs, regardless of their artistic or aesthetic merit, and 'literary' works such as brochures, lists etc including tables or compilations. The volume of these works could be considerable if the innovative concern is involved in research and development and in the manufacture, sale, promotion and distribution of the finished product. For such a concern the proper policy relating to its copyright works should be to regard all works generated as potentially valuable and thus worth protecting as such.

The key to the proper protection of valuable copyright works is to promote an awareness of the subsistence of such rights. Certainly it is prudent for an organisation to engage in a 'good housekeeping' policy for its patents and trade marks but the same is especially true of its copyright works or materials because there is no equivalent of an external register of rights. An effective policy designed to heighten the awareness of rights of copyright within any concern should include:

(*a*) an analysis of all its current copyright works;
(*b*) recording procedures of most important works;
(*c*) a review of all documentation used in conjunction with such works, such as the permitted use of them by others.

Let us look a little more closely at (*a*), (*b*), and (*c*).

(A) ANALYSIS OF CURRENT RIGHTS

6.6 This involves isolating, identifying and categorising all literary or artistic works and making adequate provision for the recording of the most valuable—ie a good housekeeping exercise.

It will be helpful again to examine the creation of copyright works within the small to medium-sized enterprise. Such a concern may or may not have already organised itself into specialist departments, but it will be clear that a number of fairly distinct stages are involved, leading to the creation of any new product. For example, in the engineering industry or in any other manufacturing industry, the completed physical product will have started life as an idea which will have found expression in a series of sketches, leading to detailed designs, models, mock-ups, production drawings, photographs and finally to the three-dimensional product based upon those drawings and designs. Today, much of the design work is often generated by the operation of computers using customised software for this purpose. 'Artistic' copyright subsists in all of the above, even though the finished product may be of a purely functional nature. If a concern is engaged in the production of standard or customised computer software itself, again the finished product usually starts out life as a concept possibly expressed as an algorithm (a mathematical representation of the instructions to be given to the computer), or more probably as a flow-chart (a visual representation of the instructions to the computer to carry out certain functions). This is followed by a series of coded instructions, in a variety of media, leading to the finished product itself, which could be in the form of a magnetically coded tape or disc. 'Literary' or 'artistic' copyright may subsist in all or any of the above. We shall discuss the relevance of copyright to computer software in a later chapter.

If a concern is structured in such a way that it does or has decided to do all its own advertising, promoting and marketing of its products, it may employ staff specifically to produce literature for this purpose. The presentation of the product might include detailed descriptions of it, its specifications, and its mode of appearance or operation. It will doubtless be designed to appear in the most appealing way, possibly with distinctive packaging or get-up, perhaps with a fanciful name to ensure that it is highly distinctive of that particular product in the market.

The designs and the text for the promotional and advertising literature together with the graphics, photographs, layout, etc all enjoy on-line literary or artistic copyright protection. The distinctive appeal through the packaging or get-up of the company's products might well be protected either as a work of artistic copyright or as a registered design, or a trade mark which the concern might later wish to register. Similarly, the name given to the product to distinguish it from like products on the market, so that it is intimately associated with the manufacturing concern, could be a trade mark which helps to build up the reputation and good will of the business, and which could be protected by registration. Furthermore, the concern might have needed outside assistance to develop its products with the result that it has commissioned further artistic or literary copyright works.

Though not all works will be of commercial value given the vast amounts of material produced in the creation of even the simplest of products, it is a prudent exercise for each department at each stage of a product's life to screen the various works created to assess their potential value as exploitable copyright works. This exercise serves to heighten an awareness of the actual quantity of right-protectable material produced and its value. In some cases, as for example with computer software, the value of the work will be self-evident, the generation of revenue of the concern depending largely upon its ability to charge royalties for reproduction or use of the software. In other cases the work produced may not be of any great significance, but yet be of commercial value to other organisations. If so, as we have seen, it could produce licensing revenue. Finally, even if the organisation has no use for the work itself, it has the right under the law of copyright to prevent others from using it. Unlike patents and trade marks there is no general requirement on the owner of the copyright to actually use the work.

I now turn to the significance of assessing, categorising and recording of copyright works in order to minimise risks.

(B) RECORDING

6.7 It is wise to implement a fairly straightforward system of recording of the works. For instance, with production drawings, the date of creation, the author, the owner, and a reference on the drawing itself as to the claimed subsistence of copyright in the work should be inserted. The appending of a small 'c' in a circle conventionally suffices to bring to the attention of any who may have access to the work, that copyright is claimed in the work, that it is proprietorial, and that it may not be reproduced in any material form except with the express consent of the owner of the copyright. This puts all parties who come into contact with the works or indeed copies of the work 'on notice' that it is a copyright protected work. This applies as much to those employed within the concern as to those allowed access to view or use the work from outside. In fact the actual marking of works with this symbol does not have any significance legally in the UK but it does protect the work in any country which has ratified the Universal Copyright Convention 1952. This, like the Berne Convention, accords mutual protection of copyright works to the nationals of the countries which are signatories to it. It acts outside the UK as a form of symbolic shorthand indicating the claim to ownership to those dealing with the work and gives a sign to those in the UK as to its likely legal status.

6.8 Stemming from the inherent uncertainties already outlined in respect of both subsistence and ownership there are obviously already good practical reasons for implementing a recording system. To sum up:

(1) It operates to heighten an awareness within the organisation of the quantity, value and importance of the variety of artistic and literary works created. It also alerts them to the dangers of infringing the copyright of others.

(2) It promotes a higher protective profile both to those within the organisation and to those outside, effectively putting 'on notice' the proprietorial interests in the work to anyone having access to it. This helps negate any possible claim by an infringer of the work who copies it that he was unaware that it was a copyright protected work.

(3) It is evidence that the author considers that sufficient skill,

labour, judgement or capital has been expended in the creation of the work to justify a claim to the subsistence of copyright and the protection accorded to such works.

(4) It establishes the date of creation of the work. Duration of protection will be either for the life of the author plus 50 years, or 50 years from first publication or public distribution of the work. At the same time it establishes the author of the work, his status and, if he is an employee, that the owner of the copyright in the work is his employer.

(5) In some cases the date of recording could be significant later in evidence against another party attempting to register the copyright property as a trade mark, where the Trade Mark registry might require evidence of use before allowing registration. Points 3 and 4 are of particular legal significance in the establishment of a claim to subsistence and ownership of a copyright work, not only in terms of the claim to exclusive use of the work, but also as evidence against an alleged infringer. As mentioned in the case of those intellectual property rights which are registrable, ie patents and trade marks, the owner of those rights is able to point to at least prima facie evidence that his rights exist and that an alleged infringer's actions are an infringement of his monopoly to exclusive use of those rights. It is not so easy in the case of copyright. Here in any action against an alleged infringer the owner basically has to prove to the court the following:

(*a*) that there is an objective similarity between the copyright work and the alleged infringer's work,[1] and
(*b*) that there is a causal connection between the two, that is to say, that the infringer has had access of some kind to that work and has actually copied it.

This means that the owner has to prove copying. If the work is the same by sheer coincidence there has been no infringement of copyright. The task is made easier for the plaintiff if he can show that there has been access by the defendant, when the onus shifts to the defendant to prove that, although he has had access in some manner or form to it, he has not copied the plaintiff's work.

In order for the owner of an intellectual property right to be able to take proceedings against an alleged infringer of those rights, he has to have some sound foundation in his claim for relief from the courts. In the case of an action relating to property he must have some proof or evidence that he enjoys title to that property. With copyright, there is no definitive register or record of either the subsistence of, or ownership in, the copyright. Here, well-preserved and authenticated original documentation relating to the property right in question, whether literary or artistic, while not being conclusive evidence either of subsistence or ownership, can go some considerable way towards deterring a defendant from claiming that there is either no copyright in the alleged work, or that, if there is, it is not vested in the plaintiff. The plaintiff could take advantage to some extent of a presumption which existed in his favour under the old Act where copyright was presumed to subsist in a work if the defendant did not put this at issue. In this case he would also be presumed to be the owner of the work;[2] however it is better to rely upon the marking of original documents. Now we can see why proper archiving of copyright materials may prove invaluable in an action for infringement. We shall see later the significance of the recording of original designs when we come to discuss registered designs and the new unregistered design right provided for under the new Act.[3]

1 *Francis, Day and Hunter v Bron* [1963] Ch 587 at 623, CA.
2 Copyright Act 1956, s 20(1) and (2).
3 Copyright, Designs and Patents Act 1988, Pt III.

(C) DOCUMENTATION ASSOCIATED WITH COPYRIGHT WORKS

6.9 In this section I am going to review briefly the sort of documentation which should be used in connection with copyright works, including contracts of employment, confidentiality agreements, the commissioning of works and the assignment and licensing-in of works. We have already looked at the licensing-out of industrial copyright works and discussed those clauses germane to the protection of the copyright work.

(i) Contracts of employment

We are now much clearer about the reasons why any innovative concern generating copyright works should ensure that its interests are at all times secured contractually. Though the old Act provided, as does the new Act, that any copyright work produced by an employee under a contract of service is vested in the employer,[1] for the sake of certainty this should be spelled out in a contract of employment with the employee.

(ii) Confidentiality agreements

It is certainly relevant to copyright, as it was with patents, to consider as a further security measure making it obligatory for every employee to enter into a confidentiality agreement. In this way the employee is placed under a contractually enforceable obligation to maintain information of the employers, which is by its nature considered to be secret, in strict confidence. This can be effective not only in restraining the employee from divulging or using secrets during the course of his employment, but also after he has ceased employment. The confidentiality agreement could be either a separate document or, for convenience, incorporated into the contract of employment. Again, although the employer might rely upon the doctrine of implied confidentiality, given the nebulous nature and the value of the copyright works, the imposition of a contractual obligation is advisable as more certain and effective.

(iii) Purchase or assignment

Some innovative concerns may not be in a position to advance further in the creation of their products because of their lack of skills, technology, know-how etc which have to be acquired outside the concern. If so they will need to arrange to have transferred to them just such technology in order to maximise their use of the markets.

There are three main methods of transferring technology in: the relevant technology could be purchased outright, with an assignment over to the company of all intellectual property rights including copyright; it could be specifically commissioned; or it could be licensed-in.

Though many small to medium-sized enterprises depend upon their own creative resources for their research and development, there usually comes a time when, in order to progress further, they need the assistance of outside help in the form of either a product, or a process, or personnel. Care must be taken in such cases that sufficient intellectual property rights are acquired for their specific needs. Much depends upon the nature of their requirements and their resources as to whether the transfer-in will be an actual purchase of that technology or whether the taking of a licence would be more appropriate. A further consideration as to whether to purchase or license depends upon whether the technology is likely to become obsolete within a short period of time.

The buying-in of technology is appropriate where it is likely to serve as a medium to long-term asset in giving the enterprise the necessary capacity or resource to produce or extend its product range. The assignment over of the technology will ensure exclusivity of the use of the intellectual property rights in it. If the transfer includes copyright works or materials, then that transfer must be in writing and signed by or on behalf of the assignor in order to effect the legal passing over of the ownership in the copyright.[2] If not properly documented the intellectual property rights in the copyright will not pass with the result that the purchaser might not be entitled to the exclusive right to use the work. If so he would be unable to sue an infringer of the copyright purportedly assigned to him. Therefore, in any negotiations for the transfer-in of copyright, it is prudent to make sure of the following:

(*a*) that the assignment is signed by or on behalf of the assignor;
(*b*) that investigation is made into and appropriate provision made for any subsisting copyright interests in the work, or an assurance given by the assignor that there are none;
(*c*) that the copyright works or materials are clearly identified, and scheduled, and that physical possession of them is obtained;
(*d*) that the assignor indemnifies the assignee against any third party claims to the ownership of the copyright;
(*e*) that if the copyright work is not yet in existence, the contract should provide for the assignment over of the work upon completion, otherwise there is always the danger that the copyright in the work will not pass.

By taking such precautions the required copyright interests may be secured and protected.

(iv) Licensing-in

Of course the concern might not need a wholesale transmission of the copyright in the work, but only the acquisition of limited rights in the copyright in order to achieve its commercial objectives. In this situation the necessary rights could be licensed-in. A copyright licence may be oral or in writing but if an exclusive licence is sought, this should be in writing.[3] In such a case the licensee enjoys all the rights of the copyright owner including the right to sue an infringer without having to join in the copyright owner to the action. Taking a copyright licence allows the licensee the right to carry out certain acts otherwise prohibited to him. The major requirements of the licence relate to the degree of exclusivity, the precise identity of the subject matter, the rights to use the work, and assurances as to title and indemnity. The licensee should ensure that he has secured sufficient rights to use the work; if not, he might be forced to return to the copyright owner to re-negotiate the terms of a new licence for such rights.

(v) Commissioning

In some cases it is an alternative to outright purchase or licence to specifically commission a work, for example, a technical drawing. If so, the party commissioned will be the author of the work and first owner of the work. In such cases, for ownership of the copyright in the work to be assured to the commissioning party, the party commissioned ought to be made contractually obliged to transfer the copyright in the completed work.

1 Copyright Act 1956, s 4(1); Copyright, Designs and Patents Act 1988, s 11(2).
2 Copyright Act 1956, s 36(3); Copyright, Designs and Patents Act 1988, s 90(3).
3 Copyright Act 1956, s 19(9); Copyright, Designs and Patents Act 1988, s 92(1).

6.10 In chapter 2 on patent exploitation we looked at the situation where the owner of intellectual property rights (in that case in an invention) wished to exploit his rights through the medium or mechanism of the licence. Many of the terms and conditions discussed there are common to most licensing situations including the present one of licensing industrial copyright. In the chapter on exploitation we concentrated on just those clauses germane to the protection of copyright.

Third party infringement and remedies

6.11 Emphasis has been placed upon the need to protect the intellectual property rights in industrial copyright, from their initial creation to eventual exploitation. In the licensing situation we saw that the copyright owner reserved certain rights of action which he could take against the licensee in the event of the intellectual property rights becoming endangered. We saw that he reserved the right to take proceedings against an alleged infringer of those rights. The owner of the copyright work has to make a commercial decision as to whether to proceed against an infringer in the light of the value of the copyright work, the nature of the alleged infringement, and the chances of bringing a successful action. If the rights are valuable and could represent a major source of income for the owner, he really has no alternative but to sue. As with any other intellectual property right, if it is seen to be valuable, there is a good chance that this will attract infringers who will wish to take the benefit of the work without payment to the original owner.

What constitutes infringement?

6.12 We have looked at the restricted acts already.[1] It is the unauthorised doing of any of these acts by a third party in respect of the work in which copyright subsists which will give rise to a claim that the owner's rights are being infringed.

It is essentially copying the work in any material form which constitutes infringement. This is not, however, restricted to copying the work in its entirety but can include the copying of a substantial part of the work. 'Substantial part' has been interpreted by the courts as being either quantitative or qualitative. Thus infringement might take place if a sizeable amount of a work is taken or where a small part is taken but this is the most significant part of the work, as for example the most important part of an industrial drawing or specification. Protection is not restricted to facsimile copying. Infringement can take place if a work is adapted in some way, for example, using someone else's industrial drawings or software and adapting them in some way without the authorisation of the owner.[2] Further, copyright is infringed where someone without the permission of the copyright owner, 'authorises' another to do any of the restricted acts.[3] The scope of this is uncertain, but its effect in the field of copyright is widespread. In Australia it has been given a wide interpretation and the provision of an unattended photocopying machine has been held to be tantamount to authorising an infringement.[4] In the USA it was held that the manufacture and sale of video recording equipment and tapes was not an 'inducement' to infringe copyright.[5] In a recent case in the UK it was held that neither the marketing of audio equipment incorporating a facility for copying pre-recorded cassettes nor the lending of recorders together with the sale of blank tapes amounts to an authorisation of an infringing act.[6]

Primary infringement takes place when there is direct infringement by copying but it is important to note that protection extends to indirect or what is called secondary infringement. These rules are designed to protect the owner of copyright from those who would profit from his work but who have not actually copied it. Thus copyright is infringed by the following acts:

(1) knowingly importing infringing articles other than for private use;
(2) possessing these in the course of business;
(3) selling, letting for hire, offering or exposing them for sale or hire;
(4) exhibiting them in public or distributing them in the course of business;
(5) distributing them other than in the course of business in a way and to an extent prejudicial to the owner of the work.[7]

Further, it is an infringement of copyright in a work to make, import, possess, sell or let for hire, offer or expose for sale or hire an article specifically designed for making copies of the work.[8] This is to prohibit someone from providing the means for making infringing copies.

There are defences open to the alleged infringer, not least of which is the claim that copyright does not subsist in the work in question, but also that the plaintiff has no title to it. Copyright, as has been explained, does not confer an absolute monopoly and it is quite possible for someone other than the copyright owner to arrive at substantially the same or similar literary or artistic work entirely independently. In this case there would be two separate copyrights in existence.

1 Copyright Act 1956, s 2(5) and 3(5); Copyright, Designs and Patents Act 1988, ss 16–21.
2 Copyright Act 1956, s 2(5) and (6); Copyright, Designs and Patents Act 1988, s 21.
3 Copyright Act 1956, s 1(2); Copyright, Designs and Patents Act 1988, s 16(2).
4 *Moorhouse and Angus and Robertson (Publishers) Pty Ltd v University of New South Wales* (1975) 6 ALR 193, [1976] RPC 151.
5 *Sony Corpn v Universal City Studios* (1984) LEXIS.
6 *Amstrad Consumer Electronics plc v British Phonographic Industry Ltd* [1986] FSR 159.
7 Copyright, Designs and Patents Act 1988, ss 22 and 23.
8 Copyright, Designs and Patents Act 1988, s 24.

Remedies

6.13 These are much the same as in any other civil action. Remedies for infringement of copyright are increased and strengthened under the new Act. New rights have been created such as the new design right; performers now have significant rights, and there are now such things as moral rights. I do not intend dealing with moral rights but briefly they are: (i) the right to be identified as the author of a work,[1] (ii) the right to object to derogatory treatment of the work,[2] (iii) the right to prevent false attribution of authorship of the work.[3] The last right already existed under the old Act, the other two rights are new.

INJUNCTION

Normally the owner will want immediate relief to prevent the alleged infringer from continuing his copying activities and will accordingly seek an injunction to stop him. Or he might wish to prevent this from happening where he suspects that infringement is about to take place. The same considerations as to the suitability of this as a remedy were discussed under patent remedies (para 3.14).

DAMAGES

Damages are available to the successful litigant. It is important to note however that if at the time of the infringement the defendant did not know or have reason to believe that that copyright subsisted in the work, then no damages are available.[4] Under the old Act what were known as 'conversion damages' were available, these being based upon the actual value of the infringing copies.[5] These sometimes resulted in the payment of considerable damages often in excess of the actual loss sustained by the owner of the work and were considered to be punitive. These have now been abolished under the new Act but the court now has new powers to make the award of additional damages where the flagrancy of the act and the benefit to the infringer should be taken into account in assessing the sum.[6]

The court has power to make orders for the forfeiture of any infringing copies of a copyright work and for any article designed for the making of those articles. It can also make an order for their delivery up to the copyright owner.[7] Further, provided that he has bona fide grounds for belief that an infringer may attempt to remove or destroy evidence which he has in his possession and which points to his guilt, the copyright owner may apply to the court ex parte for what is commonly known as an Anton Piller Order.[8] This order permits the owner to inspect and remove materials in the defendant's possession. The advantage of this is, of course, that the defendant is not given notice of the plaintiff's intentions which might otherwise provide him with the opportunity to dispose of the damning evidence.

CRIMINAL REMEDIES

Both the old and the new Act provide criminal remedies to the copyright owner. Criminal liability arises largely in the field of making and dealing with infringing articles. The penalties for breach have now been extended. Now on summary conviction the penalty is imprisonment for up to six months or a fine. On indictment where the matter is considered more serious there may be an indefinite fine or imprisonment not exceeding two years or both. These new criminal penalties extend to all types of copyright works having originally been increased to help stamp out piracy of films and sound recordings.

1 Copyright, Designs and Patents Act 1988, s 77.
2 Ibid, s 80.
3 Ibid, s 84.
4 Ibid, s 97.
5 Copyright Act 1956, s 18.
6 Copyright, Designs and Patents Act 1988, s 97(2).
7 Ibid, ss 99 and 100.
8 *Anton Piller KG v Manufacturing Processes Ltd* [1976] Ch 55.

CHAPTER 7

Trade mark creation

Introduction

7.1 I have mentioned that trade marks are often adjuncts to the intellectual property rights already discussed, in that it is often the case that the copyright or patent owner will license the use of his trade mark or marks as a part of an intellectual property 'package deal'. In this section of the book I will discuss the nature of trade marks, how they are exploited, and how like the other property rights discussed they are vulnerable and need careful protection and maintenance. I discuss these in the context of the innovative enterprise which either has or intends to apply for the registration of marks for use on manufactured products, and I deal with the substantive law and procedural matters which may give the applicant cause for concern. Later (para 9.5) I prescribe measures which can be taken to protect and maintain their value. I use the term 'trade mark' throughout, but in view of the extension of protection now accorded to services, the same considerations should apply when considering applying for registration of a mark to protect services.[1]

1 Trade Marks (Amendment) Act 1984.

What are trade marks?

7.2 They are alternative forms of registered and unregistered legal rights. We have looked at one type of intellectual property right which provides for the protection of those rights without any formal registration (copyright), and another type where the interests in intellectual property in inventions are controlled by a detailed registration system (patents). Trade marks can subsist either under the common law as unregistered rights or be registered in the Trade Marks Registry under the Trade Marks Act 1938, or be service marks under the Trade Marks (Amendment) Act 1984. The rights which can subsist under common law and statute have a common basis and a similar function but provide different forms of right. We shall compare the advantages and disadvantages accruing to unregistered and registered rights later (para 7.11).

COMPARISON WITH OTHER FORMS OF INTELLECTUAL PROPERTY

7.3 Let us compare and contrast trade marks with copyright and patents. We saw that the law of copyright existed to protect the labour, skill and judgement expended and the capital invested in the creation of original literary, dramatic, musical and artistic works. It also extended to purely entrepreneurial copyright under Part 2 of the old 1956 Copyright Act, protecting such industrial products as broadcasts, films and records.[1] Its justification is bound up with the view that a quasi-monopoly reproduction right in such works is beneficial to the community, encouraging investment not only in intellectual or aesthetic pursuits, ie, in the creation of novels, poetry, painting and other cultural endeavours, but also in industrial and commercial innovation where many so-called literary and artistic works are generated in such forms as production drawings, engineering drawings, designs, etc. It protects the original expression of ideas without protecting the idea itself and leaves open the possibility of further original expression of the idea by others.

As will be remembered, patent law is designed to encourage and protect investment in new technical information, by the grant of a monopoly right for the exclusive use of the invention embodying that information (albeit for a limited period) in exchange for the inventor disclosing it. This leads to the preservation and replenishment of the nation's stock in new and valuable inventions in technology.

In both copyright and patents, there is an underlying notion or rationale of the protection of the innovator or creator against unfair or unjust enrichment by others at his expense. Though there is no actual law or doctrine of unfair competition in the U K, often unfair competition is seen as the moral justification for these protections. Put simply, it is unfair to allow someone to take a free ride on the back of another person's labour or investment. If he wishes to compete, he must do so fairly.

1 Copyright Act 1956, ss 12, 13 and 14.

7.4 The same rationale lies behind trade marks. How then does a trade mark function? As it always operates in a purely commercial context we do not have to concern ourselves with such notions as 'author', 'work' or 'inventiveness', concepts redolent of copyright and patent law. Both registered and unregistered trade marks operate in distinct ways and may be considered as distinct property rights.

Unregistered marks are marks or symbols used by a trader on or in association with specific goods manufactured and/or sold by him. The mark is a symbol of a reputation of some kind in the goods, either in terms of their origin or quality or both. It is associated with the goods in such a way that it represents those goods. Normally, these goods have attained a reputation over a period of years and are readily identifiable, eg 'COALITE' is associated with the goods for making fires. Thus it is the trader's reputation in his goods which is protected by the mark. On this basis he claims an exclusive monopoly in the use of that mark on his goods.

7.5 By contrast, under the registration system, a manufacturer of goods can make an immediate application to the registry to have a new mark registered for them, without having used or sold them and therefore without having, as yet, any reputation to protect in respect of the origin, source or quality of those goods represented by the mark. Therefore, he has merely to satisfy the registry that he intends using that mark on them.[1] If he secures registration, he has an exclusive right to the use of that mark on those goods specified by the owner.[2] Through use, the mark becomes associated with the trader's quality of goods. The value of the mark will increase through its use on the goods. Though damages could be obtained soon after registration if the trader's rights were infringed, they would obviously then amount to very little. If he does not use the mark then his right in the registered mark is defective and the registration may be expunged, that is, struck from the Register.[3]

1 Trade Marks Act 1938, s 68(1).
2 Trade Marks Act 1938, s 4(1).
3 Tradc Marks Act 1938, s 26.

7.6 We can see that there are two separate and distinct sets of intellectual property rights which can subsist under the general legal notion of trade mark; one where the rights stem from the reputation or goodwill of a business, and the other from registration of the mark. As these are separate and distinct rights, the dealings and remedies for infringement are different in each case. Though separate and distinct they are not mutually exclusive, but could run concurrently in the same mark. For example, a manufacturer who has a reputation in specific goods manufactured and/or sold by him under a distinctive mark or name, and who enjoys an unregistered right in it, may decide to register this mark in order to have a registered right as well. If he succeeds in his application he could have his common law rights in the mark together with the additional rights accorded to him under the registration provisions of the Act. Having registered his mark he now has an exclusive monopoly in its use on, or association with, the specific goods for which it is registered and which are manufactured or sold by him or by someone whom he authorises to use the mark, such as a licensee.

7.7 A brief survey of the law explains how it has come about that there are two separate and distinct sets of intellectual property rights under trade mark law.

Originally, there were only unregistered trade marks, or 'common law' marks. The reputation built up in a mark carried by a trader's or manufacturer's goods was deemed to form a part of the goodwill of his business. This goodwill included any reputation which his business had attained in the manufacture of goods bearing that mark. The mark was thus integral to and not separate from the goodwill element of his business. The mark was used on the trader's specific goods, indicating to the world that those goods originated from a particular manufacturer and no other. Thus there was a single source of goods bearing that particular mark. If the trader produced high quality goods, then, used in association with those goods, his mark operated as an indicator of their origin and additionally as a guarantee of quality.

Such a common law mark was, and is, considered so integral to the business, that it could not, and today cannot, be justifiably transferred or licensed without an assignment of that part of the goodwill of the business with which it was so closely associated. Therefore today, any purported assignment of an unregistered mark must be accompanied by the relevant business element of goodwill to which it is attached. In the case of a common law or unregistered mark, there is no property right solely in the mark itself. Having said that, it is possible to take advantage of section 22(7) of the 1938 Act which says that in the event of someone purporting to assign a common law mark without the associated goodwill of the business, the person to whom the mark has purportedly been assigned must make an application to the Registrar within six months of the assignment having been made, to obtain directions from him to advertise the fact of the assignment. Clearly this is to protect those who rely in some way upon the identity or the source of manufacture or origin of the goods bearing the mark, by alerting them to the fact that their source or origin is no longer the same.

Because of changes in commercial practice, and in response to business needs, it became necessary to create a new personal property right in the mark itself, independent of the goodwill or reputation of the business although the 1938 Act retained these common law rights. Nevertheless even with registered trade marks, the Act made it a condition that for the mark to be used and operated as a piece of personal property, it still had to be connected in some way in the course of trade with the goods of the trader,[1] as I will later explain (para 7.12). However, this new personal property right in the mark, as registered, could be transferred by assignment or licensed without attaching to any distinct part of the business so that the mark, which if originally unregistered indicated a source or origin of the goods, no longer did so if assigned. If a manufacturer of the goods bearing the mark was an assignee or licensee of the mark, it could not be claimed that the mark operated as an indicator of the true origin of the goods. But then, what was the value of the mark if it did not operate as a guarantee of the source or origin of the manufactured goods? The value of the unregistered mark lay in its association with goods of a certain source. With registered marks the rationale behind the legislative response was to satisfy commercial practice and requirements for the mark to indicate not only source but the quality of the goods. That was its new value. It also created a personal property right solely in the mark itself, which was to have other advantages, as we will see. For with a registered mark there is a distinction between the right and the value of the right. Its initial registration and use gives the trader a right in the name distinct from its value. Then its value, which could be little initially, normally increases with use, being associated with the quality of his goods. This is different from unregistered marks which are of no legal status at all unless integrated with the reputation of the business, so the right and its value cannot be distinguished, and thus must be sold together.

1 Trade Marks Act 1938, s 68.

What is a valuable mark?

7.8 The registered or unregistered name or mark associated with the specific goods of a business can be valuable as a tradable and capital asset. We saw how the quasi-monopoly granted under the law of copyright to an original work is valuable because only the owner of the copyright in the work can reproduce the work. This gives the owner an important right in terms of the exploitation of his work. In the case of patents too the value lies in the owner's exclusive right in respect of his invention. The commercial value of the rights which subsist under trade mark law is to use a name, mark or symbol exclusively on, or in association with, a manufactured product.

Not all marks are valuable. How does one recognise a valuable mark? Obviously a valuable mark is one which has been so extensively and successfully used on goods of a specific description in a particular market that this has built up a volume of sales based upon consumer or 'brand' loyalty to the mark. Such loyalty or attraction to the goods through the mark could give the owner of the mark market dominance in those types of goods. The volume of sales and possible market dominance in a particular type of goods is achieved through the creation of a tried, tested and quality-proven product, and through the attendant skills in marketing that product. Clearly the costs and effort involved in achieving this market position and in maintaining the quality of the product have been borne by the manufacturer of the branded goods. Therefore it is fair that his investment in them should be protected by preventing others engaged in the manufacture of goods of the same type from using the brand mark or name on those goods and thus taking a free ride upon the owner's name and reputation. The rationale for protection is that only the party who has achieved, or will achieve, a particular reputation in specific goods through the use of his mark should have exclusive use of that mark.

7.9 With copyright the intellectual property right is in the nature of a negative right. The owner of the copyright in the work can prevent anyone else from reproducing that work in any material form. He does not have to use his work in any way.

However, with patents, use is important. If the invention is not worked at all, or is insufficiently worked, then indeed the owner might lose control of his intellectual property in the patent by the grant of a compulsory licence by the Comptroller. Use is also important in the case of trade marks. Justification for the continued protection of a registered mark after initial registration depends very much upon its subsequent and proper use. We shall see later that there are provisions contained in the Act which lay a registered mark open to removal unless it is actually used and so satisfies the initial legal criteria required for the original grant of protection; otherwise the mark may be removed or expunged from the register.[1]

1 Trade Marks Act 1938, s 26.

Creation and subsistence

7.10 In order to assist a manufacturer of goods which are sold under a name, mark or symbol to decide whether he should rely on accumulated common law rights or whether he should attempt to get the name or mark on to the register, it is necessary to know how unregistered rights arise and registered rights are created, and how their relative strengths and weaknesses are assessed in terms of their effectiveness as intellectual property rights.

Unregistered rights (common law trade marks)

7.11 Unregistered rights in a mark, recognised and subsisting at common law without the need for any formal registration, protect the reputation a manufacturer or trader has built up in respect of the manufacture and sale of goods of a particular kind and are rights integral with that reputation. They necessarily exist together, and with the sale of the rights in the mark go the interests in the reputation of the business. This may be a reputation built up over a long or short period of time. The manufacturer has an exclusive use of the mark in respect of goods covered by the mark, and protection could extend to cover a whole range of products. Before the 1984 Act, an unregistered mark had an advantage over the registered mark in that it could be extended not only to goods but also to services, eg garages, banking, dry-cleaning etc. But now this difference exists no longer because services are now covered by that Act.[1]

1 Trade Marks (Amendment) Act 1984.

SOME SALIENT FEATURES OF COMMON-LAW MARKS

7.12 (a) A common law trade mark covers a trader's or manufacturer's full range of goods and services if he has sufficient trading reputation in those goods or services, but he may also claim exclusive use of it in areas where it is used outside a narrow range of goods if his name or mark is widely known. Thus in the case of 'LEGO', the plaintiffs, who manufactured plastic building blocks for children, were able to prevent another company which traded legitimately with Lego as a part of their name from using that name on hose-pipes and other plastic equipment of that nature manufactured by them. It was held that the word or mark 'LEGO' was so well known to the public that use of it by the defendant would cause confusion and damage to the reputation of the plaintiff, even though there was no common field of activity by the parties. The name 'LEGO' had developed such a reputation that it had in effect become a household word.[1]

(b) Unlike the registered mark, this mark is not subject to any initial, formal, substantive legal or procedural appraisal as to its merits as a trade mark. Thus it is possible for it to subsist in names or marks unregistrable under the registered system provisions of the Act.[2] For example, the name may be laudatory, descriptive, geographic or a surname, all of which are unregistrable as new marks under the provisions of the Act. But it could well have sufficient reputation in actual use for it to subsist as a common law mark. The Act sets out the substantive legal criteria to be satisfied before entry of a mark is allowed on to the register and what can and cannot be registered is strictly specified.[3]

(c) There are disadvantages in relying on a common law mark. Dealings in it are complicated by the necessity for the mark to be associated with the goodwill of the business in some way, otherwise the right in the name cannot exist; that is, there is no actual property in the mark alone because any dealings in the mark must take account of the goodwill of the business with which it is associated. This hampers its currency in terms of its transmissibility, including licensing, as clearly use of the mark has to be transmitted with the whole or part of the assignor's or licensor's business. Indeed UK law is vague as to whether the licensing of a common law mark is valid.

This uncertainly often makes it advisable to obtain the registration of the mark as the Act provides that a personal property right can subsist in the registered mark itself independently of the business. This feature makes for its transmissibility and currency in dealings. It becomes a fluid and adaptable trading asset of a company.

(d) As an unregistered trade mark protects the reputation which the owner has built up in his goods, in order to successfully sue an alleged infringer of his mark, the owner must establish that he has just such a reputation in those goods. This could be difficult. The action is known as a 'passing-off' action, and is one where the plaintiff is put to proving complicated issues both in fact and in law.[4]

1 *Lego Systems A/S v Lego M Lemelstrich* [1983] FSR 155.
2 Trade Marks Act 1938, s 9(1)(d).
3 Trade Marks Act 1938, s 9.
4 *Erven Warnink BV v J Townend & Sons (Hull) Ltd* [1980] RPC 31, HL.

7.13 By way of comparison, these are some of the salient features of registered marks:

(*a*) The 1938 Act provides a clear framework of rules regulating the subsistence and transmission of the property rights and interests in registered marks. It provides for the creation of an intellectual property right in the mark itself. This has an advantage over unregistered marks in that the proprietor is able to deal relatively freely with the mark, enabling him to license it as a part of his overall commercial and marketing strategy. For example, he might need to manufacture goods in either the UK or abroad through a licensee, permitting him the right to use his mark on those goods without assigning any of the goodwill of his business. The registered mark is regarded as a valuable, tradable and commercially active asset of the manufacturer. The same considerations apply to assignments of the mark.

(*b*) The registration system, requiring a precise registration of the mark, and the categories of goods upon which it is to be used or is intended to be used, gives certainty to its exclusive use.

(*c*) If the owner of the mark is using, or has a bona fide intention of using the mark, he is granted an exclusive use of the mark on the goods for which it is registered.[1] Then he need only prove actual use of the mark by an infringer of the mark to obtain statutory relief. Unlike the holder of unregistered rights he does not have to prove that he has already got a trading reputation in respect of the use of the mark on those goods. It is enough that in the future he might have.

(*d*) Registration of the mark indicates to the world, and is prima facie evidence, that the registered owner has satisfied the substantive and procedural requirements of the statute, and that he is entitled to the exclusive use of the mark for the goods against which the mark is registered. This fact, together with references to trade mark registration on the face of the goods themselves, and on packaging, promotional and advertising literature associated with the goods, should have a deterrent effect upon a potential or would-be infringer. Therefore registration of the mark can assist in achieving a high protective profile for the mark.

1 Trade Marks Act 1938, s 4(1).

Let us now look at the substantive law and procedure of registered trade marks.

Registered trade marks

7.14 The Trade Marks Registry, which is a part of the Patent Office, operates a rigorous system of search and examination of all applications for the registration of marks made to it. With the small to medium-sized industrial concern in mind we now need to appraise the substantive law of trade marks and procedure in general. Such a concern could be using existing common law marks in respect of its products, or it might decide to register these and new marks in respect of its already existing and new or future products. I stress the need to advise any industrial or manufacturing concern to establish early on a specific trade mark policy directed towards the use of its presently used and proposed marks, in the light of statutory requirements for registration. This will assist the concern to achieve its commercial aims in trade mark terms. As I bring out more fully in chapter 9 on trade mark protection, policy decisions must be made to cover the obtaining of marks and also their subsequent use and maintenance. I hope an understanding of these substantive legal requirements for the registration of a valid mark will help the advisers of such concerns, or those who handle such matters within the concern, to realise the nature of the trade mark and what its function means. After obtaining registration, the mark must be handled with care, by both its owner and by anyone using it with his consent. Thus a sensible trade mark policy could be formulated to their mutual advantage. As with patents, the registered trade mark right is subject to defeasibility. No guarantees are given by the Registry as to its continued validity and thus justified retention on the register. Through inattention, non-use or improper use of the mark, in ways to be described, the trade mark owner could find himself in a position where he is no longer justified in continuing to retain the mark on the register, and the valuable rights achieved may be lost. Vigilance must be exercised by the owner to ensure that he or others do not negate these valuable rights leaving the mark exposed to predators. Unlike most other intellectual property rights, if properly handled, a registered mark could last forever, increasing in value.

Now to highlight some of the problems faced by someone wishing to apply to the Registry, and to suggest how some of these may be avoided or at least mitigated.

7.15 Before looking at the statutory requirements for a mark to be validly registered we need to consider the context in which the application is made, and examine the role of the Registrar of the Trade Marks Registry, in order to see why certain marks are viewed in a more favourable light than others. This should lead to a better understanding of the nature and function of the legal right claimed.

The general tasks of the Registrar are:

(1) to enable those applicants who satisfy the substantive legal and

procedural requirements to get their marks on to the register, by facilitating their application for the registration of new marks;

(2) to ensure that the register does not operate to the detriment of other manufacturers or traders who could have a legitimate interest in the mark and who might, without care, be unjustly precluded from using the mark as a result of that registration;[1]

(3) to help prevent deception or confusion of the public, about the use, scope or nature of the mark, or about the goods upon which the mark is to be used;

(4) to keep the register 'clean', in the sense that the proprietor of the mark continues satisfactorily to justify his claim to the mark's purity, ie its distinctive quality and its non-deceptiveness; otherwise other parties may have a better claim to the use of the mark than he does. He does not however constantly survey the register of his own accord; he must deal with such matters when others attack the registered mark for its removal and then the Registrar decides the case.

It is the duty of the Registrar therefore to balance finely the rights of the proprietor of the mark with the legitimate interests of other traders who could have an interest in the mark, and with the public, who could have certain expectations about the goods upon which the mark has been placed, eg as to their quality.

1 Trade Marks Act 1938, s 12(2).

SUBSTANTIVE LAW

7.16 Let us assume that a hypothetical industrial manufacturer has established the trade mark policy for his concern, and has decided to register (a) its existing common law marks in order to heighten its protection as already described and (b) new marks. These are, as yet, untried or tested in actual use, but the manufacturer proposes to use them on a range of products which he plans to launch onto the market either immediately or in the future. In order to do this he must ask himself at least the following three questions. In each case I supply below those considerations to be taken into account in answering them.

(1) Is what he wishes to register a trade mark?
(2) If it is, is it distinctive?
(3) Could it be considered deceptive in any way?

(1) Is what he wishes to register a trade mark?

7.17 Section 68(1) of the Act describes a mark as including 'a device, brand, heading, label, ticket, name, signature, word, letter, numeral, or any combination thereof', which is

> 'used or is proposed to be used, for the purpose of indicating, or so as to indicate, a connection in the course of trade between the goods and some person having the right either as proprietor or as registered user to use the mark, whether with or without any indication of the identity of that person'.

A traditional view of a trade mark is that it is something rather like a label appended to the goods, representing them, but not actually a part of the goods themselves—ie the mark sits on or outside the goods. Is this view right? The section quoted does not give an answer to this because it merely gives examples of the sort of things that constitute marks, and is not definitive of what might possibly have a legitimate claim to be a mark. Recent decisions have extended the notion of the mark from being a mere appendage, and have accorded rights to the packaging, colour, and 'get-up' of goods, which, in many cases, can now constitute the trade mark itself. In the case of *Smith, Kline and French Laboratories' Application*, the applicants were claiming exclusive rights to the use of specific colours on one half of a pharmaceutical capsule whereby the contents were visible through the other half of the capsule. It was held that this distinctive means of marking by colouration was capable of registration as a trade mark.[1] However, this has not been extended to the actual container itself. Proposed EEC legislation could alter this,[2] but for now the recent case of 'COCA COLA' has effectively eliminated the possible registration of a container as a trade mark. It was held there that the shape of the bottle, although distinctive, did not constitute a trade mark.[3]

1 *Smith, Kline and French Laboratories' Application* [1968] RPC 415.
2 Amended Proposal for a Council Regulation on the Community Trade Mark, Official Journal of the European Communities 1984.
3 *Re Coca Cola Trade Marks* [1986] RPC 421, CA.

7.18 Any commercial enterprise engaged in the manufacture of products should be advised to consider the possible benefits of trade mark protection, in the registration not only of traditional marks but also of those marks constituted by visual presentation and attractiveness in the packaging or get-up of the product itself. Today considerable investment is expended in the design, presentation and advertising of products to make them visually attractive and distinctive from other similar products on the market. If the 'get-up' has been used on goods for some time it could already subsist as a trade mark under the common law and thus already enjoy the benefit of protection without registration. Professional advice as to feasibility and cost of perhaps more speculative types of application should be taken from a trade mark agent.

Though there are sometimes considerations which outweigh the benefit of obtaining registration, given the certainty of the increased rights which it creates, it is always worth considering. Much depends on the concern's strategy, markets, financial resources and any possible constraints on these, as to whether its management should apply to register only those marks which it considers safe and which stand a good, rather than an outside chance of success, or whether it should embark on more adventurous, speculative and sometimes more risky applications, for example, in respect of packaging or get-up. Finally, the concern should be advised to regularly review its common law marks or potential marks as a regular feature of policy in order to consider their current adequacy of protection, usage, costs, etc, and whether they could be better protected by registration.

It is appropriate here to make reference to the Trade Marks (Amendment) Act 1984. We have been dealing with the requirements of the enterprise which creates and produces goods or products, which for the reasons already discussed, wishes to protect these with a trade mark. It may be, however, that in addition to the sale or supply of goods, complementary services are provided, as in the following cases: computers and computer services such as maintenance: motor cars and garage repair services; credit cards, travellers cheques and banking services. In these cases it will be possible to gain an additional advantage by registering the same name or mark in respect of these additional services. The Act covers not only those complementary services but also extends to the provision of services alone.

The same advantages apply with the registration of a service mark as with a trade mark, in that the registered proprietor has a definitive statement of ownership of the mark which may act as a deterrent to a potential infringer and he does not have to rely upon the common law where he has to prove an already established reputation in the mark. The Act omits brand names, headings, labels and tickets from registration as these apply to goods rather than services. The international classification of categories applies and it is necessary to fall within one or other of these, eg class 35 for advertising and business, or class 41 for education or entertainment, and it is necessary to state precisely the services which are to be covered by the mark.

(2) *Is it distinctive?*

7.19 An important requirement of the UK law of trade marks is that the mark is distinctive.[1] The need for this can be explained by looking at the function of trade marks and the rights which can be exercised by the person entitled to exclusive use of the mark.

Let us begin by asking: What are applicants trying to achieve when applying for a mark? The English language, with its common names and numbers, colours, signs, etc is our common heritage, its use our common right. Therefore we do not consider we are endangering or infringing anyone else's rights when we use a name or speak of something or someone, etc. But when an applicant attempts to register a mark he is asking the Registry to grant him an exclusive use of what may well be a common word, colour, etc, in connection with the goods of his business and thus to exclude anyone else from using that word etc in a similar context. Obviously the Registrar must prevent the grant from encroaching wholesale upon the common rights of others to use the common currency of their language. For this reason the Registrar, in following the provisions of the Act, exercises care in assessing the merits of an application in strict accordance with these provisions and requires that the mark must be distinctive. Only when the applicant has satisfied the Registrar that it is distinctive, and only when it is seen not to operate in a deceptive way, does he issue a certificate entitling the new owner to the exclusive use of the mark.

1 Trade Marks Act 1938, s 9(1)(2).

7.20 Section 9(1) of the Act states that, in order for a mark to be registrable as a distinctive mark, it must contain or consist of at least one of the following 'essential particulars':

(*a*) the name of a company, individual, or firm represented in a particular manner;
(*b*) the signature of the applicant for registration or some predecessor in his business;
(*c*) an invented word or words;
(*d*) a word or words having no direct reference to the character of the goods, and not being according to its ordinary signification a geographical name or surname;
(*e*) any other distinctive mark, such as a star, symbol, crescent, etc.

7.21 The provisions of the Act make it necessary for the following questions to be asked:

(1) Is the mark inherently distinctive?[1] and
(2) Has the word or mark through actual use in a trading context been adapted to or become distinctive?[2]

Section 9 sets out what types of item would, in its terms, be inherently or automatically distinctive or which could become distinctive through actual trading use. Thus:

—the name of a company set out in a particular manner, eg 'COCA-COLA', has automatic distinctiveness (s 9(1)(a));
—a signature is by definition a distinctive sign, provided it is a true signature and not mere handwriting (s 9(1)(b));
—invented words (s 9(1)(c)) are distinctive because they have no established meaning and are not ascribable to any known thing. This distinguishes them from conventional words of the English language;
—an ordinary English word which does not convey any meaning whatsoever when associated with the goods, either in terms of their nature or quality, will be distinctive through its lack of meaning (s 9(1)(d)). A surname or geographical name might be distinctive for trade mark purposes if used in such a way that it does not mean the name of a person or a geographic place, though these are inherently difficult to register.

If demonstration of the mark being inherently or automatically distinctive is difficult, then section 9(3) provides that evidence may be adduced to demonstrate that they have become distinctive according to their ordinary trade usage by the applicant. It must be said at this stage that very considerable use of the mark must be established in order to convince the Registry of its distinctiveness.

1 Trade Marks Act 1938, s 9(3)(a).
2 Trade Marks Act 1938, s 9(3)(b).

7.22 Now that we are clear why marks must be distinctive and what makes for their distinctiveness, let us consider the legal and practical relevance of each of provisions (a) to (e) above to an industrial concern thinking of registering its existing common law marks together with new marks which it proposes to use on its present and future product range.

(a) name of company etc and (b) signature

7.23 (a) and (b) are similar. In both cases the applicant is usually attempting to secure his trade name as a mark of his business as used on or with the goods or products of that business. In these cases, the applicant should apply for the registration of the name as it is presented in a fanciful way, such as the familiar presentation of the 'CADBURY'S' name, rather than in ordinary typographic style because of the requirement that it be represented in a special or particular manner.

It should be remembered that any existing reputation in a mark could be protected by common law provisions even if there are difficulties in obtaining registration of the trade mark. Thus, if an applicant who tried to register a name couched in a fanciful style failed to do so, because it was not sufficiently distinctive in the eyes of the Registry, he could still rely upon any reputation he had in the mark at common law.

(c) invented word etc

7.24 By definition this has inherently distinctive characteristics having no established meaning ascribed to any known thing. Necessarily, it is then a contrivance or fiction. As it is devoid of meaning when applied to a specific type of goods it will satisfy the test of distinctiveness. An invented word has been described as 'something new and freshly coined'.[1] Unfortunately, there is always the chance that the word does have a meaning, for example, it is derived from already existing words which may describe the goods, such as 'VAPORUB' ('vapour' plus 'rub').[2] It is sometimes difficult to invent a word which does not have any origin in other words and if it does suggestively describe the goods themselves then the word cannot claim to be newly coined or minted.

Those called upon to produce a new name for a new product, such as the marketing departments of industrial concerns, often mistakenly believe it desirable to invent a word for a trade mark which is fanciful and, at the same time, describes the nature or character of the goods. However, names of an attractively descriptive character could be fatal to an application, as both the registry and the courts take the view that any word which is derived from an English word such as 'PUSSIKIN' ('pussy' plus 'kin') for cat food,[3] or is a fusing together of common words such as 'UNEEDA' ('you need a'),[4] or is a misspelling of ordinary words such as 'TRAKGRIP' ('track grip')[5] is deemed not to have been invented.

Even if an applicant fails to satisfy the Registry that his word is inherently distinctive it is possible that he could demonstrate to the Registry that it had become distinctive in some actual trading context. If at the end of the day he is unable to obtain registration of the word all is not necessarily lost. He might still be able to rely for the protection of his mark upon any reputation he may have or subsequently acquire in the mark under the common law.

What, if any, are the advantages favouring an application for an invented word-mark over any other kind of mark? One advantage for the applicant is that by claiming exclusive use to a word which does not form part of the currency of the English language, his application is thereby less open to objection. Furthermore, it might eventually help to apply for the registration of what is known as 'a defensive mark'. Under section 27 of the Act, it is possible to protect very well known marks for goods of any category even if the proprietor does not trade in them. This protection is limited to invented words.

1 *Eastman Photographic Materials Co Ltd v Comptroller-General of Patents Designs and Trade Marks, Solio Case* [1898] AC 571, HL: 'Solio'.
2 *De Cordova v Vick Chemical Co* (1951) 68 RPC 103 at 108: 'Vaporub' ('vapour' plus 'rub').
3 *Quennel's Application* (1954) 72 RPC 36: 'Pussikin' ('pussy' plus 'kin') for cats' food, considered to be a word having a direct reference to the character or quality of the goods.
4 *Re Uneeda Trade-Mark* [1901] 1 Ch 550, sub nom *National Biscuit Co's Application* 18 RPC 173: 'Uneeda' ('you need a').
5 *Dunlop Rubber Co Ltd's Application* (1942) 59 RPC 134: 'Trakgrip' ('track' plus 'grip').

7.25 Clearly any commercial concern considering registering words as marks for use on its goods should be advised to exercise caution and seek registration of only those words which its investigations have established are genuinely newly coined or minted having no recognisable derivatives in the English language, ie which are totally devoid of meaning. After exercising such care, however, an applicant could advisably take advantage of some of the conflicts and disarray in this particular area of trade mark law. For instance, he might apply for the registration as a trade mark of an invented word which is not totally meaningless in the context of the type of product to which it is to be applied but which is only 'an allusion' to the character or quality of the goods. As Lord MacNaughten put it:

> 'If it is an invented word—if it is new and freshly coined . . . it seems that it is no objection that it may be traced to a foreign source, or that it may contain a covert and skilful allusion to the character or quality of the goods. I do not think it necessary that it should be wholly meaningless.'[1]

Obviously, such a judgment gives applicants more scope than they might have expected from a first reading of the provisions.

1 *Eastman Photographic Materials Co Ltd v Comptroller General of Patents Designs and Trade Marks, Solio Case* [1898] AC 571 ('Solio') for photographic paper.

(d) 'a word or words having no direct reference to the character or quality of the goods' and 'not being according to its ordinary signification a geographical name or a surname'

7.26 An applicant for the registration of actual English words (as distinct from invented words) as marks to be associated or connected with the specific goods of a business, seeks to claim a monopoly or exclusive use of a word which already enjoys a currency, and thus meaning, in the common vocabulary of the English language. An application for such a mark will not be fatal provided that the word as used will have no direct reference to either:

(*a*) the character or
(*b*) the quality

of the goods upon which it is to be used.

There is a good reason for this. As the proposed word mark must distinguish one trader's or manufacturer's goods from the same type of goods of another, it will fail to do so if it merely describes those goods in terms of their character or quality. For these are necessarily shareable by other goods. They may be 'of the same kind' simply because they share this character or quality. Therefore the applicant cannot claim that such a mark will distinguish his goods from any other goods of the same kind. The Act does not prevent any other manufacturer or trader from an honest and legitimate use of such a word on any goods of his of that type. Examples of words which have been held to have a direct reference to the character or quality of the goods are 'INSTANT DIP' (for cleaning, bleaching and dyeing preparations),[1] 'EARTHMASTER' (mechanical shovels),[2] 'TASTEE-FREEZE' (ice-cream),[3] 'WELDMESH' (welded mesh),[4] and 'FLOWSTACKA' (lifting and loading machines).[5]

It is a question of fact in each case as to whether the Registrar decides whether there has been a direct reference to the character or quality of the goods or not. He may decide that the reference is indirect and allow registration.

This was the case in the following applications; 'SHEEN' (for cotton thread),[6] 'BUSTER' (for animal food),[7] and 'CHIN-CHIN' (for alcoholic drinks).[8]

Despite the above, an ordinary English word might achieve registration, even if referring to the character or quality of the goods, if already used extensively on the goods in an actual trading context, if there is sufficient evidence that this use has achieved the required distinctiveness. But this exception does not allow registration of a word-mark of a purely laudatory nature. Probably the most oft-quoted and notable failure of this kind is the application for the mark 'PERFECTION' for soap.[9] Apart from such exceptions, any organisation deciding to proceed to apply for registration of an ordinary English word for its existing or new products should ensure that the word, as used on the goods, does not describe the character or quality of the goods, because the mere description of the goods does not make them distinctive. Though, of course, the word has an ordinary English meaning, it must be meaningless when applied to the goods. Exceptions like skilful allusions, though they might pass, risk failure.

1 *Re Seligmann's Application* (1953) 71 RPC 52.
2 *Chaseside Engineering Co Ltd's Application* [1956] RPC 73.
3 *Tastee Freez International Ltd's Application to Register a Trade Mark* [1960] RPC 255.
4 *Re Weldmesh Trade Mark* [1966] RPC 220, CA.
5 *Flowstacka Trade Mark* [1968] RPC 66.
6 *Re J & P Coats Ltd's Application* [1936] 53 RPC 355, CA.
7 *Chappie Ltd v Spratt's Patent Ltd* (1954) 71 RPC 455.
8 *Chin Chin Trade Mark* [1965] RPC 136.
9 *Re J Crosfield & Sons Ltd* [1910] 1 Ch 130, 26 RPC 561 at 837.

7.27 The latter part of section 9(1) provided that a geographical name or a surname could be considered to satisfy the requirements of distinctiveness, provided that it was not used, or intended to be used, according to its 'ordinary signification'. Put simply, this means that the name could be distinctive if it were used in such a way as to denote or signify something other than the actual surname or place name. That is, it must not be a token or sign of that actual place or name. Thus, the use of the geographic name 'South Pole' as a trade mark for pineapples could be unobjectionable. The reason for this is obvious. It is not likely to interfere with the legitimate rights of others to use the name 'South Pole' as denoting a region producing pineapples. It is use of the word in a fanciful or non-meaningful way that is most likely to find favour with the Registry. The recent decision in the 'York' case[1] indicates that applications for everyday place names face considerable problems because of possible conflicts with the rights of people of that region or place to use such place names on their goods. Registry practice is that now most geographic names are refused. Thus such applications face an uphill battle, and will probably be refused even given proof of extensive use. Further, a place name is only likely to stop being a geographic name for the purposes of the Act if it becomes of no commercial or industrial significance.

1 *York Trailer Holdings Ltd v Registrar of Trade Marks* [1982] 1 All ER 257, HL: 'York'.

7.28 Similar considerations apply to registering surnames. The Registrar looks to see whether the name is a surname in common or rare use. If common, the grant to the applicant of its exclusive use might exclude a number of manufacturers or traders of the same name from having a legitimate right to use the name on the same or similar goods. On the other hand, an unusual surname could more easily find favour. Exceptionally, even though the surname is a popular one, the trader might be able to adduce evidence of an actual trading reputation in that surname. He might, of course, be able to rely upon any common law rights in the name which he has through use, or has subsequently acquired.

(e) 'Any other distinctive marks'

7.29 This usually means those marks comprised of devices or symbols of some kind, and they may be inherently distinctive or have become distinctive through actual trading use. In one case, a coloured line woven into fabric was considered to have become a distinctive mark through use,[1] and we have seen in a more recent case that the colour presentation of the goods has been considered sufficiently distinctive for registration as a trade mark.[2]

Letters, initials and monograms fall under this heading and may be registered again providing they satisfy the test of distinctiveness.

Before discussing the next requirement of the Act, it will be useful to note here that the Register is divided into Part A type registrations and those appropriate to Part B. Part A exists for those marks which have satisfied the statutory requirements of being distinctive, these being inherently distinctive or where evidence has been adduced to show that they are in fact distinctive. It is possible for an applicant to obtain registration of his mark in Part B where he has not made out a concrete case for the distinctiveness of his mark, where his mark may be said to be only 'capable' of distinguishing his goods from those of other traders in the same goods, that is it has a potential capacity to distinguish. If such registration is allowed upon the adducing of further evidence at a later date, the owner can apply for the mark to be upgraded to Part A of the Register. The commercial upshot of this is that the applicant is given the benefit of the doubt as to the distinctiveness of his mark, with the opportunity of rectifying any defect in the distinctiveness of the mark later on, for example, through further use. The uncertainty as to conclusive distinctiveness is reflected in the Act granting him a lesser right than with a Part A registration. Thus it is that if a mark is registered in Part A of the Register and remains there for a period of seven years, it cannot be attacked on the grounds that there was some initial defect in its registration, such as for example, that it did not satisfy the requirements as to distinctiveness. If registered in Part B it does not enjoy this status.

1 *Re F Reddaway & Co Ltd's Application* [1914] 1 Ch 856, 31 RPC 147.
2 *Smith, Kline and French Laboratories' Application* [1968] RPC 415.

(3) Is it deceptive?

7.30 Let us assume that a mark satisfies the criterion of being sufficiently distinctive to justify the applicant's use of the mark on goods to the exclusion of all other manufacturers' or traders' use on those sort of goods. Then the next substantive legal requirement to be satisfied, to which the applicant should be alerted, is that the mark must not be deceptive. The Registrar is charged with prohibiting the entry on to the Register of any mark which is either:

(1) likely to deceive or cause confusion, or
(2) so closely resembles an existing mark on the Register that it could deceive or cause confusion.[1]

In order for the mark to be validly placed on the Register and retained, it must satisfy the Registrar that it is not thus 'deceptive'. The Register is designed to reflect commercial realities. Any mark proposed to be placed on the Register must not impinge or impose upon the possible legitimate interests of others in that mark, nor be allowed to operate to the detriment of those who rely upon it as does the consumer of the goods bearing the mark.

1 Trade Marks Act 1938, ss 11 and 12.

The interests that the Registrar take into account, in order of priority, are as follows:

(i) The public interest

7.31 The public are the ultimate consumers of the goods bearing the owner's mark. The effect on the buying public may be to deceive them into thinking that the goods enjoyed some special, significant or additional recognition or quality by virtue of the presence of the trade mark. So a mark which misrepresents the nature of the product, appearing to be associated with some special quality, trade connection, or the approval of some institution or association which it does not have, is considered to be deceptive. Thus 'ROYAL WORCESTER', for use on corsets, was refused registration as this suggested royal patronage of some kind which was not the case.[1] The word 'VITASAFE' was refused for a vitamin preparation as this would suggest in the minds of the public consumer some degree of guarantee of safety of the product.[2]

The Registrar takes account of 'any matter' under section 11 which he considers is likely to have a deceptive effect. He also considers whether any mark is the same as, or similar enough to, a mark already on the Register, such that its use on the same type of goods in the market might lead to the public being deceived or confused. Thus, he conducts a search of the Register to see whether any newly proposed mark conflicts with any earlier registered ones in order to avoid such risk.

1 *Re Royal Worcester Corset Co's Application* [1909] 1 Ch 459.
2 *Vita Safe Trade Marks* [1963] RPC 256.

(ii) The interests of other manufacturers, traders and mark owners

7.32 Section 12 of the Act dealing with this aspect of deception charges the Registrar with prohibiting the registration of marks either identical to, or which resemble, those already on the Register. The reason for this prohibition is as follows: an identical or similar mark to one already registered for the same type of goods would cause confusion in the market place by allowing the same or similar goods to be sold under an identical or similar mark and so negate the registered proprietor's rights to the exclusive use of the mark.

Exceptionally, the Registrar might exercise a discretion given him under the Act, and register identical or similar marks where this is justified, on the strict proviso that the risk of confusion to the public in the ultimate use of those marks is minimal.

7.33 The general rules allowing his exercise of this discretion are as follows:

(*a*) Where the applicant for registration of the same or a similar mark can prove that he too has used that mark in trade both honestly and concurrently with the registered owner, even if there is an already existing mark on the Register.[1]

Provided the applicant, as concurrent user, can produce sufficient evidence of trading use, the Registrar might allow the registration to succeed. In such a case, however, he could impose some limitations on the use of the mark if it were likely to cause confusion in the market. This regulation enables the Registrar to ensure that a prior registration of a mark does not interfere with the honest and legitimate interests of other manufacturers and traders who may have a genuine interest in the mark. Of course the parties might have to limit their claim to a more restricted use of the mark. They may no longer be given an exclusive use of the mark on goods of that class or type or they may have to modify the subsequent appearance of the mark after the application has been processed. That is, the already registered proprietor of a mark and the applicant could be forced to compromise both in respect of their claimed exclusivity of the use and ownership of the mark. Then it is possible that neither party gets what is asked for in registering the mark. In commercial terms, what they get sometimes suffices, sometimes not.

(*b*) Again, the Act allows the Registrar to exercise his discretion when dealing with separate and concurrent applications for registration of the same or similar marks in respect of the same type of goods.[2]

In this case, he first seeks to establish who has priority of use and takes into account the actual degree of use that each of the parties has made of the mark in trade. He could refuse to allow any registration to proceed until the parties come to a satisfactory agreement as to how the mark is to be used. His aim is to achieve a balance between legitimate interests in the mark and to ensure that any use of the mark or marks does not deceive or confuse the general consuming public. Compromises can be painful. Applicants should consider carefully just what the effects of such compromises could be on their interests.

1 Trade Marks Act 1938, s 12(2).
2 Trade Marks Act 1938, s 12(3).

7.34 By way of summary therefore, any concern considering making an application for registration of either an existing common law or of a new mark, is well advised to ascertain the state of the register beforehand by conducting a search, which should show if there are any identical or similar marks already there or which are pending a decision by the Registry as to their suitability. This will also indicate on which goods it is proposed to use such marks. In the light of this and any other commercial information which the applicant may have at his disposal, he is then able to make a reasoned decision as to whether to proceed or not. Even if there is an existing mark on the Register in the same kind of goods for which he proposes to use his mark, he might still be able to adduce sufficient actual trading use of the mark to be able to claim an honest concurrent use of the mark. If the value and importance of the mark to his concern warrant it, he might be prepared to proceed and to accept possible limitations on the use of his mark. Such practical commercial considerations, together with the Registrar's appraisal of the strength of any possible objections to the mark, help him decide whether to proceed further or whether it would be wiser to drop his application and seek a new and hopefully less contentious mark. Obviously he must decide whether his organisation can afford to spend its time and money and other resources on a potentially contentious application, and accept the attendant uncertainty inherent in such an application.

I set out in the next chapter the sort of matters which an organisation should consider in establishing its trade mark policy and those measures which can be taken to increase the chances of its securing registration of its required marks. But by now it is clear that a proper understanding of the legal nature of trade marks and their commercial significance could help those small to medium-sized concerns from making costly mistakes in making applications which stand little chance of success.

Procedure

7.35 Because all trade mark applications claim important rights, and because the law so demands, the Trade Mark Registry operates a rigorous vetting system. After processing a claim, dealing with opposition to it and eventually satisfying itself that the claim is valid, it issues a certificate entitling the applicant to the exclusive use of the mark on the category of goods specified in the certificate. From that moment the Registry maintains a definitive Register of all the interests, rights, and dealings (if notified) in that mark. Obviously, such applications should not be undertaken lightly. Before applying for the registration of a number of marks the applicant should be advised to consider carefully what his concern could achieve by it. He should not proceed in an ad hoc or haphazard manner, applying just for individual marks, but properly co-ordinate and plan an integrated policy designed to achieve a particular commercial objective which includes the role played within it by his trade marks.

Trade mark policy

7.36 Thus, before deciding upon this policy, he should review the following:

(1) the concern's current registered marks;
(2) its common law and unregistered rights;
(3) its past, present and future goods upon which the marks have been or are to be appended;
(4) its past, present and future markets or territories in which the marked goods are to be sold including foreign markets;
(5) its present and future use of the marks by others; ie where the marks are or are proposed to be appended to goods manufactured by others under licence.

Supplied with this management information, the applicant can form a proper trade mark policy to suit the concern's precise requirements.

A well thought out trade mark policy thus entails considering the past, present and future commercial requirements of the concern and should operate in conjunction with its sales and marketing arm as a direct response to their needs which should help determine policy. An active policy of this kind, incorporating its trade mark rights as an aspect of it, can be used in many different ways; for example to support a new product drive where a distinctive mark could help focus attention on and thus ensure the future recognition of the new product, or to promote a drive into some new market or territory. The aim of such a policy should be to help pave the way for new products and to protect old and new products by deterring potential infringers of existing and new trade marks.

7.37 Having appraised the market function of trade marks the concern should establish the precise markets where the goods are to be manufactured or sold. As with patents, the exclusive right only operates nationally. Protection in other jurisdictions requires registration in that national territory; thus applications for the registration of the mark should be made in those territories if the product is to be either manufactured or sold there.

7.38 Applications to the Registry can be made by individuals, firms or companies, either themselves or through the services of a trade mark agent or legal adviser who is able to assist and advise on the processing of these both in UK and foreign jurisdictions. Trade mark agents especially have valuable experience of the legal, procedural and commercial vagaries of foreign jurisdictions, and their services are particularly useful where some jurisdictions are more rigorous in considering the merits of applications for registration than others; though the UK is probably the most stringent of all.

What is needed to proceed in the UK Registry?

7.39 In the UK it is not necessary, unless the Registrar has doubts, to provide the Registry with precise details of the way in which the mark is to be used. The UK is a signatory to an international convention for the international classification of goods which exists for the convenience of international trade marking.[1] This sets out categories of goods and services for which registration may be made in classes eg class 16 (paper articles), class 35 (business services). A separate application must be made for use of the mark on each category of goods or services in any individual class.

Upon receipt of the application, the Registry carries out its own search of the Register of existing and pending marks, to see whether the mark, as proposed to be used, is identical, or similar, to any mark on the Register on that class of goods. If the mark does not conflict with any other registered mark, then the Registry examines the mark in accordance with the substantive legal criteria, that is to say, it considers whether it is something which does or might constitute a trade mark by being either, as is said 'inherently or actually adapted to distinguish', and whether the application is invalid because 'deceptive' in some way.

On completion of his examination the Registrar notifies the applicant of any objections he might have, given these substantive requirements. At this stage, if there are any objections, he may recommend to the applicant suitable modifications to the mark which would make the mark acceptable to the Registry, or he may simply refuse to grant it.

1 International Classification of Goods and Services Nice Agreement 1957.

7.40 Careful appraisal is needed of any objections made by the Registrar, to see whether these are acceptable in the case of suggested modifications, or surmountable if he claims there is a flaw, eg that the mark is not distinctive. The applicant can then choose whether to:

(1) abandon the mark;
(2) modify the mark as suggested by the Registrar, or even suggest a suitable modification himself in the light of the nature of the objection;
(3) continue with the application, but disclaim those parts which the Registry have found objectionable;
(4) withdraw the mark if the objection is based on the grounds that there is insufficient use or reputation in the mark to justify

its acceptance. He could withdraw the mark, use it in the market place for such time as is necessary for it to achieve a reputation and become distinctive, and then apply for registration at a later date;

(5) withdraw the mark and rely upon any common law reputation there may be in the mark;

(6) adduce sufficient evidence to prove that though not inherently distinctive it has in fact been adapted to distinguish in an actual trading context.

Clearly the commercial decision to be made as to whether to abandon, modify or proceed should be influenced by the nature and force of the Registrar's objections, the ability of the applicant to overcome those objections and the commercial importance and value of the mark.

Even if the applicant is unable to reach a satisfactory result in his dealings with the Registry because it continues to object to the registration of the mark, he can still apply for a hearing before the Registrar where the merits of the application are more fully explored. Yet a further appeal against a refusal to register by the Registrar is possible to the court or to the Secretary of State.

7.41 If the applicant is successful in satisfying the criteria established for validity, then the Registry advertises the mark in the *Trade Mark Journal*. This system differs materially from the investigation and examination under the patent system. With patent procedure we saw that third party interests could only be entertained in the form of informer advice submitted by an interested party or objector to the Patent Office during the prosecution of the patent. If a challenge was made as to the validity of the patent this would have to take place after the grant of a certificate by the Office. However, in the case of trade marks, any objector may lodge opposition proceedings with the Registry within one month of the placing of the advertisement by the Registry in the Journal.[1] Indeed, the function of the advertisement is to alert those who may have an interest in the mark, such as an honest concurrent user, to the fact that the applicant is making a claim to an exclusive use of the mark. Opposition proceedings are similar to those held under a hearings procedure. Both parties are given an opportunity to state their case as to the interest they claim in the mark or the objections which it arouses. Such a provision ensures that the system does not operate to the detriment of those who may have a legitimate interest in the mark, and who might otherwise be unjustly excluded from using it.

1 Trade Marks Act 1938, s 18.

Ownership/title

7.42 Before going on to deal with the exploitation of trade marks it is useful to see what sort of problems may arise which may impede the title to, and thus exclusive use of, a mark. Certain precautions should be taken to ensure that title to the mark is secured by its proprietor. As we have seen, anyone can apply to register a trade mark, providing he is using or intends using the mark on goods.

If a firm needs to use a name on products created by it, it should first try to reach agreement between its constituent members as to the ownership and use of the mark. This removes possible conflict and uncertainty as to where the rights reside in the use of the mark if the firm or partnership dissolves.

If the marks are to be registered in the name of a company, it will be their registered proprietor, and they will form a part of the company's assets. If they are to be used by a group of companies, it is advisable that they are registered in the name of the parent company for two main reasons:

(1) Its subsidiaries could use the mark without having to enter into a trade mark licence agreement, because at common law use by the subsidiary is deemed to be use by the parent company.[1]

(2) If the mark or name is registered in the name of a subsidiary company the mark could be vulnerable in the event of a take-over of the subsidiary by another company. The acquiring company would automatically be entitled to the assets of the subsidiary including all its intellectual property rights. This would give the predator company all the exclusive rights in the mark which the subsidiary had once enjoyed. This could happen to a subsidiary company operating either in the U K or in a foreign jurisdiction. Obviously these are situations to be avoided.

1 *'Bostich' Trade Mark* [1963] RPC 183.

7.43 Even so, the sort of ownership problems which often arise in an innovative concern involved in the generation of copyright works and patentable inventions are rare in the field of trade marks.

New names or marks generated by a concern designed for use on its new manufactured products will usually emanate from the publicity, marketing or sales departments or some special group charged with the creation of new names as a part of its function. It is unlikely that there will be claims to ownership of the trade marks by any party from within the organisation itself as the mark will be designed for use upon the concern's own manufactured goods. However, it is still wise to avoid problems of the ownership of trade marks by including relevant clauses in contracts of employment as I have already described in connection with other intellectual property rights emanating from the concern (see paras 3.9 and 4.14).

7.44 Other problems relating to title, ownership, and interest in trade marks, whether registered or unregistered, can arise with joint ventures, the licensed use of the trade mark by others, and use of the mark abroad. These problems are often due to neglecting to care for trade mark rights at the commencement of a transaction or use.

As a registered mark gives an exclusive right to use a name or mark on specific goods, if in any commercial joint venture an agreement has not been made between the parties to the venture as to the use of the mark on new products, then both parties could later be excluded from the right to its exclusive use or only have a right to its use with the consent of the other party or parties. Clearly, the existence of a number of equal claimants to the mark tends to dilute the strength and distinctiveness of that mark and thus its value.

It is important to note at this stage that the owner of a registered mark who allows the use of his mark by others under a licence or user agreement which he registers at the Registry, is deemed at law to be using that mark himself; but use by someone else without registration—eg by a manufacturing licensee, an agent or distributor—is not deemed to be use by the registered proprietor. If the latter, this could have the effect of associating the mark in the mind of the public with that of the user and not the owner, and then the user would build up a reputation of his own in the mark, to the detriment of the registered proprietor. Therefore, it is crucial to ensure that each permitted user of the mark enters into a written licence or user's agreement, which is then registered at the Registry.

The claim to exclusive use of the mark extends only to those jurisdictions in which the mark is actually registered. If the mark is only registered in the UK, this will not protect the proprietor's use of the mark in another legal jurisdiction. Therefore care needs to be taken in allowing use of the mark abroad where (a) there is no system of registration, and (b) there is no rigorous examination system for validation leading to ownership of the mark. If the applicant is intending to use the mark in foreign markets, where the mark is registrable, he should apply there, whether for use either by himself in that foreign jurisdiction or for use by others whom he intends licensing. In this way he protects his mark from potential infringers, and at the same time prevents a licensee of the mark from claiming ownership of the mark by being the first to use it.

CHAPTER 8

Trade mark exploitation

Introduction

8.1 Before examining some of the commercial reasons which make it desirable or necessary for a trade mark owner to license the use of his mark, we need to know the legal position on licensing which must be taken into account.

Because the Trade Marks Act made it possible to trade in the mark without the attachment of a relevant part of the business, the practice of registering trade marks expanded. By registering its marks, a manufacturing or trading concern was able to adopt a more flexible trading policy. Gradually, the trade mark became an indicator of the quality, not of the origin of the goods. There need now no longer be a single source or origin of the goods, as they can be manufactured by any number of licensees of the mark; goods can now and in the future be multi-sourced. The consumer of the goods thus has no guarantee as to their origin, which was the original function of the trade mark. Is there any guarantee as to quality, in return?

8.2 Section 28 of the 1938 Act charged the Registrar with the duty to satisfy himself that any use of the trade mark should not be contrary to the public interest.[1] Therefore it is a statutory condition of licensing that the parties to a licensing agreement apply to the Registrar giving particulars of the relationship between the licensor and the licensee, showing the proprietor's degree of control over the permitted use of the mark and whether there are any other permitted users. Further, the type of goods upon which the mark is to be used must be given, together with details as to whether there are any restrictions on the use of the mark, the duration of use, and any other material information.[2] Thus the Registrar ensures that the proprietor of the mark has a built-in contractual quality control in any licensing arrangements with those who wish to manufacture the goods and append the mark. In this way to some extent the public interest is protected. The consumer has legitimate expectations in terms of the quality of goods he expects to obtain when purchasing marked or branded goods and the proprietor has the right to see this expectation is satisfied. Though nothing requires him to do so, his interests in the reputation of his goods would seem to assure his control.

1 Trade Marks Act 1938, s 28(5).
2 Trade Marks Act 1938, s 28(4)(a) to (d).

8.3 It is only if the Registrar ensures that the Register is kept 'clean'—ie legitimate valid marks and legitimate users or licensees alone are registered there under agreements imposing strict quality control—that use by the licensee can constitute use by the proprietor. Thus the owner can claim continued use of his mark and at the same time ensure that his mark is properly used. The public interest is protected, as well as the owner of the mark.[1]

1 Trade Marks Act 1938, s 28(2).

Why license?

8.4 In the normal course of events a trader or manufacturer of goods, who is the owner of a registered mark, produces his goods, appends his mark to them, and distributes these for sale through either his own or others' wholesale or retail distribution outlets. If he finds that there is a demand for his goods at home and possibly abroad, and he does not have the capacity to satisfy that demand, he might need to use the spare capacity of others in the same manufacturing industry. Provided he enters into the requisite registered users' agreement with quality controls to satisfy the Registrar, and this arrangement is registered,[1] he can permit others to manufacture his goods and append his mark to them and so enjoy the following benefits of both a legal and commercial nature:

(1) He is able to claim use by his licensees as use by himself, thus preventing an attack on the mark based on non-use.
(2) Contractually he can oblige his licensee to use the mark correctly thus preventing attacks on the mark based on its becoming descriptive or non-distinctive or in some way misrepresenting the goods.
(3) He penetrates foreign markets without having to manufacture there and enjoys the accrual of reputation and goodwill to his business, generated through the use of his mark on his quality

goods and through the advertising and promotion of the goods. This assists him in a still further penetration of the market by any subsequent product range which he might develop. Thus he is helped to establish a presence in a foreign market and create a brand identity and loyalty of substantial value.

These are only some of the legal and commercial advantages of pursuing a licensing policy and particularly of licensing a registered mark within the context of such a policy, but they at least give some indication of the value of the licensing of trade marks.

In summary then: A sound licensing policy helps expansion and protection of a manufacturer's goods. It enhances the reputation and goodwill of the business and establishes and encourages long-term brand loyalty. Properly managed, trade marks are valuable assets and commercial tools of a company, while conversely, indiscriminate licensing or mismanagement of the mark can result in the dilution and negation of its value, and even in total loss.

1 Trade Marks Act 1938, s 28(4).

8.5 We shall look shortly at the sort of clauses which should appear in a typical registered user's agreement and which are designed to protect the trade mark.

As with the other intellectual property rights discussed, the trade mark is at its most vulnerable when it is entrusted to the care of and exploitation by others. Even so, as we have seen, there are commercial reasons why the owner would want to license his mark. Therefore it is important that we now examine protective clauses relating to the use of the mark, which should be incorporated into a typical registered trade mark user's agreement, and take note of the care required in drafting them. The aim of such documentation licensing intellectual property is to ensure the owner of the intellectual property is still able to exercise and retain control of that property, though the rights of use might, at times, be temporarily in the hands of others.

Registered user's agreement

8.6 The owner of the mark will draft the agreement, keeping in mind the following:

(1) The owner's need to exercise control over the production of the goods which will eventually bear his mark. By doing so he

satisfies the section 28 provisions of the Act. That is, (a) if sufficient control is exercised by the owner of the mark, use by the licensee of the mark on his manufactured goods will be considered use by the owner; (b) controlled use by the owner helps defeat a claim that the mark was wrongly on the Register because of the non-use of the mark by the proprietor, and (c) control of the quality of production ensures that the owner's mark is not being placed upon goods of inferior quality so exposing it to attack on the grounds that use of it had become deceptive.

(2) His need to avoid any expression suggesting that (a) the licensee could be the owner of the mark or (b) the licensee has acquired rights in the mark through his use of it, by explicitly stating this in the agreement.

(3) The advantages of obliging the licensee to use the mark precisely. Uncontrolled and vague use of the mark obviously leads to it being used generically and thus losing its distinctive quality.

8.7 Let us now look at some of the clauses which should be included in a typical trade mark user's agreement.

(1) THE PARTIES

The right granted is personal to the licensee. If the licensee is a company and needs to allow its subsidiaries use of the mark, the owner should ensure that the licensee is in control of those companies and holds itself liable to the owner for any breaches of the licence. In this case it will be necessary for each subsidiary to take a licence from the licensor as under UK law it is not possible to sub-license a trade mark. Therefore, the same considerations would apply where the licensee wishes to allow third parties to use the mark. Each third party needs to enter into a separate licence with the licensor.

By way of contrast, if a parent company itself is the registered proprietor of a trade mark and this is used by its subsidiaries, there is no need for the subsidiaries to take a licence from the parent company, as use by the subsidiary will be deemed to be use by the parent company.[1]

(2) THE MARKS

These should be scheduled, setting out precisely the way in which they should be used when applied to manufactured products, labelling, advertising or promotional material relating to the sale of products. No other form or manner of use should be permitted. This prevents generic use of the mark leading to its loss of distinctiveness, a subject I shall deal with in greater detail later. The licensee should be obliged to either append a 'TM' or 'R' symbol to the mark as the case may be, and to make reference to the proprietor's rights in the mark each time it is used, thus preventing the licensee from claiming proprietorship or from gaining any interest in it through its use to the detriment of the legitimate interests of the owner.

(3) TERRITORY

This should be clearly designated to show the area for either selling and/or manufacturing the goods to which the mark is to be appended. The owner of the mark should register this in the relevant jurisdiction for that area, or at least have an application pending, for the reasons already discussed.

(4) DURATION

The licence should provide for the automatic termination of the right to use the mark in the event of the licensee breaching a material provision of the licence. This should be independent of any other agreement the parties may have entered into. However, the mark will normally be a part of a package arrangement relating to the manufacture or sale of the owner's goods and the trade mark agreement will thus stand or fall by those other arrangements as well.

(5) EXCLUSIVITY

The owner will grant a licence which will reflect the agreement reached with the licensee on the exclusivity required in terms of the manufacture and sale of goods upon which the mark is to be placed.

(6) PRODUCT CONTROL

The quality or product control clause serves two main commercial and legal purposes.

First, commercially. As the licensee is obliged to produce goods of the same quality as the owner of the mark, if he fails to do so the owner of the mark is entitled to terminate the licence. Otherwise of course the licensee could damage the mark by producing inferior goods which would become associated with the mark to the commercial detriment of its owner, exposing it to attack on the grounds that it had become deceptive. Clearly the consuming public could be confused as to the quality of goods it should expect from those bearing the mark.

Second, sufficient control of the quality of the production of the goods allows the owner of the mark to take advantage of the provisions of section 28, as use by the licensee is deemed to be use by the owner, thus preventing attacks based on non-use.

The owner of the mark cannot leave it to chance that the licensee will adhere to the quality of production obligations in the agreement. As well as obliging the licensee to regularly submit samples of the goods bearing the mark, for inspection, he should also provide that he sends samples of all trade and promotional literature used by him associated with the sale and marketing of the goods to ensure that the mark is being properly used. In reviewing all samples of goods, promotional or advertising materials sent to him showing the mark, the owner should make sure that in each case there is a reference to his proprietory interests in the mark, lest any goodwill generated by it accrue to the licensee and not to the owner.

(7) REMOVAL OF MARKS

The licensee should be obliged to remove all the labels or marks on any goods and from any other materials upon which the mark is attached in the event of the licensee abandoning its use or being unable to produce goods conforming to the standard quality required. He should also be under an undertaking not to attempt to use the owner's marks again.

(8) ALTERATION OF MARKS

The licensor should reserve the right to alter the mark in any way, eg to update its design, or to change the category of goods upon which the mark may be used.

(9) RIGHTS OF ACTION

The proprietor of the mark should not undertake to enter into legal proceedings in respect of it, as this could be commercially onerous. It is enough that he should reserve the right to do so, retaining and reserving all rights of action in respect of the mark; for example, to take proceedings in respect of any infringement of the mark by others, to defend any proceedings for infringement of another's trade mark, and to settle any matter. It is a commercial decision as to whether the mark is worth protecting or not, to be taken at the relevant time.

After these safeguards have been inserted to protect the mark, the agreement must be registered by the proprietor of the mark and the proposed registered user must apply in writing to the Registrar providing him with information about the proposed use of the mark, together with any additional information which he may require as requested by him. Thereafter, all provisions, active and operative, must be monitored to ensure strict compliance with the terms of the agreement.

1 *'Bostich' Trade Mark* [1963] RPC 183.

CHAPTER 9

Trade mark protection and maintenance

Introduction

9.1 We have examined the nature of trade marks, the criteria to be satisfied in order to obtain a trade mark and the procedures involved. In this chapter I now seek to draw together the threads of the previous two chapters on trademarks and prescribe measures which the innovative concern can implement to prevent the negation of the value of its trade marks. Again, if implemented, these can assist in the creation of a controlled environment both within and outside the innovative concern.

I retain the same notion of 'protection' as I have throughout. It is to be understood in terms of the sort of measures which can be taken by manufacturing and trading concerns to minimise their risk of loss of their interests and rights in their intellectual property.

9.2 Unlike patents and copyright, trade marks, upon payment of the requisite fee for regular renewal after every seven years, can virtually last forever and need never be a wasting asset of the proprietor. This gives them their peculiar value.

In order for the mark to gain this value and for the proprietor to properly justify his exclusive use of the mark, it is vital for him to understand that his mark is only a claim to an exclusive right, which could be defeated.[1] Registration establishes only a prima facie evidence of the validity of the mark. Initial grant of the right only means that the claimant has shown, so far as the Registry is aware, that he is entitled to its exclusive use. However, the Act does provide that registration as the proprietor of a trade mark shall be taken as prima facie evidence of the validity of the original registration of the trade mark and of all subsequent assignments and transmissions of that mark. Thereafter the Registry cannot guarantee the mark's absolute or continued validity. Only the court can issue a certificate of validity in any subsequent proceedings when this is in question.[2]

The Registry takes the view that if any of the initial criteria justifying the grant of the monopoly right no longer apply to the mark, then it should be removed or 'expunged' from the Register.[3] Therefore there can be no guarantee of the continued validity of a mark which is on the Register. Obviously, we must consider measures that might need to be taken in order to prevent such expungement and loss of the mark. Let us get a better idea of how the mark could degenerate in this way.

1 Trade Marks Act 1938, s 46.
2 Trade Marks Act 1938, s 47.
3 Trade Marks Act 1938, s 33.

Reasons for expungement

9.3 The main reasons for expungement are as follows:

(1) that the mark is not being or has not been used,[1] or
(2) that it has been used improperly, meaning that it has either lost its distinctive quality[2] or
(3) it has become deceptive.[3]

Another ground for removal is sometimes that, quite simply, it was incorrectly placed on the Register in the first place. The reason for expungement in each case is clear. If the mark is not used, then the basis of the original grant has disappeared, eg that it has been and will continue to be so used on goods, or that there was such an intention of use. If it is used in such a way that it is no longer distinctive, if for instance the word is now used to describe goods in a generic sense—eg as aspirin and linoleum have been—then it could lose its distinctive quality. If it further becomes deceptive, then this is a misrepresentation of the goods to the public. For example, this could happen where either intentionally or unintentionally the mark registered is used in such a way as to give a misleading impression to the consuming public of usually the origin or quality of the goods. Thus in one case where there was a registered mark for the use of the word 'HAVANA' for cigars, it was held that use of that word on cigars manufactured in Brazil made the mark deceptive.[4,5]

1 Trade Marks Act 1938, s 26.
2 Trade Marks Act 1938, s 32.
3 Trade Marks Act 1938, s 11.
4 *Newman v Pinto* (1887) 4 RPC 508, CA.
5 *Re Fuente's Trade Marks* [1891] 2 Ch 166, 8 RPC 214.

9.4 Let us now look at each of these.

First, any defect in the original registration can only be raised within a period of seven years of registration given that it is likely that any defect would be revealed within that period in any case.[1] The objection can only be made by 'a person aggrieved'—someone with a sufficient trading interest in the mark. The seven-year period provides the Registrar with the chance to consider any interests more adequately, if need be, by allowing someone to lodge an objection with him and so covers the possibility of him not having taken into account all outstanding matters or interests in the mark at the time of application.

Second, although initially satisfying the criteria for validity, the mark now fails to do so and thus should be removed from the Register.

1 Trade Marks Act 1938, s 13(1).

Let us now examine these:

(1) NON-USE

9.5 The basis of the initial grant was that the mark was either in use, or there was a bona fide intention to use the mark. Therefore it follows that the Registrar may remove the mark if either:

(*a*) the proprietor had no intention of using the mark when he applied for registration and in fact he has not used it since registration, or

(*b*) at the date of any objection to the Registry, there has been no bona fide use of the mark on the described goods. The Registrar looks at the position which prevailed during the previous five years.[1]

Therefore use is crucially important in the UK registration system as it was with common law marks where use built up the owner's reputation in the mark. Under the registration system actual or intended use of the mark must be shown because it is a function of the trade mark itself to distinguish one manufacturer's or trader's goods from that of others by the trade mark owner's use of the mark on his goods. As registration denies that use to others, the exclusive use or monopoly given to the registered proprietor must continue to be justified, and shown to be legitimately required.

If the owner does not use the mark, he is thus presumed to have abandoned it. Were the case otherwise, highly distinctive marks could be stockpiled in a company's portfolio, excluding the possible rights of others to use those marks while not being used by the company itself. Directly after registration, immediate use of the mark prevents such a presumption arising of the abandonment of the mark. And, as use under a registered user's agreement is deemed to be use by the owner himself,[2] a properly regulated licensing policy ensures the continued legitimate use of the mark by the proprietor, though the Registrar's power of removal of the mark remains always a discretionary one. So use by the owner and use by others under a registered user's agreement can rebut any allegations or objections made to the Registrar on the grounds of non-use.

1 Trade Marks Act 1938, s 26.
2 Trade Marks Act 1938, s 38.

(2) NON-DISTINCTIVENESS

9.6 Under the provisions of section 9, one of the requirements for registration was that the mark contained, or consisted of, what is called 'an essential particular', meaning a word such as an invented one or an ordinary one having no direct reference to the character or quality of the goods, and that it was distinctive as is said, 'inherently or actually'. Thus, if a word-mark became used as the name or the description of goods in a generic way—as is sometimes the case with the use of the word, eg, 'HOOVER', as a name for vacuum cleaners generally—then it lost its initial distinctive quality which first justified its registration. If this happened then it would no longer be eligible to remain on the Register. It is not use by the public which counts in the Registrar's consideration of loss of distinctiveness, rather it is the way in which that word or mark is used and viewed by those in the same trade or industry.[1] Therefore it is advisable that the proprietor of a trade mark vigilantly monitors which members of the same manufacturers, trade or industry use the mark. Of course, vigilance means making sure that no-one is trying to achieve sales by an infringing use of the mark on their goods. But it also means looking out for the way in which other traders refer to the mark in relationship to the proprietor's goods, trade or brand name, in trade or other magazines; for example, when comparing his goods with similar ones on the market.

1 Trade Marks Act 1938, s 15(1).

(3) DECEPTIVE

9.7 Should the use of the mark on a proprietor's manufactured or traded goods become deceptive in any way, that is, if it is used in such a way that it operates as a misrepresentation in some way to the public, then this may justify the Registrar removing the mark from the Register.

Measures to be taken to protect the trade mark

9.8 Having decided upon a trade mark policy and strategy in conjunction with the sales and marketing departments, the concern is now in a position to register its chosen names. As registration operates to protect the mark on specific goods only if used correctly, otherwise it is open to attack and possible expungement, I now prescribe measures to form a part of a general policy to increase an awareness of the nature, function and value of the proprietor's mark. The aim of such a policy is to maintain and increase the protection of the mark by avoiding its negligent use.

Such measures are to be implemented in order to produce a protective environment necessary to the proper use and thus maintenance of the mark.

(*a*) Given that non-use of a registered mark is fatal to the continued justification of retention of the mark on the Register, it is essential to ensure that any mark, prevailing or newly registered, is used upon the goods. A new mark should be used immediately after registration. Reasonable commercial use will suffice to rebut allegations of non-use.

Further, it is advisable for anyone contemplating registration of a brand new mark to use the mark before proceeding to register it, provided that he is reasonably confident that it is a distinctive mark or capable of being made distinctive. This may assist in establishing a claim to first use of the mark where another party is seeking to register the same or a similar mark.

(*b*) Careful records should be kept of the mark, unregistered or registered, the precise way in which the mark is used, the dates of registration and in which jurisdictions, and the precise category of goods on which the mark is used. Most jurisdictions will require regular renewal fees to be paid and care should be taken to update these.

(*c*) Special efforts should be made to keep internal records of the commercial use of the mark with details of the volume of sales of goods bearing a particular mark in the various territories in which the goods are sold. This may be difficult, but it will assist in adding to management information about the state of use of the marks.

(*d*) A detailed schedule of all those licensed to use a mark should also be kept because use by a registered user legally counts as use by the owner.

(*e*) As we have already seen, evidence of the actual use of a common law mark can be used in an application for registration of that mark in the UK if it is not inherently distinctive. Keeping details of unregistered marks is as important as keeping details of registered ones.

Proof of trading use in the UK or other jurisdictions or territories helps support applications for registration in those foreign jurisdictions which require evidence of the use of the mark as a prerequisite for registration; eg as in the USA. Money spent on obtaining a mark and its subsequent maintenance and exploitation—such as renewal fees, advertising and promotion—may assist in the adducing of evidence of use of the mark, particularly where the mark has appeared in extensive advertising campaigns in respect of a product bearing the mark.

Records of the annual trade mark budget should be kept. The certificate itself should be filed carefully and examples of actual use of the mark on products and promotional materials as future possible supporting evidence.

Measures to prevent dilution of the mark

9.9 I now outline measures to be taken to prevent diluting the strength of the mark through its improper use as this may result in attacks on the mark, expungement and subsequent loss of rights because it has become non-distinctive, descriptive of a generic type of goods, or it has become deceptive in some way.

In any manufacturing or trading concern some are entrusted with, and have access to, the use of the mark. Usually it is the function of the advertising, sales and marketing departments to ensure that the mark is given a high profile in order to promote its products. Normally it will be found on the trader's or manufacturer's letter-heads, work manuals, advertisements, the packaging of the product itself, training literature, and used in internal and outside magazines. But even before any such uses are allowed to be made of it, it is wise to establish a vetting procedure within the concern to ensure that such uses will not dilute or degenerate the mark in the ways I have described. All internal personnel, retailers and distributors of the goods handling the marks should be briefed as to the precise manner in which the mark is to be used in order to ensure that it retains its distinctive quality and is not used so as to suggest that it is but an ordinary word in the English language. As we know, it is quite easy for a mark like 'DAIQUIRI',[1] though distinctive, to fall back into the common language so as to suggest that it is not distinctive but is generic, meaning that it is only a type of rum drink. This degeneration from use in a distinctive to a generic use can apply equally to any common law rights in the mark as well as the registered rights. The same fate has befallen such former trade marks as aspirin, cellophane, and milk of magnesia.

The appearance of the mark must be emphasised to retain its distinctiveness; for instance by the employment of capital letters or speech marks encapsulating the word or mark. Use of the letters 'TM' denotes that the mark is unregistered and 'R' in a circle denotes that it is registered. They should be used in close proximity to the mark itself, and should be referred to elsewhere in any narrative in which it appears as a mark of the company, usually with a clear and unequivocal statement of the concern's proprietorial rights in the mark.

1 *'Daiquiri Rum' Trade Mark* [1969] RPC 600, HL.

Misuse of the mark by others

9.10 Use of the proprietor's mark by others normally arises in two distinct situations:

(1) When another manufacturer or trader refers to the proprietor's goods when marketing his own goods, (eg '"X" brand films are suitable for use on "Y" brand cameras') where the mark is not used in a trade mark sense, ie is not actually on the goods themselves.
(2) When the proprietor has agreed to permit the use of a mark on manufactured goods under a licensing arrangement. In the case of use by another trader, this should be carefully monitored. In the case of use by a licensee, the owner must ensure that any use of the mark is monitored, controlled and properly made to avoid diminishing its strength.

9.11 Further protective measures:

(*a*) Any party who has referred to the mark incorrectly must be made aware of the identity of the registered proprietor and advised as to the correct manner in which to refer to it.

(*b*) It is possible to advertise in a trade journal—as is commonly done in the USA—to the effect that the manufacturer or trader is the registered proprietor of the mark, and that if it is to be referred to at all, then it must be so in a specified way, in order to indicate that it is a trade mark and is not being used generically. (*a*) and (*b*) help to prevent others in the same field of trade or manufacture as the proprietor from claiming that his mark has assumed a generic meaning in that particular trade or industry, which, if not refuted, might justify an application for its being expunged from the Register.

Let us now turn to the third type of user of the owner's mark—the unauthorised user or infringer.

Infringement and remedies

INFRINGEMENT

9.12 A mark is deemed to be infringed

> 'by any person who not being the proprietor of the mark or a registered user thereof using by way of permitted use, uses a mark identical with it or so nearly resembling it as to be likely to deceive or cause confusion, in the course of trade, in relation to any goods in respect of which it is registered, and in such manner as to render the use of the mark likely to be taken either—
>
> (*a*) as being used as a trade mark; or
>
> (*b*) in a case in which the use is use upon the goods or in physical relation thereto or in an advertising circular or other advertisement issued to the public as importing a reference to some person having the right either as a proprietor or as registered user to use the trade mark or to goods with which such a person as aforesaid is connected in the course of trade.'[1]

The above means that the proprietor of a registered trade mark can prevent anyone using a mark which is identical to the registered mark on the type or category of goods which the proprietor manufactures or sells in the market, and for which it is registered. Or, if someone is using a mark so similar to the proprietor's that the public will be deceived by its presence in the market for those sorts of goods then this too will be an infringement of the mark. Thus no-one can claim that he is doing nothing wrong by using a mark which is not the same as, but is only similar to the mark. Similar means so nearly resembling the mark as to be likely to deceive or cause confusion between the registered mark and the mark in actual use. The legal basis of this right is of course that it is only the registered proprietor who has the exclusive use of the mark upon the goods for which it is registered. It is important to note that it is only an infringement of a registered mark if that mark is used upon goods for which it is actually registered. Any further claim to rights in the mark on goods for which it is not registered must be substantiated by proving a reputation in those goods associated with the mark.

The use of the mark must be in relation to goods. However, this has been held to extend to use on the container in which the goods are normally sold such as wrappers, labels, boxes, etc. Further, infringement might take place if only a part of the mark is used, but usually only if an essential feature of the mark has been used.

'Importing a reference' means the use of the mark by someone other than its owner, not in the sense that he is implying that his goods are associated with those of the owner of the mark, but rather that he is selling his own wares, be they branded goods or not, by reference in some way to the trade mark owner's brand name or mark. This may not be use of the trade mark owner's mark in a deceptive way but it is considered to be an unfair practice. Use may be either on the goods themselves, on their packaging, or in physical relation to them by being displayed on them, or it could be in an advertising circular to the public and so not on the goods themselves.[2]

1 Trade Marks Act 1938, s 4(1)(a),(b).
2 *Bismag Ltd v Amblins (Chemists) Ltd* [1940] Ch 667, 57 RPC 209, CA.

9.13 Taking the measures suggested in the previous sections will obviously help deter infringers by achieving a high level of awareness, maintenance and thus protection of the mark. But if a mark becomes valuable, even these measures are unlikely to prove sufficient. There will always be those unscrupulous enough to use on their goods either the mark, or something similar to it to the market detriment of its owner, taking a free ride on the owner's reputation in the mark attached to those goods, and deceiving the consumer into thinking that he has purchased goods whose quality is guaranteed by the mark. As with any type of intellectual property matter, it is a commercial decision as to whether to take proceedings against an infringer or not. However, inactivity is often fatal to the survival of the mark. Obviously if the infringement continues the proprietor could lose his position of market dominance. If the goods of the unauthorised user are of a particularly low quality, his mark will become equated with this low or inferior standard. This will lose the owner valuable custom and brand loyalty. Worse, if the infringement continues he exposes his mark to potential expungement from the Register on the grounds that it is causing confusion in the market and has therefore become deceptive.

REMEDIES

9.14 The usual civil remedies apply. The owner may obtain an immediate injunction to stop the infringer from using the mark on the goods in question. He can apply to the court where there is a strong argument that an infringement is likely to take place, that it has actually commenced, or that an infringement is likely to be repeated. Injunctions can have serious commercial effects and consequently they are not granted lightly. As we have seen with patents and with copyright, the owner of the right has to have an arguable case before grant of an injunction. The grant of an injunction will have the effect of limiting any damage which may have been caused to sales of the trade mark owner's goods and to any reputation which he may have in his marked goods.

In addition to an injunction the owner of the mark can claim damages based upon lost sales and in appropriate cases damage to reputation. An alternative is to ask the court for an account of profits which is a remedy granted at the court's discretion and is not automatic. Given that the mark has been used in an offending way the owner can ask the court for the erasure of the mark from the goods upon which it has been used and for delivery up of those articles in order that this can take place. If it is not possible to erase the mark he can ask for an order that the goods bearing the mark be destroyed.

Further, a certificate as to the validity of the mark can be obtained from the court if this question has been at issue.[1] Like every successful litigant, the owner can claim the costs in having had to bring the action in the first place.

The new Copyright, Designs and Patents Act 1988, while making no reference to trade marks in its title, amends the Trade Marks Act 1938 by providing for a new criminal offence, that of fraudulent application or use of a registered trade mark. An offence occurs if someone with fraudulent intent applies a mark identical or similar to an already registered trade mark to goods, or to material used or intended to be used for labelling, packaging or advertising or selling, hiring or offering to sell or hire the goods or the material. Fraudulent intent means acting for gain for oneself or another or intent to cause loss to another in such a way that the goods will be accepted as being genuinely connected in the course of trade with the person entitled to the trade mark, and the defendant does not reasonably believe that he is entitled to use that offending mark.[2] The penalties on a conviction are: on summary conviction, a term not exceeding six months or a fine; on indictment, an unlimited fine or imprisonment for a term not exceeding ten years.

1 Trade Marks Act 1938, s 47.
2 Copyright, Designs and Patents Act 1988, s 300.

CHAPTER 10

Designs

Introduction

10.1 Next in our practical guide to intellectual property law we must look at the law of designs which has been touched upon in our discussion of copyright. The protection of designs combines some of the principles of copyright law with the features of a registration system. Its abolition has been advocated on a number of occasions, but it will continue to serve a useful function under the new legislation.[1] Therefore we must clarify what the function is of this final piece of armoury within the context of intellectual property law by recapping very briefly on the features of those rights which the law has sought to protect under this umbrella heading of intellectual property.

1 Copyright, Designs and Patents Act 1988, Pts III and IV.

Registered designs and the intellectual property law system

10.2 Patents protect the new and inventive concept, notion or idea underlying and embodied in an industrially applicable invention. Innovation is good because the nation's industrial assets are restocked and replenished by the incentive of the grant of a monopoly to the inventor to exploit that invention.

10.3 Trade marks protect the reputation built up by a trader in his goods represented symbolically by the mark. What is protected is the mark as applied to industrially manufactured goods, not the goods themselves, and we have seen that often the get-up or appearance of those goods may be capable of constituting a trade mark—for example the coloured capsule—but not as yet the actual physical container of goods, such as a bottle.[1,2]

1 *Smith, Kline and French Laboratories' Application* [1968] RPC 415.
2 *Coca Cola Trade Marks* [1986] RPC 421, CA.

10.4 Copyright protects the original expression of artistic, literary, musical and dramatic works, irrespective of their artistic or aesthetic merit. As we have seen, copyright does not protect the idea itself but the original material expression of an idea. It is not a monopoly right as it is possible for another party to arrive at the same or substantially the same or similar work entirely independently. Copyright is designed to prevent copying. It has an entrepreneurial function. It protects the labour, skill, judgement, capital and investment in the creation of original works or products, without the need to register the results of that investment.

The justification for such protection is that it is unfair to copy someone else's work thereby profiting from it. The quasi-monopoly is necessary to ensure recompense for the expenditure of labour involved, to recoup on the costs of production of the work or goods, to encourage innovation for the good of industry and society and to prevent industrial and cultural stagnation.

10.5 The intellectual property system has to satisfy the needs and requirements of a number of interested parties, such as the manufacturer of goods or artefacts, the creator of works, materials or ideas, and the consumer, so that no one group benefits at the expense of others. Manufacturers wish to make technological advances available to as wide a market as possible, the creator wants to recoup on the labour involved in his efforts to create new works and products, and the consumer wants access to the latest consumer goods as cheaply as possible. The aim is to balance these interests by providing varying degrees of protection to the innovator but ensuring that he does not abuse the grant of such rights to him by unfairly exercising his monopoly position within the market.

10.6 Before we can understand why there is a separate law for designs, and why it is not covered by the above three—patents, trade marks or copyright—we need to examine the present law of designs, what is required for registration under the Registered Designs Act 1949, and the procedure involved.

Creation and subsistence

(A) SUBSTANTIVE LAW

The Act provides that a registered design protects a design considered novel, for a period of 15 years from registration. Section 1(3) of the Act defines design as follows:

> 'Design means features of shape, configuration, pattern or ornament applied to an article by any industrial process or means, being features which in the finished article appeal to and are judged solely by the eye, but does not include a method or principle of construction or features of shape or configuration which are dictated solely by the function which the article to be made in that shape or configuration has to perform.'

Thus the law is clear and consistent, relating to designs which may be said to have an essentially aesthetic feature.

The design must be one which is to be applied industrially, which must have 'eye-appeal', and must not be dictated solely by its function. Eye appeal is considered to be an appeal to the immediate customer. If the aim of a design is to carry out a function more effectively, with no consideration of the appeal of the design to the ultimate consumer, it is deemed to be 'dictated solely by function', and is thus unregistrable.

Furthermore it is a requirement of the Act that to be protected under its provisions the design must be both novel and original. 'Novel' in this case means that the design has not already been registered, published or disclosed in any way.

One important feature of registered designs is that like patents, if there is not a reasonable use of the design taking place after registration, anyone may apply to the Registrar for the grant of compulsory licence to use the design.

(B) PROCEDURE

All applications for the protection of designs are dealt with by the Patents Office. The requisite forms, the application fee, an illustration of the design and a statement of novelty must be filed by the applicant. As in the case of patents and trade marks, a search is carried out of already registered materials to see if there are any existing registrations. If not, a certificate is issued giving the applicant a monopoly, ie an exclusive right to the use of that design. As in patent law, this means that there can be no claim by another party to an independent creation in the same or similar design, which is different to the legal right granted under the law of copyright. That gave a right to prevent copying and not the right to prevent independent creation. The grant is for exclusive use of that design for a period of five years, though it may be renewed for a further two terms of five years, making a total of 15 years in all. The Register contains the names of the proprietors of the designs, and as with patents, any dealings are registered, such as the assignment of the right, or any licences granted for use of the design.

10.7 Why, with such an armoury of intellectual property rights available to the creators of new industrial innovation, is there this special right in respect of designs?

The system of registering rights in designs arose because the traditional copyright protection extended only to literary works. Therefore pressure was brought to bear to legislate in order to protect also those engaged in innovative design. The shape of new designs to be applied industrially were given a monopoly right of protection of 15 years. To prevent duplication by the ensuing Copyright Act of 1956 and to prevent the rights becoming cumulative, section 10 of that Act effectively provided that if a design was registered, or if it was applied industrially, then the owner of that design could not rely on copyright protection under the 1956 Act.

Clearly, if the rights in the design are registered they should not be duplicated, but what if the design was applied industrially but its owner in fact was not able to obtain registration of his design because it was in respect of a purely functional article? In this case he would have neither protection under the Registered Designs Act nor under the Copyright Act. This seems unfair. Indeed, it was held in one case that this situation was unfair, and that someone who had a design who was unable to register it because it was not a registrable design, should be able to rely on the Copyright Act.[1] Unfortunately this had a peculiar effect. It gave the designer who had an unregistrable design 50 years' protection instead of the 15 years protection under the Registered Designs Act for a design which was registrable. He was thus better off in terms of the duration of protection of his design than someone who was able to register his design.

Another question arose about the position of someone who had a registrable design, in that the design was not dictated by its function and generally satisfied the requirements of the Act, but who for good reasons did not actually register it. This might be the case where the design depended upon seasonal factors, such as in the design of toys, or where the designer had so many designs that the cost of registering them was prohibitive. The Design Copyright Act of 1968 attempted to solve this problem by providing for a new copyright in designs which could be registered but which were not in fact registered. The design was granted protection for a period of 15 years from the date of first sale of an article embodying that design.

Recently the position of the law of designs was confirmed in the case of the protection which may be extended to functional articles based upon original copyright drawings. Functional articles were protected for the life of the author plus 50 years with the exception that where they were spare parts required for the purpose of repair of equipment, any other person could manufacture that spare part and supply this to the owner of the equipment.[2]

1 *Dorling v Honnor Marine Ltd* [1965] Ch 1, [1964] RPC 160, CA.
2 *British Leyland Motor Corpn Ltd v Armstrong Patents Co Ltd* [1986] AC 577, [1986] RPC 279, HL.

10.8 If I describe the work of a designer, we can see whether his type of work has special features which warrant this grant of a specific monopoly right, and whether what he does could not be covered by the already existing intellectual property laws of copyright, patents or trade marks.

The designer's work falls into two main areas of activity:

(1) he may be engaged in the design of, or employed to design, an industrial artefact specifically to appeal to the eye of the consuming public, this appeal having little or nothing to do with the actual function of the article, such as wallpaper, fabrics, toys, etc; or
(2) he may design something where the main feature of the article is not to appeal to the eye of the consuming public. This is a technical design which will, for instance, make an industrial artefact, such as a crankshaft or cylinder head for a car, work better. In this case he could be either designing something completely new or perhaps engaged in solving a design problem which has beset that particular area of industrial artefacts. His endeavours might result in a better crankshaft or a better cylinder head.

The designer is pre-occupied then with the appearance of things and how this relates to the way in which they work. What is common to both situations is that considerable time, skill, labour, judgement and investment go into his design products. It is reasonable that this innovation is protected from those who might profit by copying them.

What legal protection is appropriate to design products?

10.9 Fewer problems are posed by the first category of designs because it is generally acknowledged that the efforts involved in the design of something which has a specific quality or feature which appeals to the eye, has meant the expenditure of labour to produce a product somewhat different to those protected under the general law of copyright. Copyright protects the appearance of something whether it has eye appeal or not and it therefore does not need to be considered aesthetically pleasing or attractive. There is no requirement for a copyright work to be novel, it has only to be originally expressed. Thus it is the novelty and the eye appeal features of designs which are specifically protected as monopoly rights under the Registered Designs Act 1949. The Act does not provide for the registration and protection of something which has been designed purely with the function of the article in mind.

10.10 Is this protection appropriate to the second category of designs: functional articles?

Such goods often result from considerable innovative efforts on the part of the designer. They may be entirely new artefacts or the result of his efforts to overcome design problems or defects in other already existing designs. The designer may have incorporated into his design new concepts, or novel features of a practical and technical kind. As it only covers the appearance of the design, the designer cannot turn to the Registered Designs Act 1949. A crankshaft is not the sort of item or article which is purchased because of its aesthetic appeal. It is unlikely to be a visual feature of the vehicle. It is purchased only in the hope that it will carry out a specific, perhaps improving function, within the car. In this case if the design is one which advances the state of the art in whatever technology it is operating, in that it is new, involves an inventive step and is capable of industrial application, then the underlying idea or concept in the invention might qualify for a patent. But if it is obvious to the notional addressee of the patent application, to the technician skilled in that art, or, if it has been disclosed or anticipated, then it will fail to qualify. Whether it satisfies sufficient criteria to claim to be a new invention or not is, in each case, a question of technical judgement. What if what the designer has achieved does not quite suffice to claim the protection of a patent? Despite there being some novel idea, concept or feature embodied in his final design, it fails to enjoy patentable status. Furthermore, because the design has been dictated by its function and not its appearance, it will not qualify for registration as a design under the Act either. Is there no other protection available to its designer?

Relevance of the law of copyright and proposals for reform

10.11 At this stage it might be profitable to look at what commentators such as the Whitford Committee of 1977 and later committees have said about the function and role of the design of functional articles in industry, whether they should be protected, and if so why and how. In particular they have asked whether such designs should be protected by copyright or whether they require special treatment.

(1) THE WHITFORD REPORT 1977[1]

This placed the role and function of designs firmly within the prevailing economic context. Its position was as follows: although the designer needs to recoup on his costs and labour in the creation of the design, a grant of a monopoly for the protection of a purely functional article would stifle competition, frustrate the supply of much needed spare parts and inhibit the development and improvement of industrial products. It was argued that the present uncertainty in the law had been partly brought about by the actions of the motor car industry. In order to bolster up its flagging revenues on car sales it had used the law of copyright to prevent others from producing spare parts for motor vehicles. It had claimed copyright in the creation of three-dimensional motor car parts initially represented in two-dimensional drawings. Therefore a resulting three-dimensional industrial article, a spare part, itself constituted an infringement of the copyright in an original drawing. The grounds for this lay in the provisions of the 1956 Act which provides that 'reproduction' in the case of an artistic work includes a version produced by converting the work into a three-dimensional form or, if it is in three dimensions, by converting it into a two-dimensional form.[2] For some years the spare parts industry had produced spare parts for vehicles considerably cheaper than similar ones produced by the motor industry. Should the motor manufacturer, or any other manufacturer, be able to use the law in order to restrict the manufacture of spare parts, and thus result in their maintaining a high pricing policy for the supply of those spare parts to the purchasers of their motor cars or other products? This would seem unfair.

In reviewing the law of copyright Whitford considered the position of designs and divided them into two types, categories A and B. Category A comprised those designs where the appearance of the article influences the purchaser eg 'wallpaper and carpet patterns . . . toy figures, china figures, pottery, crockery, cutlery, furniture and other similar articles'.[3] Category B reflects the purely functional, purchased because it is able to do a particular job, eg 'propellers, aerofoils and replacement parts in cars and other machinery to which no decorative additions had been made'.[4]

For a category A type design, provided it was only the appearance which was protected, and not any underlying idea or principle, the committee favoured a grant to the designer of a period of monopoly protection for 25 years from the date of first marketing articles embodying the design. There was no unanimity about what the law should do about functional articles. But if any protection was accorded for category B designs then there should be compulsory licences made available if the market for such goods was not satisfied in the UK. Any rights granted to the designer in respect of those sorts of designs would be conditional on there being adequate provisions to prevent abuse of those rights, rather similar in substance to the provisions relating to patents and designs already registered under the 1949 Act.

(2) THE GREEN PAPER 1981

What further commentaries have there been on the state of design law? The 1981 Green Paper[5] committee believed that only true inventiveness should be rewarded and feared industrial stagnation if monopolies were allowed for the purely functional form of an article. It felt that there should be a 'common pool of experience from which all can freely take'[6] and it concluded that there should be no protection for purely functional forms save those which were patentable.

The 1983 Green Paper Committee[7] decided that there should be some protection for the design of functional articles, but only if that design qualified as being novel.

(3) THE WHITE PAPER 1986

Let us now look at the proposals of the 1986 White Paper.[8] The Paper's conclusions are based upon the generally held belief that innovative designs, costly to produce, and denied patent status, should qualify for some form of protection. It considered that copyright gave an excessive degree of protection quite outside the requirements of the designer's needs which were basically to recoup on his design costs.

It explored other possible forms of protection as follows:

(i) A registration system

It decided against extending the registration system to cover functional designs as this would impose additional costs on the designer applicant and also on the resources of the Patent Office which would have to process these.

(ii) An unfair copying law

Such a law would be something of a European import. It is like copyright in that there is no registration involved, but it introduces the idea of a matter being actionable on the basis of any act of competition contrary to honest practices in industrial or commercial matters. It was felt that this would introduce an untried and untested legal doctrine into UK law and so would not instil the requisite need for certainty.

(iii) An unregistered design right

It favoured a 'modified copyright' approach in the proposed grant of an unregistered design right, the modification being that the more objectionable features of copyright, such as 50 years' protection, would be absent and a lesser right than full copyright protection granted.

This lesser right would:

(*a*) protect functional designs;
(*b*) give the designer of functional articles a 'lead-time' in the market;
(*c*) entitle the designer to recompense for his design expenses;
(*d*) encourage investment in design;
(*e*) reduce the possibility of monopolies;
(*f*) benefit industry;
(*g*) benefit the consumer.

The features of the right?

(1) no registration to be involved;
(2) protection to be against the copying of the original design;
(3) protection to be for ten years from the first marketing of the product to which the design has been applied;
(4) licences of right to manufacture the protected articles to be made available during the final five years of the term, with the proviso that licences may be issued earlier if there has been abuse of the exercise of the right contrary to the public interest.

The right to come into existence on either of the following events:

(*a*) the first making of the article embodying the design or
(*b*) the first expression of the design in any independent form eg from a drawing or a computer.

How was this to interface with the Registered Designs Act 1949?

(1) the unregistered design right to apply to both functional and aesthetic designs;

(2) a possible 15 year monopoly in respect of purely aesthetic designs only;
(3) functional articles which incorporate aesthetic designs not to be denied registration under the Act, but only the aesthetic element of the design to be protected by the registration;
(4) no registration as a design for articles where:
  (*a*) it could not be shown that the aesthetic appearance of the article would be a material factor taken into account in its purchase
  or
  (*b*) the article was an integral or a working part of a further article, unless the appearance of the two articles are substantially independent, such as presumably a spare part for a car.

Thus only genuinely aesthetic designs were to admit of registration with 25 years' monopoly protection, the protection of functional articles to be given limited copyright or modified copyright protection under an 'unregistered design right'.

1 'Copyright and Designs Law' (1977, HMSO) Cmnd 6732.
2 Copyright Act 1956, s 48(1).
3 Chapter 3, para 167.
4 Chapter 3, para 168.
5 'Reform of the Law relating to Copyright, Designs and Performers' Protection' (1981, HMSO) Cmnd 8302.
6 Chapter 1, para 13.
7 'Intellectual Property Rights and Innovation' (1983, HMSO) Cmnd 9117.
8 'Intellectual Property and Innovation' (1986, HMSO) Cmnd 9712.

The 1988 Act

10.12 The Act provides for a new unregistered right and amends certain sections of the Registered Designs Act 1949. It should strengthen the distinctions between copyright works, aesthetic designs and designs for functional articles, these distinctions having become blurred over the years.

THE DESIGN RIGHT

What is created is a new intellectual property right which is a personal moveable property right in original designs.[1] 'Original' means that it is not commonplace in a particular design field.[2] 'Design' means the design of any aspect of the shape or configuration of the whole or part of an article, to include internal or external shape or configuration.[3] The legal requirement is that it is original and that one of two things has been done to it, either:

(*a*) that the design is registered in a design document, or
(*b*) that an article has been made to that design[4]

Either establishes subsistence of the right. The recording of the design in a design document simply means 'making any record of a design whether in the form of a drawing, a written document, a photograph, data stored in a computer, or otherwise'.[5] In other words a record is made of it.

How long does the right last?

The design right expires:

(*a*) 15 years from the end of the calendar year in which the design was
  (i) first recorded in a design document or
  (ii) an article was made to that design, whichever first occurred or
(*b*) if articles are made available according to the design, within five years of the date of either recording the design or making of an article, then ten years from that date. Thus there is effectively 10 years' protection from the first marketing of an article bearing the design.[6]

What rights are conferred and upon whom?

The exclusive right is to reproduce the design for commercial purposes, by making articles to that design, or by making a design document recording the design for the purpose of enabling such articles to be made.[7] Examples of indirect infringement of the right would be authorising its use for commercial purposes, importing, possessing, selling, letting or hiring or offering an articlc which the alleged infringer knows or has reason to believe is an infringing article.[8]

The designer is the person who creates the design and is its first owner unless it is created in the course of employment, in which case it belongs to the employer. If the design is commissioned it is the commissioner who owns the design. The right is transmissible as personal or moveable property and there may be partial assignment of the right thus permitting licensing. Any assignment of the rights in the design must be in writing and signed by the assignor.

Exceptions to the right

There are important exceptions to the right the most significant being the 'must fit', 'must match' provisions.

First, the design right does not apply to the feature of shape or configuration of an article which:

(i) enables the article to be connected to, or placed in, around or against, another article so that either article may perform its function ('must fit') or
(ii) are dependent upon the appearance of another article of which the article is intended by the designer to form an integral part ('must match')[9]

These exceptions seek largely to exclude spare parts from the protection of design right. Thus if we take the example of a part of a car such as a wing or body panel, then under the first exception, 'must fit', the design of the part will not gain design right protection because it will be designed so that the features of shape or configuration enable it to be connected to another article or articles so that either article may perform its function. Under the second exception, 'must match', the designer will intend the article to form an integral part and be dependent upon the appearance of another article. So the new design right will operate to give protection to the design of functional articles but not if they are designed to fit or match with other articles.

HOW DOES THIS NEW RIGHT INTERFACE WITH COPYRIGHT?

If copyright subsists in a work which is either a design or the artistic work includes a design, the design right is not infringed if there is an infringement of copyright in the work. Thus the design right exists independently of any copyright in the work.[10]

ADDITIONAL FEATURES OF THE RIGHT

Licences of right

In an effort to ensure that there is no abuse of the new right which protects purely functional articles the Act provides that licences of right shall be made available in the following circumstances:

(i) In the last five years of the life of the design right any person can apply to the owner for a licence of right, and if the terms are not agreed between the parties, these will be settled by application to the Comptroller of Patents.[11]
(ii) If a reference is made under the Fair Trading Acts to a monopoly existing in respect of an unregistered design, to a

merger situation, to an anti-competitive practice, or to a course of conduct which operates against the public interest, then licences of right are available.[12]

(iii) Where the owner of an unregistered design is unknown and reasonable inquiries have been made, a licence may be granted.[13]

Thus the Act should ensure that there is a sufficient term of protection granted for the research and development costs to be recouped on the design and creation of functional articles. It should also prevent abuse of these rights through the potential creation of monopolies which might operate against the public interest by allowing others the right to use them under reasonable licensing terms or by the imposition of compulsory licences by the Comptroller.

REGISTERED DESIGNS

The Registered Designs Act 1949 has been amended to make a clear distinction between design right and purely aesthetic designs.

The law itself remains largely the same. A method or principle of construction and the features of shape or configuration of an article which is dictated solely by its function are still not registrable.

Provisions similar to the 'must match' provisions under the design right also apply. The features of shape or configuration of an article which are dependent upon the appearance of another article of which the article is intended by the author to form an integral part are not registrable.[14]

Further, a design may not be registered in respect of an article if the appearance of the article is not material, that is, if aesthetic considerations are not taken into account to a material extent by persons acquiring or using an article of that description.[15] This would presumably cover such articles as spanners or hammers.

Amendments have been made to the period of protection available for truly aesthetic designs. The right subsists initially for five years and can be extended by a further four periods of five years making a total of 25 years' monopoly right in that design.[16] The Act further provides for the protection of computer-generated designs. In this case the person by whom the arrangements necessary for the creation of the design are made will be the author.[17]

Briefly, to summarise: there is provision for a two-tier system of designs, one system where purely aesthetic designs are registered in a public register with protection for 25 years and the other system where protection lasts for a period of ten years from the date of commercial manufacture of articles bearing the design.

1 Copyright, Designs and Patents Act 1988, s 213(1).
2 Ibid, s 213(4).
3 Ibid, s 213(2).
4 Ibid, s 213(6).
5 Ibid, s 263(1).
6 Ibid, s 216.
7 Ibid, s 226.
8 Ibid, s 227.
9 Ibid, s 213(3).
10 Ibid, s 236.
11 Ibid, s 237.
12 Ibid, s 238.
13 Ibid, s 248.
14 Ibid, s 265(1).
15 Ibid, s 265(1),(3).
16 Ibid, s 269.
17 Ibid, s 269.

10.13 In conclusion, the Act's measures should:

(1) protect and encourage investment in design and innovation
(2) bring some certainty and consistency to the law of designs
(3) prevent the law of copyright being used to protect purely functional designs
(4) provide sufficient protection to give designers a lead-time in the market
(5) recognise that what are created as designs, although functional, and not protected by patent or copyright, are worth protecting
(6) prevent the growth of a monopoly position in the spare parts market
(7) stimulate industry
(8) ensure, in the event of the grant of the right being abused by the holder, that licences of right are made available
(9) ensure that design costs are recouped adequately
(10) help make sure that the consumer is able to take advantage of a greater range and variety of goods at a reasonable price and that he is not held to ransom with highly priced protected spare parts
(11) maintain the balance between, on the one hand, the possibility of over-protecting an intellectual property right, and on the other, under-protecting it
(12) clarify and strengthen the distinctions between the protection available for artistic copyright works, designs which are functional in operation and those which have achieved a higher degree of aesthetic quality which thereby gain additional rights.

CHAPTER 11

EEC competition law

Introduction

11.1 No book about intellectual property rights and their exploitation would be complete without at least some mention of possible fetters which might be imposed upon their exercise. What follows is a thumb-nail sketch of the law in this complex area and an attempt to alert the reader to the dangers inherent in the exercise of his intellectual property rights.

Under UK law there are some inbuilt safeguards to ensure that any intellectual property rights granted by the state operate for the benefit, not only of the owner of such rights, but for industry and the consumer. Thus the non-use of a trade mark or its improper use can result in its expungement from the Trade Marks Register. Likewise, as we have seen, in some circumstances a patent may become subject to compulsory licensing by the Comptroller. Thus under the substantive law there exist some fetters upon the exercise of these rights.

11.2 Are there any other legal, economic or political principles which may yet further override the exercise of the rights of the individual holder of intellectual property?

One economic principle developed in recent years is given by the free market economy, namely, that there should be free trade to include the free movement of goods, capital, people and services across national frontiers. This is thought to operate as a stimulus to both trade and the economy, resulting in the creation and production of a greater variety of consumer goods at competitive prices. The result of adhering to this principle has been the creation of policies designed, both nationally and internationally, to provide laws where these desired effects may be brought about through an increase in competition and in the removal of restrictions on the movement of goods. The UK has its own policy some of which is provided for by the Restrictive Trade Practices Act of 1976 and the

Competition Act of 1980 which, as the names imply, attempt to provide a regulatory system whereby competition in trade is promoted and preferred against restrictive practices. The main UK legislation is the Restrictive Trade Practices Act of 1976 which makes it necessary to register agreements which try to impose terms or conditions which are unduly restrictive of trade. This shows a national concern to eradicate practices which may operate to restrict trade.

Further, the European Community has established very definite objectives to remove trade restrictions between member states and has enshrined basic principles in the Treaty of Rome itself. The EC Commission is entrusted with achieving these objectives. It has exercised its legislative powers in the promulgation of regulations which are immediately and automatically binding in each of the member states of the Community and which have direct effect in each member state and upon the exercise of the rights of owners of intellectual property.

Nothing has been of more significance to the UK in preventing restrictive practices flowing from such agreements than the European Community policy on competition and the free movement of goods. The main relevant provisions are contained in Articles 85, 86, and Articles 30 to 36 of the Treaty of Rome. Let us glance at developments in this field which may be of importance to the innovative enterprise, which on the one hand needs reassurance of the subsistence of its intellectual property rights, and on the other hand wishes to exercise these rights itself or permit others to do so, and let us look at what fetters are imposed upon such exercise.

Subsistence of rights

11.3 The Community attempts to create a legal regime where holders of intellectual property rights can ascertain with clarity and certainty the range, extent, and general enforceability of their intellectual property rights within the Community. The aim is to harmonise those laws of the individual nation states where they have delegated competence to the appropriate Community organs.

Exercise of rights

11.4 Article 36 of the Treaty of Rome confirms the existence and validity of national intellectual property rights and these have been upheld by the Commission and the European Court. To achieve harmonisation requires the balancing of a recognition of the subsistence of intellectual property rights throughout the community while at the same time ensuring that their exercise is in keeping with the avowed principles of competition and the free movement of goods. How far has the Community achieved this balance as it concerns the interests of the owner of intellectual property rights? What rules must the owner of intellectual property rights be aware of in planning their exploitation lest he fall foul of the law? First:

Article 85

11.5 This article deals with anti-competitive agreements or practices. It covers agreements or practices between traders in whatever form which may affect trade between the member states of the Community which restricts or distorts competition within the Community in some way. The Article sets out the sort of acts which could breach the rules:

(1) direct or indirect fixing of purchasing or selling price or other trading conditions;
(2) limiting or controlling production, markets, developments or investment;
(3) sharing markets or sources of supply;
(4) applying dissimilar conditions to equivalent transactions;
(5) making the conclusion of a contract subject to supplementary obligations not connected with the subject of the contract.

However, some acts prohibited may be permitted provided they improve;

(*a*) production
(*b*) distribution
(*c*) technical or economic progress

and provided they are for the benefit of the consumer generally. The Commission has developed an 'effects doctrine' which means that in any particular case it looks at the effect which the agreement or practice has on trade within the Community.

HOW DOES THE SYSTEM OPERATE?

The Commission is empowered to look at written or oral agreements between organisations and indeed at such things as concerted practices which might exist under a 'gentleman's agreement'. Thus if a group of companies have an understanding between themselves to maintain a high pricing level for a particular commodity, if this affects trade and distorts competition within the Community, this will be contrary to the rules.

When establishing a licensing policy it will be important to consider whether what is proposed might fall foul of the anti-trust provisions outlined above.

Further, the Commission can look at individual clauses of agreements to assess whether these are anti-competitive. It will be useful to look briefly at some of the sorts of agreements and clauses which have given rise to problems.

Agreements

One sort of agreement which could offend is the exclusive distribution agreement. This occurs where only one party is allowed to sell and distribute the goods of a manufacturer. This limits the sale and distribution of goods thus restricting their free circulation.

Another is the exclusive licence. This restricts the possibility of the grant of licences to others and therefore is inherently anti-competitive. This is especially so where the exclusive licence is for a patent and the relevant product market in which the patented product exists is highly specialised. If the exclusive licence is between competitors then this could have a serious effect upon trade.

What sort of clauses might offend?

So far as patent licensing was concerned there was considerable uncertainty amongst licensors as to what sort of clauses they could include in their licences. To make the legal position more certain the Commission issued a block exemption Regulation in respect of the licensing of patents.[1] This was designed to set out clearly the sort of clauses which would or would not be likely to offend if included in a licensing agreement. For example, clauses prohibiting the licensee from challenging the validity of the licensor's patent, requiring the licensee to pay for patented goods after the patent has expired and tying-in the licensee by making him purchase goods not essential to the existence of the patented product have been considered unduly restrictive. This certainty makes it easier for the licensor to plan the licensing of his patents in a sensible way without fear of breaking the law.

1 Regulation No 2348/84.

Article 86

11.6 Article 86 takes effect when the owner of the intellectual property right attains a dominant position in a relevant product market, and subsequently seeks to exercise his right in a manner which, according to Community principles, appears to be an abuse of this position. The same sort of types of act which are likely to contravene Article 85 apply here. An organisation is in a dominant position where it is dominant in a relevant product market. In considering such matters the Commission first looks at the specific market in which the organisation is operating, eg, in the manufacture of a particular chemical. It then decides whether there is any competition in this market and whether it has achieved a position of dominance in that market. Finally, it looks to see whether it is abusing any such position of dominance in some way. For example, in the case of patents this could occur where there has been the imposition of unfair purchase and sale conditions, or if the owner of the patent tries to tie-in the licensee to purchasing from him alone the raw materials for the production of a patented product. It is important to note that it is not the subsistence of a monopoly right via the patent itself which offends the Article, nor indeed is it the fact that there is a dominant position situation; rather it is the abusive exercise of the right within this context of dominance. Further, it must be noted that the dominant position may arise as the result of the concerted action of a number of concerns.

Articles 30 to 36

11.7 Articles 30 to 36 deal with the principle concerning the free movement of goods and services. Here the Community has developed what has become known as the 'exhaustion of rights' doctrine. This attempts to stop the owner of intellectual property rights preventing the free circulation of goods within the Community. It operates as follows: it is possible for the owner of a national patent right, for example, to prevent anyone from using, selling, or importing any patented articles; he can enforce this right in the courts. The right is one granted under the patent and the exercise of these rights is not in itself objectionable. However, once a patented product has been sold either by the owner or by someone permitted to do so under licence within another part of the Community, then the strict enforcement of his patent rights becomes forfeited and his rights are said to be exhausted, that is, they are inoperable. Thus if the patented product is sold under licence in any of the member states of the Community the patent owner's national patent rights cannot be used to prevent the import of these products into the UK. Thus the patent owner is only protected against the importation of his patented goods on the first marketing of his product and thereafter he cannot rely upon his national patent rights to prohibit the import of goods which have been lawfully placed in the market of the Community. He is thus unable to prevent their free circulation.

11.8 What are the consequences of breaching the rules? The Commission can and does impose quite heavy fines against concerns which offend against the regulations. Another consequence is that individual clauses in agreements may be rendered inoperable and indeed the whole agreement may be rendered void and thus inoperable. The consequences of this could be disastrous. It is prudent therefore to consider carefully the possible effects of breaching the regulations when planning the exploitation of any intellectual property rights.

11.9 In the chapters relating to the exploitation of the various intellectual property rights under discussion, I have referred to those clauses which might evoke interest in an EEC dimension and which should therefore be considered carefully.

Part 2
New challenges to copyright

CHAPTER 12

Information technology

Introduction

12.1 'Information technology' is an umbrella term for a gradual convergence of technologies which include word-processing (computers and software), micro-electronics (chip technology), electro-magnetism (conducting medium), and telecommunications (cable and satellite). It also embodies developments in optical technology, such as print recognition (photocopying), conducting materials (optical fibres), and storage technology (optical discs). Each of the above developments has taken place within its own specific field of technology but they have now become co-ordinated and merged in the creation of a separate and unified technology known as information technology.

What is this new technology?

12.2 Let us examine some of the background and development of this phenomenon in order to place the present problems and changes in the law of copyright within the context of the advances made in the convergence of these technologies. This will illustrate the way in which new technology has led to the erosion of the protectability of intellectual property rights in copyright.

12.3 Computers and computing are hardly new phenomena, the first fully digital computer having been made in the USA in the 1930s. What is new however is that the same computing capacity of that first computer, large enough to fill a room, can now be contained on a single micro-chip. The original development of computers was to establish a method of processing raw data in such a way that it could replace the drudgery of the repetitive, tedious and mechanical processes of the brain when engaged in certain activities, just as machines replaced some types of physical labour in the Industrial Revolution.

The data processing machines of today are capable of processing, storing and retrieving data in vast quantities and at phenomenally fast speeds. The physical scale of the machines has been reduced, while their processing capacity has been scaled upwards in terms of volume and speed largely due to the development of micro-electronic circuitry. This has meant that very fast and densely packed electrical conducting components can be placed on a single silicon chip.

Developments in the field of telecommunications, for example, in the technology of opto-electronics, have led to the ability to distribute processed data through the normal system of telephone wires or through cable using the latest data distribution technology of optical fibres.

The final link in the chain of new technological distribution systems is the development of satellite technology, which has made it possible to transmit and disseminate processed data over great geographical areas. The scale, quality and volume of distributable data increases enormously with each new development in information technology.

Developments in science and technology have now transformed early forms of simple telephony into a technology with the ability to interconnect data processing machines for the creation, processing, storage and distribution of data. This data can be in the form of vocal, pictorial, textual and numerical information.

How does the technology work?

12.4 Information technology, that is, the application of new and advanced communications technology to information in some form, operates in the following way:

(1) There has to be an input of some kind; generally this may be either text or graphics. Initially these normally subsist in a traditional medium, for example, paper and print or other tangible medium. In order for them to become a part of any transmission system, they have to undergo a conversion from that tangible form into one which is capable of forming part of the transmission. In other words, they must be reduced or converted into some common communications denominator. Today the common denominator used for the handling and transmission of data in information technology systems is the electronic digital signal. For example, by the use of electronic devices the information contained in an original piece of text can be embodied in an electronic signal. In this electronic or electro-magnetic state it can be processed, stored, retrieved, and transmitted along suitable electronic distribution

systems. This is a vital stage in the process—the original material must be converted into a series of electro-magnetic pulses—it must undergo a 'digitising' process. In its digital electronic form it can be stored in electronic memories, such as on optical discs, magnetic tape, or for example, in 'bubble' which use magnetic bubbles to store the information.

(2) Access to this stored data and its eventual transmission will again be via electronic equipment. The stored data can be further converted for transmission by using a variety of distribution media, such as telephone wires, co-axial cable, or optical fibre cable. It can also be transmitted by any number of conducting and transmitting media, such as microwave radio signals, terrestrial broadcast, or satellite transmission.

(3) The final stage in this process is for the information in digital form, carried by the distribution medium or contained in the transmission medium, to be converted back into a human understandable form. Clearly, the electronic digital signal must be reconverted in such a way as to reconstitute the original form of the data before it was converted into digital form. Thus, if the information originated as a piece of written text, then the conversion of the digital information must be such that it can be reconstituted in the form of readable characters. For example, the signal will be reconstituted in such a way that the original piece of text will appear on a visual display unit of a computer terminal (VDU), a cathode ray tube such as a television set (CRT), or indeed may be reconstituted via an electronic printer which will reconstitute the text in a tangible written textual form. The output phase of the process takes the form of the information contained in the digital message being re-converted to a human understandable form. This enables the recipient to understand the information contained in the binary digital coded form of the signal.

Developments in signal delivery will soon make it possible to transmit and deliver information on a cable capable of carrying all types of signal whether of sound, voice, text, or graphics. Thus the common language of information technology—ie digital electronic signals or pulses—will soon be conveyed on a common medium. With the 'band-width' of cable systems, that is, generally their information carrying capacity, increasing due to developments in fibre optics, an even greater density of data will be capable of being transmitted with great clarity and speed.

Commercial considerations

12.5 At present enormous sums of money are being invested in the science and technology of information technology. Investment comes from government, industry, individual enterprises and a variety of other research and development sources. The UK is further engaged in research projects such as Esprit conducted under the auspices of the European Community which has a budget for development specifically in this field, and to which the UK contributes.

In the light of the decline of our older manufacturing industries and technologies where the UK is now a net importer, there is a strong movement in the direction of creating industries which are geared to serving the international information technology market. There is keen investment and activity in the development of the technologies themselves—ie in computers, software, satellite, etc—and also in the creation of such information or intelligence services which are valuable and tradable commodities in their own right. Precise and accurate information plays an increasingly important part in industrial and commercial operations and whole industries employing considerable numbers of personnel are concerned with the generation, storage, recording, processing, reproducing, conveying and transmitting of information in numbers and words. The advent of the new technologies, together with planned liberalisation through policies of telecommunication de-regulation, has meant that there is now, more than ever before, the means to create, process, reproduce and distribute accessible data or information in vast quantities, of high quality and at considerable speed.

Legal considerations

12.6 I will now examine the impact that these technological developments have had in the field of intellectual property law and in due course detail the provisions for change proposed in the government's 1986 White Paper[1] and now enacted under the provisions of the new Copyright, Designs and Patents Act 1988 ('the new Copyright Act').[2] These changes have largely been prompted by the failure of the law to respond quickly enough to the considerable impact which these new technologies have made and continue to make on the owners of intellectual property rights.

1 'Intellectual Property and Innovation' (1986, HMSO) Cmd 9712.
2 Copyright, Designs and Patents Act 1988.

The impact of information technology on copyright

12.7 The prevailing rationale behind intellectual property law is this: a grant of monopoly or quasi-monopoly rights to those engaged in innovation of some kind operates as a reward for the investment and effort expended by allowing exclusive rights to the exploitation of the innovation. This acts as an incentive to continue to invest effort and capital in further innovation. This is to the public good as it ensures a flow of new ideas, inventions and products. The rewards granted to the innovator are reflected by the benefits which the innovation confers on the consumer. Through continual innovation, the consumer in a modern society enjoys a greater variety of new, well-designed, safer, more efficient, time and labour saving, and ultimately cheaper, consumer durables. The stimulus or incentives towards creating new technological advances and developments has meant the following: an increase in sophistication in new products; a resulting eventual decrease in their cost; and an increased and widespread use of the technology. By and large this is true of most technologies, but perhaps no truer than of those developments which have taken place in the whole field of information technology. As techniques, skills and technology advance in, for example, computer hardware and software, so the costs of purchasing that technology eventually reduce. Thus, at one time, computers were used only by those organisations which had the money to purchase them and the space to accommodate them. With developments in micro-circuitry, the application and use of the computer has become widespread and pervades just about every aspect of our daily lives both at work and at play.

12.8 The expectations of the consumer are now such that he considers he has a right of access to the latest benefits of modern technology, which, not unnaturally, he wishes to harness for his own individual use. This is true in the field of information technology, where the ability to access, manipulate, reproduce and use information has been made simple. The information which the individual may wish to access, use, or reproduce may be in the form of textual or graphic material. It might be a textual work embodied in digital form on a magnetic disc, or a piece of video material, again digitally encoded, say on a piece of magnetic tape. It could be in the form of a sound recording embodied in digital code on a magnetic disc or tape. Access to, and reproduction of, such materials is often carried out by a simple operation involving little skill and at minimal costs. The cost will normally only relate to the purchase of the equipment used for reproduction itself and to the physical medium upon which the material is reproduced. Because they have invested money in, for example, a video recorder, a record player, a cassette recorder, a computer, or photocopier or other form of reprographic device, the public consumers of information will want the fullest possible access to the sort of goods which are the natural concomitants to such technology, such as software programs, without which the machines themselves are useless. The goods or materials they require and to which they could believe they should have unrestricted access, are often materials in which there are intellectual property rights, namely copyright. As well as software, these include films, records, pre-recorded cassettes, video tapes, video discs, etc. Alternatively, the recording medium itself may be left blank, the consumer deciding what material he wishes to record on it from whatever source is available to him. Thus the machines themselves are produced to serve a dual function: to play pre-recorded copyright materials or to record or reproduce other works or materials which could well be copyright protected. The new technology of information technology has thus created a situation where it is now possible for the owner of an inexpensive machine to copy or reproduce materials fixed in the medium which the machine is geared to operate, virtually at will, and at very little cost, save the price of the actual medium upon which the recording or reproduction is made, eg the tape or disc.

To the consumer this represents a fair use of the technology in which he has invested. He considers that, as it is designed to fulfil a particular function—to reproduce or copy materials—he should be at liberty to do so with impunity. However, the copyright owner is unlikely to concur. Without rights to restrict usage, the mass reproduction of his works would represent a loss in terms of revenue or royalty which he would otherwise have achieved were it not for the fact that they were reproduced in a manner or form outside his control.

The role of copyright in traditional industries

12.9 Copyright, as we have seen, is the right of the owner of the intellectual property in a work to prevent others from reproducing his work or material without his permission. This includes single or individual copying, or multiple copying. Prior to the advent of the new technologies which have made widespread copying possible, it was possible for the owner of copyright interests to enjoy some comfort and certainty, in the knowledge that the legislature had produced sound laws designed to ensure that his rights and interests in his work, whatever it was, enjoyed protection. This was also true of concerns such as publishers, engaged in the exploitation of such works. This comfort stemmed from the fact that the work would normally subsist in a readily identifiable medium over which it was possible to exercise a degree of control. If we take the example of a book or magazine produced under the traditional technology of printing, we can see that copyright subsisted in an artefact which existed in a tangible medium. The product was readily identifiable, ownership in the work could be ascertained without great difficulty, and its unauthorised reproduction readily discovered. Loss or commercial damage caused to the copyright owner could be calculated, that is, based on the number of units sold illicitly by the party who had reproduced the work without the consent of the legitimate owner of the copyright in the work. Thus, in this paradigm case, we see how the law of copyright could operate quite effectively on behalf of the rights owner, due largely to the fact that the intellectual property rights were embodied in a work in a controllable medium. This certainty of the subsistence of copyright in a work, together with the ability to protect it, engendered a feeling of confidence in the law and acted as an incentive to further investment in innovative ventures. Thus the publishing industry amongst others was underpinned by, and could rely upon, the law of copyright to protect its investment in its commercial interests. The economic balance between the creator of the work, the investor in its exploitation, and the consumer was maintained and the copyright owner could expect a fair return upon his investment and labours.

The imbalance

12.10 With the advent of the new technologies what has occurred is that there is now an imbalance between the traditional and legitimate rights and interests of the copyright owner and the modern consumer. What has been produced in a tangible form, such as a book or magazine, can now be either reproduced by very fast optical reprographic machines or reduced into digital form and multiple copies made of it. The creators of works on films, video and computer software are in a similar position. Valuable works can be reproduced virtually at will and at very little cost. Thus not only are the creators of works in the older type of technological media at risk from illicit copying, but also those whose industry is engaged in the creation of works in the newer media. They are even more at risk, as the new media lend themselves to easy reproduction. Not only is the medium of creation and reproduction drastically altered, but also the means of distribution which now includes cable, terrestrial transmission and satellite. Whatever the information, and in virtually whatever form, modern technological processes and systems exist which can reduce it to a form of digital electronic pulses, fixed in such a medium as to make access, multiple reproduction and rapid distribution a comparatively easy task.

What should the law of copyright seek to achieve?

12.11 Clearly, in order for the creators or innovators of new works to continue to create and innovate they need the comfort of a copyright law which will do at least one of three things.

First; to make it possible for the creator/author/artist to say with some certainty that the work which he has created in a particular medium is one which is protected under the law of copyright, ie that copyright subsists in the work. This becomes of increasing importance as more information is created in new forms of media. In the case of a work initially subsisting in digital form, such as in the memory of a computer, prior to the Copyright (Computer Software) Amendment Act 1985, there were doubts as to whether such a work would be accorded copyright protection. This meant that there was a possibility that the creator of such a work was not protected. Further, even if a work did exist in a legally recognised material form, such as the physical text of a book, if that text was reproduced in a digital form—eg into a form where it subsisted as electro-magnetic pulses on a computer disc—this may not have constituted reproduction in such a manner as to infringe the copyright in the original work. Vast quantities of information are created at present in the digital medium and stored in data-bases without ever having been commended to the form of a traditional text. Clearly, it is important that copyright be seen to subsist in such works.

Second; once there is certainty as to the subsistence of the right, its effective practical protection is required. Here there are problems too. With new technology, even if it is decided that a work exists in what we might describe as a tangible material medium—eg, as above, the work being created on magnetic disc and placed in a data-base—its subsequent reproduction, transfer and future use might be virtually undetectable. In this case, the medium is one which is also virtually uncontrollable, and if so, not easily protectable. In such a case, if the law of copyright is such that it is ineffective, then the owner of the work will have to rely largely upon what protection he can gain in terms of the contractual use of his work, or, if possible, try to apply some technical protection. This problem is highlighted in the field of the audio/video medium with the advent of digital audio tape or DAT.

Third; if the creator is to have an incentive to continue his creative endeavours then he must be able to rely upon some form of legal mechanism which will ensure that he can obtain some reasonable recompense for the investment of time, labour, skill, judgement, investment, etc in his work and thus be able to enforce his strict rights against infringers. Later I detail the magnitude of the problem of the unrecompensed copyright owner. Suffice it to say now that many industries which have traditionally relied upon the law of copyright to underpin their investment have found that the new technologies have seriously undermined those investments and interests. While their rights are recognised at law, the law is powerless to protect them by the exercise of the strict enforcement of those rights. In this case where the traditional mechanisms have failed, new mechanisms must be worked out.

In the light of the above we will have to consider later the proposals recommended by the White Paper and the provisions of the new Copyright Act to see whether they offer a solution to these acute problems as they hope to do, and whether they would be able to protect and defend the holders of copyright interests.

The new technologies which we have been talking about confront both the legal profession and those industries which are underpinned by the protection of copyright with new problems, and it is these that I am now going to discuss.

12.12 The main provisions of the new Copyright Act stem largely from the recommendations of the government's 1986 White Paper. Part 2 of the White Paper[1] deals exclusively with the government's proposals for the reform of the law of copyright based upon the recommendations of earlier reports, including the Whitford Report on Copyright and Designs Law 1977,[2] the Green Paper on the Reform of the Law relating to Copyright Designs and Performers' Protection 1981,[3] and the Green Paper on the Recording and Rental of Audio and Video Copyright Material of 1985.[4]

1 'Intellectual Property and Innovation' (1986, HMSO) Cmnd 9712.
2 'Copyright and Designs Law' (1977, HMSO) Cmnd 6732.
3 'Reform of the Law relating to Copyright, Designs and Performers' Protection' (1981, HMSO) Cmnd 8302.
4 'The Recording and Rental of Audio and Video Copyright Material' (1985, HMSO) Cmnd 9445.

12.13 Copyright subsists as we have seen in any original literary, artistic, dramatic or musical work, providing protection in the form of an exclusive reproduction right lasting for a period of 50 years from the end of the year of the author's death with certain exceptions. It is designed to give 'on-line' protection to the labour, skill, judgement and investment in the creation of original works. It protects both artistic or literary works satisfying some aesthetic criteria and those of a purely functional or commercial nature, thus importantly extending to the design of industrially applied products or artefacts. Entrepreneurial copyright under Part II of the old 1956 Copyright Act protected the investment of those engaged in the exploitation of original Part I authors' or artists' copyright works or of the products generated by a particular industry thus protecting the investment in such materials as films, broadcasts, phonograms etc. The common law has extended copyright protection to a very wide range of works in a variety of media as we have already seen. Whole industries—often referred to as 'copyright industries'—such as computer software, film, record and broadcasting industries, often place reliance upon copyright alone to protect their investment in the creation, production and exploitation of original works. Their investments are underpinned by it. It is on the protection of their copyright that I now concentrate, having discussed the problems generated by the sort of works and materials of the average innovative industrial concern which qualify for copyright protection in Part 1 of the book.

Why copyright works are susceptible to the new technologies

12.14 A main disadvantage of copyright is that because it is not a system of registered rights, the creator of an original work or an innovator has no definite statement of his rights and instead often depends upon the general level of understanding of copyright protection within his particular field of endeavour. This was the case with computer software before the 1985 Act. Where there is uncertainty of the subsistence of copyright in his work, the creator looks to a consensus of opinion that copyright protection does or does not subsist in a particular type of creation or in a particular medium; hardly satisfactory given the rather nebulous or amorphous nature of copyright. Obviously the owner of the rights in any original work, from whatever source, benefits from making an initial assertion of the subsistence of copyright in it and claim to his ownership, even if legally this is strictly not necessary.

12.15 The nebulous character of the nature of copyright is nowhere better illustrated than in the increasing difficulties presented to the law—and to the new technological industries—by the problem of determining the sense of the expression 'material form'.

The 'material form' provisions of the 1956 Act were important in two ways:

(1) To the very subsistence of copyright in a work. The law is clear enough: for copyright to subsist in a work it must be expressed 'in a material form'. But what does this expression mean? Questions have arisen as to whether a work expressed in any other new technological medium, for example as a hologram, is in a 'material form' or not? If not, then any works created in that medium are not protected by the law of copyright.

(2) For a work to be infringed, the owner of the copyright in the work has to prove that the work, or a substantial part of it, has been reproduced in a material form. What if the work is in the form of a printed page of text and is thus automatically copyright protected; would the copyright in the work be infringed if it were then converted in some way into electro-magnetic pulses and fixed on a disc or tape in the memory of a computer or again if it were reproduced in a completely new technical medium? The material form provisions relating to computer software were discussed extensively at international legal level,[1,2,3] culminating in an intense lobbying of Parliament, and the introduction of a Private Member's Bill, soon to be followed by an Act of Parliament marking the end of considerable speculation and uncertainty. The problem of the meaning of the expression 'material form' is illustrative of the kind of conceptual problem faced by the creators or innovators of works in any new medium, let alone in the medium of electro-magnetic pulses, though I discuss it in more detail largely in relation to computers in the next chapter.

1 *Northern Office Microcomputers (Pty) Ltd v Rosenstein* [1982] FSR 124 and the 'Apple' cases.
2 *Apple Computer Inc v Franklin Computer Corpn* 714 F2d 1240 (1983).
3 *Apple Computer Inc v Computer Edge Pty Ltd and Suss* [1984] FSR 426, Aust FC; revsd [1984] FSR 481.

Proposals for reform

12.16 In order to get a better understanding of how the present problems have arisen, to appreciate the reasoning behind the provisions of the new Copyright Act and to decide whether they are adequate, it will be useful to start by looking at the Whitford Report 1977.[1] This report considers the lessons which can be learnt by the law, posed by considerable technological advances made between the Copyright Act of 1956 and its review of the law of copyright in 1977. These advances have moved at such a pace that the law has been able to respond only haphazardly in response to the fears of those whose intellectual property rights are deeply affected by such advances. We have already examined the nature of some of the technological changes which have taken place in order to get a better perspective on the question of whether the changes in the law of copyright are adequate. That is, do they give the owners of copyright the certainty in terms of subsistence, ownership, protection and the reward of recompense which they require for their individual rights and for the industries affected?

1 'Copyright and Designs Law, Report of the Committee to consider the Law of Copyright and Designs' (1977, HMSO) Cmnd 6732.

12.17 The Whitford Committee's brief was to review the whole of the law of copyright and registered designs. The report itself was a thorough examination of the law and it made recommendations for sweeping changes. It recommended that such changes be incorporated into a new Copyright Act. This new legislation would have to place copyright law, in the words of the Report, on a 'plain and uniform basis'[1] and, following the evidence submitted to it by interested parties, it decided that

> '. . . it is inherent in the nature of the rights which copyright protects and in the myriad and prospectively unlimited ways in which such works may be utilised, that legislation which seeks to define extensively and precisely the detailed limits of control and free use will be out of date and virtually unworkable before such legislation comes into operation.'

It recognised that the 1956 Copyright Act was beginning to look out of date by the time of the Report. The Act had sought to cover in too great a detail the sort of activities which would attract copyright protection, in terms of the then state of the technological art. Clearly technology had moved on apace, and the detailed language and provisions of that Act were having to be applied tortuously to novel situations where works were being created in various new media not contemplated by the Act when it was passed. Thus, under its provisions, the owner of computer software would be put to proving to the court that his software program constituted a 'literary' work under the prevailing precise language of the Act, and should therefore be accorded protection. The Report highlighted quite clearly the defects of the Act and advocated that any new copyright law to be promulgated should seek to establish more general principles of protection rather than itemise specific terms or categories, such as whether such a work was a literary or artistic work etc; the principles of protection would then remain long after any specific categories of activity or media rights had ceased to be relevant.[2] This would remove the present need to torture the English language in an attempt to encompass new forms of works in a hitherto unknown medium. The significance of this is clear as the proposals of the White Paper and the provisions of the new Copyright Act show. Any new Act must protect the creation of works in any presently known medium and be sufficiently broad to encompass the creation of works in any new or, indeed, as yet unknown medium. This will not only protect new works created in a new medium, but will also protect from unauthorised copying existing copyright works which might subsequently be expressed in that new medium as this would constitute an unauthorised act of infringement.

1 Whitford, para 43.
2 Whitford, para 43(1), p 12.

12.18 Whitford further foresaw that with the advent of the new technologies, the enforceability of rights in some cases may become a serious problem irrespective of increased civil or criminal remedies or sanctions being made available to the copyright owner, because of the problem of detection. In these difficult cases mechanisms other than the enforcement of strict rights of copyright would have to be brought into play to ensure a fair return for the innovator in his investment. Thus, if the copyright owner was indeed in the unhappy position where, although he could point to the subsistence of copyright in his work, he was unable to enforce his strict rights, then the law would have to make some provision for this commercial fact of life. Later we will see the sort of compensation schemes suggested by Whitford and later reports on the problem of the unenforceability of rights. The Whitford Report was important because it focussed attention on the actual practical, commercial and industrial problems encountered by a considerable diversity of copyright owners. It proposed practical measures as solutions to their practical problems. To some extent it also foresaw the direction that copyright law would have to take in the future, if it were to ensure a continuation of investment by industries dependent upon the law of copyright for the protection of their industrial and commercial assets.

12.19 Some of Whitford's proposals have already been put into effect. Certainly the last few years have seen a steady flow of legislation in the field of intellectual property law, sometimes as a result of the intensive lobbying of those with interests in the various and very widespread copyright industries. Legislation has taken place, at least on an ad hoc basis.[1] In some cases this has been to confirm that copyright does subsist in a particular type of work (Copyright (Computer Software) Amendment Act 1985), and in others to increase the sanctions which could be imposed upon those who infringed the rights of the copyright owners.[2]

1 Cable and Broadcasting Act 1984.
2 Copyright Act 1956 (Amendment) Act 1982.

12.20 The gradual increase in the level of awareness of the crucial influence which the law of copyright plays in the whole field of industrial innovation and the fact that whole industries rely upon the form of protection which it affords, culminated in the proposals for change contained in the government's White Paper of 1986 and in the changes now effected by the new legislation. The White Paper attempted to set out changes which it hoped would streamline the law of copyright and designs. It followed many of Whitford's recommendations in seeking to make the law more consistent, in ensuring a greater degree of certainty in the subsistence of rights and enforceability of these rights, and perhaps most importantly, where the enforceability of these rights cannot be guaranteed, in ensuring there is in force some effective legal mechanism so that the legitimate rights of copyright owners are properly recompensed for the investment of labour and capital which they have made in the creation of their work.

12.21 In a recent report,[1] copyright was placed at approximately 2.6% of the Gross Domestic Product of the UK, which suggests in the words of the preface to the report that 'in size they thus exceed the motor car and food manufacturing industries and approximately equal the chemical and man-made fibre industries'. This figure does not include the products of the computer software industry. Copyright is a valuable commodity.

Whitford pointed the way to a reform of the law of copyright, dealing largely with the impact which modern technology has had on the rights of copyright owners. Since Whitford, technological advance has moved even more rapidly than possibly even Whitford himself envisaged; and in many cases, where Whitford hinted at impending problems arising from the new technology, the problem has not only manifested itself but has become acute.

1 Jennifer Phillips, 'The Economic Importance of Copyright', published by the Common Law Institute of Intellectual Property Limited.

12.22 Much of the rest of this book will be taken up with a discussion on the emergence of information technology as a technical and commercial phenomenon and, most importantly for this book, what these developments have meant in terms of its impact on the owners of different types of copyright works and whether the latest changes in the law provided by the new Copyright Act will be adequate to ensure the protection necessary. Information technology is without doubt the fastest growing area of convergent technologies, and it is likely to continue virtually unabated. Its impact upon the law of copyright has been profound, and it presents the law with a challenge. Any amendments of the law have to take account, not only of problems posed by the current state of the technological art, but of possible or potential future developments in the whole field of information technology. The law has to deal with issues such as the ownership of rights of computer-generated works, the issue of rights in the products of parallel processing, of expert systems, and in due course the legal status of the output of machines capable of mimicking the activities of the human brain which exhibit what is known as artificial intelligence. I will discuss these particular matters further in the final chapter of this Part, entitled 'The Future'.

CHAPTER 13

Computers

Introduction

13.1 Computers and computing form the basis of information technology. Developments in these fields have raised questions as to the adequacy of copyright for the protection not only of the products of the technology, such as software, but also for the protection of information or data which is converted for use in computers and is accessed, manipulated and transmitted in this medium. This raises fundamental questions about subsistence, authorship and ownership, and what constitutes infringement of both programs and data. In this chapter I intend looking at these problems and how the law of copyright has responded to the challenge posed by them, whether sufficient has been done legally to assure the necessary protection, and if not, whether the proposals in the government's 1986 White Paper and the reforms actually effected by the new Copyright, Designs and Patents Act 1988 go some way towards remedying the remaining defects in the law.

13.2 Copyright 'works' in the UK are not confined to what might normally be considered literary or artistic works in the aesthetic sense, but include the considerable variety of artefacts which are generated by a host of industrial concerns. As we saw, the 1956 Copyright Act provided that works which have the quality of having had time, energy, skill, judgement and capital invested in their creation enjoy copyright protection. This has been extended to the most mundane of creations, such as street directories, racing score cards, etc. Indeed, in this country it is the investment of money and labour involved in the production of the work which copyright protects. This is not true of some legal jurisdictions such as that of West Germany where there are stricter standards of aesthetic judgement applied if a work is to be accorded copyright protection. Those concerned with the creation or generation of copyright works in the UK industrial and commercial context may take some comfort from the fact that their interests are properly served by the law and their rights in this respect are accorded a degree of certainty.

13.3 But for a number of years the legal status of computer software was uncertain. The main question was what to make of the 'material form' provisions of the 1956 Copyright Act.[1] It provides that protection is accorded to original works which are fixed in a material form. It protects the work if it exists in one form and is then reproduced in any other material form.[2] To gain the protection of copyright it is crucial to establish that the form in which the work is originally fixed is 'material'. But what does it mean for a form to be 'materially' fixed? An obvious paradigm material form is the textual inscription of a work on paper. But the days of the book are being superseded; the question arises, what else counts as such a form? As we have seen already, it has been debated[3] by the courts whether the fixing of digitally encoded information by means of electro-magnetic pulses on to a magnetic disc or tape amounts to the fixing of a work in a material form so that it could claim the protection of copyright. As I said in the last chapter, the solution to this problem, for computer software at least, was resolved by the passing of the Copyright (Computer Software) Amendment Act of 1985 which provided the software industry with a degree of protection for its programs and allowed that fixing a text in electro-magnetic form does count as being a material form for the purpose of copyright protection.

1 Copyright Act 1956, s 49(4).
2 Copyright Act 1956, s 2(5)(a).
3 See 'Apple' cases in footnotes 2 and 3 to para 12.15.

13.4 Though they are not exactly new technological industries, the effects of broadcasting, cinema, and phonograms became widespread and their economic value highlighted as a result of intensive lobbying for the protection of their products by those who had made considerable investment in them. The Copyright Act of 1956 recognised their increasing economic importance within the UK industrial context, and extended the law of copyright to underpin their products. At the time of the Act, computers were in use, but only by organisations with sufficient money to purchase them and space to accommodate them. Therefore there was no computer lobby to speak of, and it was only in the early 1980s that lobbying of the legislature produced the required statutory recognition of intellectual property rights in computer software culminating in the passing of the 1985 Act. By then the industry had grown worldwide, and the value of the product could not be denied. It was not only the value of the labour and investment in the product itself which at last was recognised, but also the overall effect which such a product could have upon industrial performance generally in terms of investment, jobs, revenue generated by the industry, new industrial ideas, and the impact of these in stimulating already existing industries, making them more competitive. Thus national and international use of the product justified its eventual acceptance as a commodity to be accorded intellectual property rights and in due course some of the necessary protective legislation was passed. More of it was promised in the 1986 White Paper and there are additional provisions in the new Act.[1]

1 'Intellectual Property and Innovation', Cmnd 9712.

13.5 I now propose to give a brief exposition of the technical features of, and the commercial and legal problems posed by, this product. I will discuss the problems of software protection in the light of the inadequacies of the old Act and conclude by appraising the changes effected by the present legislation.

The technology

(1) WHAT IS SOFTWARE?

13.6 Having already described the function of a computer as an element of information technology, it is time to consider the technology involved.

There is no universally accepted definition of 'a program'. It is generally considered to be a series of instructions for controlling and conditioning the operation of a computer in order to make it perform certain desired tasks.

It is usual to divide computer programs into two specific types: the operating program, and the application program. Without programs the computer has no function. It must be told what to do by the operator. In order that it may have some general initial instructions, it is normally equipped with a set of instructions already which set out the types of functions and capabilities which are required of it. This will be the operating program and these instructions are in the form of an electronic code. Often an adjunct to many homes in the UK, the normal personal computer has an operating program which provides that the computer has the capacity or capability to function as a word processor, display graphics, play games, etc. The initial role and function of the operating program can be set out in the actual electronic circuitry of the program itself, on a microchip, or on a program disc or magnetic tape upon which the instructions to the computer are encoded, and which has to be physically loaded on to the computer. In most cases this type of program is supplied with the computer and produced by the computer manufacturer himself or by a software house which produces that type of program to run on a series of compatible machines to give them a standard set of capabilities.

After determining the range of functions which the computer could perform, the computer must be instructed to perform a specific function in a particular way as incorporated, for instance, in a program such as a word processing package. This is arranged by the use of an applications program, normally physically loaded on to the computer. These again are produced by the computer manufacturer or a software house producing a whole range of software programs to run on a variety of standard and specific machines in conjunction with their operating programs.

13.7 A simplified explanation of the technical make-up of computer programs is as follows:

A program whether operating or application may exist

(1) as a written text;
(2) as electro-magnetic pulses on magnetic tape;
(3) as electro-magnetic pulses on a disc;
(4) as a pattern of electrical charges or circuit within the surface of a micro-chip (sometimes called 'firmware').

(2) HOW IS SOFTWARE DEVELOPED?

13.8 Computer programs, like so many other technological developments, do not exist in vacuo, but are often the response to a particular need or requirement, or the solution to a problem which is often approached initially in terms of a suitable mental model of the problem as stated. Thus to gain some visual concept of a problem and its possible solution, the model of the flow-chart is often used. This states the problem, and in diagrammatic form indicates the form and direction which the solution should take in a practical illustration. From this is developed what is called an algorithm, which sets out the various practical steps to be taken to create the program. During these stages of production of the software program there are a variety of works which could satisfy the original requirements of material form under the old 1956 Act as a literary work (the algorithm), or an artistic work (the flowchart).

Thus, were any of these reproduced in a material form, in all likelihood the copyright in them would be infringed.

13.9 Let us now go one stage further in the process. We have seen that the software program is something which gives instructions to the computer to carry out a particular job or function. Clearly, something which exists in a substantial material form, such as an inscription on paper, cannot be used to drive, operate or instruct an electronic device, such as a computer. It is necessary to convert this language represented by the inscription into a language which the machine understands. This is done by converting the written language into digital binary electronic pulses which represent the machine language. Special forms of program called 'compiler' or 'assembler' programs exist in order to carry out this conversion. When the conversion has been completed by the compiler or assembler program what we are left with is the finished product which is capable of giving instructions to the computer. The original written code, called the 'source' code, has in effect had all the information contained in it converted into digital binary code, which is now machine readable, i e understandable, as it exists in the form of electronic pulses. This goes under the title of the 'object' or 'machine' code. The computer is merely an electronic device, and in order for it to be instructed in some way, the ordinary language instructions which we give it must be converted in some way into a language which the machine also 'understands', i e can use, which is in the form of electronic media, such as the binary digital electronic pulses referred to. Applications programs can then be applied or loaded on to the machine, again containing information in digitally encoded electronic form which the machine can understand. For the machine to then operate meaningfully, all data or raw materials which require processing in some way must be introduced electronically into the machine, usually via an electronic key-board. The operating and application programs are directly instructed by the user of the machine to process the raw data. Thus the activities of the various programs and the raw material fed into the machine are electronically interactive. The data can be processed, accessed, manipulated, and then put into memory, either inside or outside the computer, and in due course retrieved and re-manipulated at will. Then it can be distributed or transmitted in the form of digital binary electronic pulses through conducting wires and cable. As we know already, the final stage in the process is the re-conversion of the electronic digital binary pulses into some tangible readable form by means of the electronic printer, or on the screen of a VDU or CRT.

Legal considerations

13.10 Let us now look at the sort of legal problems which this sort of activity has engendered and at the fundamental challenge which it has posed to the law of copyright. So how does the law apply to the computer and its software?

The computer—the machine itself—could be protected as an invention under the law of patents provided it was novel and involved an inventive step, and its design could be protected under the law relating to registered designs. Copyright protects software. But is something like a pattern of electrical charges within the surface of a micro-chip a piece of software, and so protected by copyright? Or is it hardware—part of the machine itself—and so protected under patents? Such a problem illustrates the difficulties in determining which intellectual property rights best protect a given item requiring such protection and why it is often misleading to call 'software' all the different ways in which instructions may be given to a computer. There is no definition under the Copyright (Computer Software) Amendment Act 1985 nor is one offered under the new Act. Even so, copyright has assumed and maintained its importance in the protection of diverse technologies all subsumed under the general heading of software. This is especially so given that the Patents Act 1977 expressly excludes the patenting of computer programs per se, although there have been cases where software has been held to be a patentable invention where the program was integral to some novel industrial invention.[1] It will of course be a question of fact in each case as to whether the criteria for patentability are satisfied.

1 *Re Burroughs Corpn's Application* [1974] RPC 147.

Some problems

(1) SUBSISTENCE

13.11 Difficulties occur in any attempt to employ legal notions or principles of copyright to the processes described. However, from the above brief description of the technical processes involved in the creation and production of a piece of computer software, it will be seen that there are a series of artefacts which are produced to which copyright protection might be accorded. The Copyright Act of 1956 was designed to protect any original literary or artistic work in which sufficient labour, skill and judgement was expended. That

Act provides that a 'literary work' includes 'any written table or compilation'.[1] 'Writing' includes 'any form of notation, whether by hand or by printing, typewriting or any similar process' and a literary work is 'made' when it is first reduced to writing or some other material form.[2,3]

The main problem faced by the courts in interpreting the 1956 provisions in the UK, and comparable provisions elsewhere, where there has been no specific legislative provision for the protection of computer software,[4,5,6] has been in deciding whether a program, which is first expressed in the form of invisible magnetic patterns on a disc or tape, constitutes writing or other material form sufficient for the Act. In order to claim protection for this sort of program, the paradigms employed were the flow-charts and algorithms originally used as the original expression of the program. It was said that these were original artistic and literary works, the material form of which was expressly provided for under the Act. Thus anything having an analogous form ought to be automatically protected as there are no further requirements of the Act such that a work has either literary merit or is intelligible to the human brain. In the past, telegraphic codes which were unintelligible to the human brain have been accorded protection as copyright works, and this is the case today, provided that the communication conveys information of some kind.

So much for programs created inside the computer based upon flow-charts and algorithms. What other problems are there which relate to subsistence?

In the description given of the function of the computer, flow-charts and algorithms were seen to be a part of the primary process in the production of a software program. The next process was to convert this information into a form which would give understandable instructions to the computer. The information which existed in coded form now had to be converted into machine code, i e a coded pattern of digits suitable for consumption by the computer's central processing system. As we have seen, the conversion is carried out by what is called the compiler or assembler program which is lodged within the computer. How can we characterise this in legal terms? The courts have held that, when the source program incorporating the original instructions to the computer is converted by loading this into the computer, what happens is that the original literary work subsisting in the source code is 'adapted' by being 'translated' under the terms of the Act;[7] that is, it is the same work, only it now subsists in another material form. An adaptation of a work is as protected as the original work itself.[8] The translated work will then be accorded copyright protection as being derived from the original. Thus the feeding of the copyright source program into the compiler of a computer which automatically translates it into object or machine readable, i e understandable, code will thus be considered to be a restricted act. The final product, created via the source code and the compiler—i e the machine readable, digitally encoded object code program—is itself a derivation or adaptation and thus will attract copyright protection.

1 Copyright Act 1956, s 48.
2 Copyright Act 1956, s 48.
3 Copyright Act 1956, s 49(4).
4 *Northern Office Microcomputers (Pty) Ltd v Rosenstein* [1982] FSR 124 and the 'Apple' cases (below).
5 *Apple Computer Inc v Franklin Computer Corpn* 714 F 2d (1983).
6 *Apple Computer Inc v Computer Edge Pty Ltd and Suss* [1984] FSR 426, Anst FC; revsd [1984] FSR 481.
7 Copyright Act 1956, s 2(6)(a)(iii).
8 Copyright Act 1956, s 2(5).

13.12 These were the kinds of arguments needed for those engaged in the creation of computer software to claim that what they were doing amounted to the creation of an original literary or artistic work in a material form to gain the protection of copyright.

There was further uncertainty when the object code, that is, the machine readable code, was not derived through the adaptation by translation of an original literary work such as a written source code based for example on a flow-chart or algorithm, but was created by direct digital input, for example via another computer, or when it was typed or 'keyed' straight into the computer's memory. The only way in which this type of program could possibly be protected, since it did not satisfy the material form provisions initially—i e it was not originally fixed in a material form as either a literary or artistic work—was to make sure that at the end of the process of creation there was a physical print-out of the completed program. Copyright would subsist in this printed material form automatically as a literary work. Any reproduction of the electronic digitally encoded program could be protected as representing or constituting a 'translation' or 'adaptation' of the literary work in print-out form.[1]

In order to understand the currently enacted reforms in this complex area, it will help to look at some of the commentaries and recommendations for change made in the last ten years beginning with the Whitford Report 1977.

1 Copyright Act 1956, s 2(6)(a)(iii).

13.13 The Whitford Committee in 1977,[1] reviewing the law of copyright, considered that the labour, skill and judgement and the considerable investment involved in the creation of these programs, required effective legislation for their protection. In order to effect this and so encourage further investment in this increasingly important field, it suggested that the same basic law of copyright should apply to computer programs as to other works and that no special provisions were needed for software programs. The report of the committee suggested that copyright should subsist in any original work which is fixed in such a way that the recorded information can be reproduced. This meant that it became immaterial that the program may not be visible to or readable by the human eye, or directly understandable by the human brain. Nor should it matter what original form it was in or in which form it was first fixed, that is, whether it was in written or other form, or indeed whether derived from a written source code or not.

The Green Paper of 1981[2] agreed with Whitford that all uncertainty should be removed and the law made explicit in new legislation in order that computer programs should attract protection in the same way as literary works. This meant all works were protected in any form from which they could, at least in principle, be reproduced.

1 'Copyright and Designs Law' (1977, HMSO) Cmnd 6732, chapter 9, pp 124–133.
2 'Reform of the Law relating to Copyright Designs and Performer's Protection' (1981, HMSO) Cmnd 8302.

Let us look at the statutory provisions made so far to see whether these have dealt effectively with the problem of subsistence in computer software.

13.14 First there was the Copyright (Computer Software) Amendment Act 1985 which is now repealed by the new Act. The main provisions of this Act were as follows:

(1) computer programs attract copyright protection in the same manner as literary works;[1]
(2) a work directly created in a computer—e g by typing in from the keyboard without its first having been written on paper—attracts copyright protection;[2]
(3) criminal remedies were increased against commercial piracy of programs;[3]
(4) a version of a computer program which is to be converted into or out of a computer language or code, or into a different computer language or code, is an adaptation of the program. Thus if the original code is written in one language and this is then converted into another language, this will be deemed to be an adaptation by translation;[4]
(5) the reduction of any work to a material form includes references to the storage of that work in a computer.[5] Thus storing a

work in a computer is a form of reproduction requiring the copyright owner's consent.

It must be said that the Act was essentially a codification and declaration of the prevailing common law position on computer programs.

The 1988 Act

The Act confirms the present legal status of computer software, namely, that copyright subsists in such programs as literary works. 'Literary work' means

> 'any work other than a dramatic or musical work which is written, spoken or sung, and accordingly includes–
> (*a*) a written table or compilation and
> (b) a computer program'.[6]

Copyright does not subsist in a literary work unless and until it is recorded in writing or otherwise.[7] 'Writing' includes any form of notation or code, whether by hand or otherwise and regardless of the method by which or medium, in or on which, it is recorded.[8] We can presume that this would normally include such operations as 'keying in' electronically in which case a program which is first expressed in invisible magnetic patterns on a disc or tape would gain the protection of the Act.

It is further confirmed that converting the source code into machine readable object code is a restricted act and there is specific provision that in relation to a computer program a 'translation' includes a version of the program in which it is converted into or out of a computer language or code into a different computer language or code.[9] This means, for example, that any unauthorised reverse and re-compiling to produce a different machine code form of the program would be a restricted act.

Additional protection is provided. Reproducing a work in a material form now specifically includes storing the work in any medium by electronic means.[10]

Duration of copyright for computer programs remains the same as for any other literary work.

Thus the Act strengthens and confirms the subsistence of copyright in computer programs; it gives certainty of protection for those who invest in their creation.

The legal problems surrounding databases highlight the inadequacies of the old Act when we now look at the amendments of the new Act.

1 Copyright (Computer Software) Amendment Act 1985, s 1(1).
2 Ibid, s 2.
3 Ibid, s 3.

4 Ibid, s 1(2).
5 Ibid, s 2.
6 Copyright, Designs and Patents Act 1988, s 3(1).
7 Ibid, s 3(2).
8 Ibid, s 178.
9 Ibid, s 21(4).
10 Ibid, s 17(2).

(2) DATABASES

13.15 Databases pose special problems for the law of copyright. They are a comparatively novel phenomenon in the UK. Statute law has been uncertain, and there is no case law to assist. Databases have certain features which are similar to computer programs. They both contain digitally encoded information. But there are material differences which make it unsatisfactory to consider a database as just another form of computer program. The 1985 Act dealt with the legal status of computer software but did not specifically deal with databases. Let us look at the 1956 Copyright Act and then at the provisions of the new Copyright Act to see whether databases are now adequately protected or not.

The 1956 Act

Databases were probably protected by copyright as a literary work under the 1956 Act, s 48 which provides that a literary work includes any written table or compilation. There is certainly authoritative case law to support this position. It has been held that the labour, skill and judgement which have been expended in the form or arrangement of a compilation could be sufficient to restrain the copying of such compilation.[1] Normally what has been capable of protection is the arrangement of the work, that is, the assembly of the facts in some meaningful way. This includes the effort taken to select these facts as they are incorporated in the arrangement, together with the effort, labour and expense involved and the investment generally made in such a creative, innovative endeavour. Facts alone are incapable of protection.

The 1988 Act

The new Copyright Act indirectly confirms the subsistence of copyright in databases by providing that a compilation is to be specifically considered a form of literary work.[2] Thus directly referred to, computer software and databases are both sub-sets of literary works. This should give database owners the certainty they need to protect the products of their investments.

Given the subsistence of copyright in a database, how does this differ, if at all, from a traditional copyright work, such as a compilation like a street directory?

With a traditional work there is often one author, the work is readily identified, it is often accessed only once (for example by sale), and a requirement of a sufficient degree of originality is required. In the case of the database there are normally several authors contributing to the contents, and the identity of the database constantly changes in order to serve the needs of the individual users. Furthermore, there is usually no originality involved in the creation and updating of the database. As it is the subject of continuous creation it poses questions as to its identity—what is to be protected? When this is decided, for how long would be appropriate? Obviously it is important to the owner or compiler of the database that these questions are answered. Later we shall see whether the law has done so adequately. I shall also look at the legal position of copyright works including computer software which is loaded on to databases, and the uses to which copyright works may be put.

1 *British Broadcasting Co v Wireless League Gazette Publishing Co* [1926] Ch 433.
2 Copyright, Designs and Patents Act 1988, s 3(1).

13.16 There is some likelihood that digitally encoded information will remain one of the main methods of conveying information for the foreseeable future. Enormous quantities of information are currently stored in databases where materials—many of which are copyright protected—are created, stored, accessed, manipulated, transmitted and displayed by the use of a variety of digital processors. These databases might be archives within commercial or industrial, private or public concerns, where the information is used both internally and externally, accessed and used via the medium of the processor. Or they may exist remote from the user and be accessed by him by arrangement. How can this information, much of which could have an intellectual property content as copyright works, be protected? Let us consider some of the specific problems relating to digitally stored information.

What are the problems which face the owner of a copyright work such as a written text which is converted into digital data, or a copyright work already subsisting as digital data, such as a computer program, which is then loaded and stored on to a database for eventual use by those other than their owner?

(a) loading and storing

13.17 The database is quite simply a base or bank in which information is electronically stored. The actual facility is provided by the owner of the database who stores the information in digital or electronic form, and supplies a service to those who require this information, usually for a fee. It has some of the features and functions of a library or archive. Often the database is one which specialises in the storage and continual update of the sort of information which will be of value to a particular body of subscribers. There are a number of databases specialising in such diverse activities as scientific, legal, technical, medical, and financial information, e g Stock Exchange prices and indices. The information is continually updated. Where the information is of a financial nature this will be virtually on-stream and immediate.

Prior to offering his services to subscribers, the database owner obtains permission from the owners of any copyright works to be used, to load those works or materials to form the substance of the database, on to the database. This could include artistic, dramatic, musical or literary works—literary works to include here computer programs. These works may exist in digital form or require conversion into that form for inclusion in the database. Those who allow their works to be placed in databases do so under the grant of a licence to the database owner and for a fee appropriate to the use to which the information will be put. Thus only the party who can claim the subsistence of copyright in his work is able to claim compensation for its use in being loaded and stored on to that database. We have already examined the possibility of the owner of a computer program being unable to claim subsistence of copyright in his work if it had been created digitally and had not been expressed in a material form such as a textual print-out. If this problem had not been overcome by the 1985 Act and the position confirmed by the new Act then the owner of such a program would also not have been able to protect his asset from inclusion on such a database and from the subsequent free exploitation by the database owner and his subscribers to it. The database owner would have been able to load the program on to his databank with impunity. This illustrates the importance of subsistence as being essential to protection and the vulnerability of such works.

Let us look to see how the problem relating to loading and storing developed and what recommendations have been made to resolve it. The basic question is: would the feeding of a program or data into the memory store of a computer be to reproduce it in a material form or not? We can understand this question better by reviewing some of its crucial history.

The Whitford Committee: 1977

13.18 The Whitford Committee, while reviewing this question, was of the opinion that the feeding into store of such a work did constitute a reproduction of that work in a material form. The Committee recommended that any subsequent legislation make such an act one of the restricted acts. Further, it recommended that explicit provision be made so that compilations of data and computer programs should themselves be treated for copyright purposes as literary works. Thus, in his preparing it for use with a computer, if someone invested in the setting up of the collection and compilation of data, provided that there was a sufficient degree of skill and/or labour involved in the preparation, then this would be protected as a literary work itself. The 1956 Act and case law made it quite clear that copyright exists in the compilation of useful information.[1,2]

1 Copyright Act 1956, s 48(1).
2 *Kelly v Morris* (1866) LR 1 Eq 697.

The Green Paper: 1981

13.19 The committee which issued the Green Paper of 1981 agreed with Whitford. The act of loading a program into a computer should be a restricted act, and provision made to extend copyright protection to works subsisting as computer programs, and literary, dramatic, musical, or artistic works stored in a database. This was then confirmed by the Copyright (Computer Software) Amendment Act 1985 which provided the certainty required, making it clear that loading and storing a work in a computer is a form of reproduction requiring the copyright owner's consent.[1] Further assurance was to be expected if the proposals of the 1986 White Paper were to be adopted and become law, as it stated that the provisions of the 1985 Act should be retained in any new legislation extending protection to the loading and storing of computer programs or works created in an electronic medium.

The 1988 Act

This provides that the copying of a work is an act restricted by copyright. Copying in relation to a literary work means reproducing it in a material form. This includes storing the work in any medium by electronic means.[2] Thus storing a work, such as a computer program, in a computer will constitute an infringement of copyright. It will constitute copying it. The Act therefore confirms that it is an infringing act by copying to load and store a copyright work in any medium by electronic means. This means that the database owner must obtain authorisation of the copyright owner to incorporate a copyright work in his database.

1 Copyright (Computer Software) Amendment Act 1985, s 2.
2 Copyright, Designs and Patents Act 1988, s 17(1) and (2).

(b) Problems relating to accessing the database and the transmission of data

13.20 Once stored, what happens then to the digitally generated information? Once loaded onto the computer database, the data is stored in memory until accessed by someone who requires it. He will normally have taken out a subscription with the database owner in order to use it, rather like a magazine subscription. This information in digital form, supplied on payment of the necessary fees as appropriate to the nature and value of the information to the user, may be transmitted in the same digital form direct to the user's printer. Or, it might be copied on to a magnetic tape, cassette, or direct into the memory of a dedicated micro-computer.

What legal problems, if any, are inherent in this operation? The database owner has acquired a licence from the owners of copyright works, whether these are in digital or other form, which he needs to include in his information system. Under the old Act the database owner probably enjoyed copyright in the compilation of that database as this involved the expenditure of labour, skill, time, energy, know-how and capital in sufficient quantities for it to qualify as a 'literary work'. The information, which forms the content of the transmission to the user, is probably the subject of copyright interests, as not only the original materials loaded on to the database qualify for protection, but also the database itself. The act of transmitting such data could be seen as a form of reproduction of the data itself. The nature of a database is that the data provided in the service to the subscriber is to be used by him. However, in law it is unclear what rights the user has in respect of that copyright protected data and what rights remain to, or are reserved by, the original creators of the copyright works and the database owner. This lack of clarity is often critical, not only for the present users of such information systems, but also for potential future developments in the field. The use of databases and computerised information systems will proliferate in an information technology age. The legal rights of the creator of the original contents of the database, the compiler of the database, and the user should be firmly established on a basis of certainty, so that each of the parties concerned enjoys some degree of this certainty in their dealings with each other. Without it, there will be a disincentive for the creators of copyright works to place their innovative works on the database and a corresponding disincentive for database operators to invest in the setting up of such information services.

13.21 Given that the database owner must obtain permission to store a work on his database and that the database owner has a separate copyright in his database, what rights does the user have in respect of the material or information transmitted to him and for which he has paid? In order to answer this question we need to look at the reasons why someone would want to use the information on a database. The two main areas concern 'broking' and 'downloading'.

(i) Broking

In this case the subscriber does not use the content of the information himself. He operates as a 'broker' in the passing-on of information, perhaps accessing it in electronic form, or obtaining it in a written or printed form. In either case, whatever his intentions, after paying for it, he obtains what counts as a 'reproduction' of a copyright work. He might operate as a broker. Alternatively he might adapt it in some way or re-combine it with other information so that when it is received by the user it is in an entirely different form. In either case he too is likely to charge a recipient for the information. Is this activity one of reproducing the work according to the law? If so, then strictly speaking the copyright owner, whether the creator of an original work included in the database or the database owner himself, should be able to prevent this kind of activity, as the user is reproducing and exploiting the work for his own commercial benefit, riding free on the back of the copyright owner's expenditure, investment etc. To secure his position legally the database owner has had to contractually ensure that he includes in his licence with the user the precise permitted use of the data, the extent of any additional selling or activities by him or other re-use, and the use of the data with any other works which he intends including with it, for example, if it is to be merged with data accessed from another database. He has also had to clarify the payment basis, whether this is to be per frame, or related possibly to an on-sale royalty, per print-out or whatever. Other charges may relate to the duration of use of the data, any exclusivity granted in respect of that data, and any services provided such as hardware or maintenance services.

However, it may be that given the nature of the use of the information that for all practical purposes there is reached a point where there is said to be an 'exhaustion of rights'—that is, that the exercise of any form of legal control over it is impossible given its amorphous nature.

(ii) Downloading

If the user 'downloads' or transfers parts of a database into the memory of his own computer for his own use, then he is not broking the information; he requires it in the memory of his computer purely for his own personal use. Examining the problems relating to the loading and storing of copyright material in computer databases, the Whitford Committee recommended that such information be protected by the law of copyright[1] but it did not deal with the legal status of information which is accessed, nor with its subsequent manipulation by the personal user. Indeed this problem was not dealt with satisfactorily in the 1981 Green Paper,[2] nor the 1985 Copyright Act, nor the 1986 White Paper. Given that there was no specific or general legal guidance on how much of the database could be transferred, how long such information ought to be allowed to be kept and what acts were permitted to the user, these were thus matters which had to be included by way of specific contractual conditions in the licence with the user in order to leave no doubt as to the rights of the user vis-à-vis the owner. The owners of copyright material had of course also to consider carefully the sort of restrictions which they might wish to put upon the use of their works in their contracts with the database owner. Clearly they would have to rely upon the contractual conditions which they wished to impose for the protection of their rights otherwise the user could have unrestricted use to reproduce their works.

The 1988 Act

Does the new Act clarify the legal nature of broking and downloading and give certainty to the interests of the owner of those original works which are incorporated on a database, to the database owner and to the user of the database?

The position of the owner of copyright in original works has been strengthened under section 17 which as we have seen provides that a work is copied if it is stored in any medium by electronic means. It certainly would seem to strengthen the database owner's position by confirming the subsistence of copyright in the database as a compilation. Thus under the general principles of copyright law the reproduction of the contents of the database or a part of it is a restricted act.

The Act also deals specifically with the problems of access and use of an electronic database. Section 17(2), as we have seen, provides that the storing of a work in any medium by electronic means is a reproduction in a material form. This will not only protect the owner of an original work which is to be placed on a database but will also extend to the position where someone wishes to store the database or a part of it in computer memory. This act would require the authorisation of the owner of the copyright in the database.

Under the general law of copyright it is a restricted act to issue copies of a work to the public.[2] The Act also provides that 'commercial publication' means making works available to the public by means of an electronic retrieval system.[3] Under these provisions the database owner has an exclusive right to issue copies of his work (the database) to the public and to make the work available to the public by means of an electronic retrieval system. This means that under the law of copyright he now has the right to control the copying of his database and to prevent someone else from commercially exploiting this by onward re-sale of all or parts of it. This strengthens his commercial position as he alone may profit from his investment in his database.

Further, the copyright in a work is infringed by a person who without the permission of the owner transmits that work by means of a telecommunications system, if he knows or has reason to believe that infringing copies of the work would be made by means of the reception of the transmission in the UK or elsewhere.[4] If therefore information in the database is downloaded to a user who then seeks to exploit this by onward re-sale by electronic means, this will be an infringing act. We see therefore that the rights of the database owner are increased by the new Act, not only by confirming the subsistence of copyright in his database, but by ensuring that he has legal control over the contents, their use and exploitation.

1 Whitford Report, paras 511 and 512.
2 Copyright, Designs and Patents Act 1988, s 18(1).
3 Ibid, s 175(2).
4 Ibid, s 24(2).

(3) USE

13.22 Copyright legislation exists to restrict or restrain reproduction of an original work, ie by copying. Therefore it is no infringement to use a copyright work in such a way that it is not actually being reproduced. But what is meant here by 'reproduced'? If a computer software program is used on a computer does that use constitute a 'reproduction' of the program? Could it be argued that use of a program must in fact involve the reproduction of that program, in that the instructions already contained in the computer itself are reproduced in the running of the program? The law itself is unclear.

Whitford[1] was undecided as to whether, and if so to what extent, the owner of a work in which copyright subsisted could or should have a right to control the use of the program. However, most on the committee argued that a 'use right' should exist, and that there should be an explicit restriction in respect of the use of the computer program to control or condition the operation of the computer. After all, the creator of a work such as a computer program should be allowed sole exploitation of it as is a creator of other works, and the use of the program should secure the author his return on his investment. Thus certainty of the rights of the author in respect of the use of his works needed securing by legislation.

But these arguments did not convince members of the committee which issued the 1981 Green Paper. On the contrary, they were persuaded that it was up to the copyright owner himself to negotiate and secure what rights he could in an initial agreement allowing the user the right to load that program on to the computer. If he wanted to control the use to which his program is put he should ensure this in his negotiations with the proposed user of the program. Thus any creator of a computer program negotiating with a potential licensee is in the position where he can control the right to load the program on to a computer, i e he can decide whether to grant a licence for the use of the program or not. In order to maximise its exploitation he ought to restrict its use at this point. For example, if the potential licensee requires a licence to use the program upon more than one machine, as in a net-working system where a single program may be used on or used to control any number of computers, then, as owner of the program, he should contractually provide for an appropriate payment to be made for such multiple use of his software. Without this contractual claim to payment for use of the software to control a number of machines, the user would not have to pay for each use as he would not be considered to be copying the program on each occasion.

The committee did not support the notion of a 'use right', nor was one included in the subsequent 1985 Copyright (Computer Software) Amendment Act and no provisions were made for one in the 1986 White Paper either.

The 1988 Act

The new Act makes it the case that copying in relation to works of any description includes the making of copies which are transient or incidental to some other use of the work.[2] This means that storing a work in any medium and making copies which are transient are infringing acts. Transient might describe the situation where a program is held in volatile machine memory; such would often be the case when used in a multiple networking system. In effect the provision gives the owner of the copyright in a program the exclusive right to use the program.

Further, secondary infringment will be the unauthorised transmission of a work by means of a telecommunications system.[3] The combined effect of the two provisions ensures that, if there is the networking of programs and these are made available to a large number of terminals, this activity can be regulated by the copyright which the owner enjoys not only in the program but also in its use.

1 Whitford Report, para 499.
2 Copyright, Designs and Patents Act 1988, s 17(6).
3 Copyright, Designs and Patents Act 1988, s 24(2).

(4) DISPLAY

13.23 One output feature of a computer is where electronic data exists in the form of an electronic message appearing on the screen of a CRT or a VDU. As much of this information needed by the user will appear fleetingly on a screen for the foreseeable future, it is vital to be clear about its legal status and protectability. But, to date, this remains unclear. The law was clear about the old technologies. If you view the pages of a book in a library you are entitled to use the information contained or displayed in it because copyright does not protect information but only prevents people from reproducing the work or a part of it in any material form. The Whitford Report was silent about the matter, but the 1981 Green Paper addressed itself to the problem of output in the form of printed text or VDU display.[1] Members of the Committee decided that there was no problem if the program was printed out as hard copy, as this fell into the traditional area of copyright protection as a literary work. However, if not, they did not believe there should be any specified protection for the mere display of the work on the VDU as this was analogous to the reading of a book, which entailed no reproduction of the work itself. By reading a book and using the information in it, you are not said to be 'reproducing' the copyright work. Thus the position is that if the output of electronic data is in printed form, this counts as a reproduction of the work; but if the same work is accessed in a transient or fleeting form via its display on a VDU screen, this is considered to be analogous to the reading of a book and therefore does not constitute a reproduction of the work.

At present this view of the matter prevails and it will remain the position for some time as neither the 1985 Copyright Act nor the 1986 White Paper dealt with the matter and the new Copyright Act does not seem to have specifically addressed the problem.

1 Chapter 9, para 6, p 33.

(5) PROBLEMS OF AUTHORSHIP AND OWNERSHIP OF COMPUTER-AIDED AND COMPUTER-GENERATED WORKS

13.24 We now come to one area which has received little or no attention from those committees investigating the state of copyright protection. It is an area which required urgent attention because of the considerable developments taking place in the whole field of computer-assisted and computer-generated works largely associated with the emergence of artificial intelligence and expert systems which we shall look at in more detail in a later chapter. The central question to be asked is: 'Who is the author and therefore the copyright owner of the results of using a computer with interactive software?' An answer to this question becomes urgent as computers become more sophisticated and their functions more analogous to the human brain. Computer programs are designed to instruct a computer to carry out certain tasks. Computers are interactive. Programs which instruct the computer do not operate on their own, but require some kind of input from the user. Raw data is inserted into the computer in digital form and the computer is required to carry out certain tasks with that data. In the simple case of word-processing the authorship of the work is fairly clear—it is the party who is using the computer where the skills and invention of the human user constitute the identity and ownership of the final work, and who thus enjoys copyright in that work. The substance of the created work is predictable in that it is the human agent who has directed the course of events. But what about a situation where the output is not the result so much of a human agent engaged in the activity of fashioning an individual work, but rather of two or more programs being used on the computer or computers interactively to produce results which cannot be predicted with any degree of certainty? Who is the owner of the eventual output of the computer? Is it the creator of the program that controls the computer; the originator of the data upon which the computer operates, who is also the user; or is it the person responsible for running the computer to produce the work? It would impede the exploitation of the work not to know the answer to this question, not to have a clear notion as to who is to count as the author and owner of the eventual product. The government initially decided that the legal principles laid down by the 1956 Copyright Act sufficed to settle such problems and that no new ones would be required. This is why none were offered by the 1986 White Paper Committee for new legislation. However, the new Copyright Act makes provision for ownership of computer-generated output and it is hoped that this will give the certainty required. I shall look at the changes in the law at the end of this section. First, let us see why the government has decided against its earlier recommendations not to legislate in this area, and the arguments which must have led to this decision. In order to understand why these proposals have been made I mention some of the points raised by earlier committees which discussed these problems. These matters are likely to be highly relevant in the future as I shall show in a later chapter (chapter 17, p 280).

13.25 What are the problems with computer-aided and computer-generated works? Partly the question is a conceptual one: just what is to count as 'authorship'? How does a computer rank in the function of authorship—as an instrument of an author like an author's pen? Or does it function more in terms of providing a half-written manuscript which someone has only to complete? When programmed, does the computer already contain a completed work, which the user, making of this completed work yet another one, simply performs with a further copyright work in addition to the first? These questions are not going to disappear and require legal definition if particular cases are to be determined according to clear legal principles. Some guidelines were required.

The Whitford Committee understood this need. It took seriously the issue of who should be the author, and therefore the owner, of a work produced with the aid of the computer. It likened the computer to the slide-rule or the paint-brush, ie to a tool in the hands of the party using it.[1] This meant that the authors were those who devised the computer program and the person responsible for the original data put into the computer, giving them joint authorship and ownership in the work. This also gave them all the problems of joint authorship in that neither would have complete control of the exploitation of the work.

By contrast, the 1981 Green Paper committee believed that if anything should be regarded as a mere tool, it should not be the computer itself, but the computer as programmed.[2] This meant that the author turns out to be the person responsible for running the data through the programmed computer in order to create the new work, and not the person who devised the program nor the person responsible for the input of the raw data. Obviously, the different models chosen by the two committees embody different principles of guidance as to where copyright resides, and come up with importantly different answers. Who should own the results of the use of a computer running a program on computer-aided design if the computer is already programmed to assist in the construction of a new design of some kind of manufacturing item? Far from disappearing, such questions can be expected to increase in the expanding use of computers in such activities as: parallel processing (the operation of two or more devices performing simultaneously on one particular task, for example the creation of another piece of software); the emergence of expert systems (the creation of a knowledge base containing the codified knowledge of experts); and in the development of artificial intelligence (the creation of systems which mimic the activities of the human brain). In all of these activities the role of the computer software itself is of a highly interactive and creative nature, either with other programmed computers or with human beings. The operator of the computer could not have gained his results without the use of the program.

Even so, after considering the responses to the 1981 Green Paper, the White Paper committee[3] concluded that there was so much variance in practice that it could not recommend any solution which could apply generally and which would be fair. No specific provisions were required. The question of the authorship of computer output would have to be left to the relevant parties to negotiate, any arrangement to be determined under the general law of contract.

1 Chapter 9, paras 513–517, p 132.
2 Chapter 8, para 7, p 35.
3 Paras 9.6, 9.7 and 9.8, p 51.

13.26 Until there were special legal provisions to guide people using computer software programs capable of producing copyright works as to who is to count as their owners, parties to agreements had to rely on the general law of copyright given in the 1956 Copyright Act and determine answers to these questions themselves with absolute clarity and certainty in their specific case, in order to avoid subsequent disputes.

The 1988 Act

The new Copyright Act breaks new ground by attempting to provide a proper legal framework for the authorship and ownership of computer-generated works. It provides that 'author, in relation to a work, means the person who creates it'[1] and 'in the case of a literary, dramatic, musical or artistic work, which is computer-generated, the author shall be taken to be the person by whom the arrangments necessary for the creation of the work are undertaken.'[2] The wording is the same as that used for establishing the authorship of films under the old Part II entrepreneurial rights of the 1956 Act. It will be a matter of commercial usage in the business as to who the person referred to might be. Though it is too early to tell what effect this provision will have it is however a bold step and gives some degree of certainty to those businesses investing in the creation of works which are largely computer-generated. For instance the telecommunications industries, which create large databases of telephone directories that are continuously updated from a variety of sources by use of interactive software, will gain copyright protection for their investment in such computer-generated products even though necessarily there is no human author involved. Subsistence of such copyright only extends to those works where there is no human author involved.

If at any level of creation of the work there is someone who might be considered author, whether as an employee or someone commissioned to input into the creation of the work, then because there has been some human involvement in the creation, the resulting work might not be protected. It would be prudent therefore for the party who considers that he is the person who makes the necessary arrangements for the creation of the work to ensure that at all stages he enjoys copyright in all the assembled elements. There could always be other individual claims to authorship in the future.

The new Act confirms the subsistence of copyright in computer-generated works and gives some certainty to those who invest in such products. These provisions reflect the growing need to protect and encourage investment in the increasingly important range of products arising from developments in artificial intelligence and expert systems which I discuss in a later chapter (chapter 17, p 276).

1 Copyright, Designs and Patents Act 1988, s 9(1).
2 Copyright, Designs and Patents Act 1988, s 9(3).

Protection of computer programs generally

13.27 I leave to more specialised books the task of dealing in detail with the contractual terms of the software licence which are important as a means of protecting the intellectual property rights in the product and in maintaining its value, and I look only briefly at some of these. The measures to take in order to protect intellectual property rights in copyright were set out extensively in earlier chapters and can be equally applied to the creation, exploitation and protection of computer software as a literary copyright work.

Computer software licensing is now firmly established as a means of transferring technology. Most licensing in the past related to patents, trade marks and the traditional artistic and literary copyright for use in exploitation in plays, films and television medium. However, with the considerable growth of computer software and specialist houses providing it, the issue of ownership and protection of software has become crucial for the recoupment of the substantial costs in creating it. Licensing therefore has been seen to be the best means of exploiting and protecting this product; as the creator retains ownership in it, he can contractually control its use, and he can maximise his profits further in this way.

The following is not designed to be a full exposition of the ways in which computer software can be protected in the licensing context, as clearly the contractual terms of any licence will be negotiable between the parties. However it is hoped that it will alert the reader to the main points to be considered when engaged in the licensing of software.

13.28 We know from Part 1 of the book that various measures can be taken by small to medium-sized enterprises to protect their intellectual property rights and that copyright protection applies generally to organisations creating and generating computer software programs. Wisely, such innovative concerns should ensure that all the measures relating to confidentiality are properly implemented, both when employees are under contracts of service to produce the product, having access to it in its various stages of development, and when the software is exposed to the gaze of those not within the employ of the concern, such as those under contracts for services, or potential licensees of the software.

Though software should be treated in exactly the same way as any other type of copyright material, it must be remembered that it is difficult to protect, so extra vigilance should be exercised in the event of the actual business being concentrated on the creation and production of software alone and not any other product. With a small software house the labour and capital expended in its creation is considerable and the ability to protect the product often crucial to the survival of the concern. The difficulty in protecting software resides in the context of modern technology which has made it possible to reproduce or copy it at a fraction of the cost of actually producing the original article. Detection of its use can be difficult largely because of its technical nature; it can be done but it requires considerable determination, not to say money, to pursue an infringer successfully; this means that prevention is always the best policy to begin with. Further, the copyright owner should also examine alternative ways of protecting his software, and not necessarily rely only on copyright.

13.29 For instance, although it is true that the Patents Act 1977 does not include computer programs as the sort of materials normally considered suitable for patenting, the Patent Registry has not entirely excluded the possibility of patent protection extending to them, provided they are not claimed per se, but as a method of use in a novel and inventive way. Patents could be granted where software subsists as a form of circuitry of the machine itself and is thus considered to be a part of the machine. In such cases the claim is that the ability to make the machine operate in a particular way, through the adaptation of the machine itself, is novel and involves an inventive step.

13.30 Trade mark rights can also be employed in the context of software protection. We saw how trade marks operate as a marketing tool to distinguish one product from a similar product in the market, to help create a high protective profile for copyright works generally, and to deter potential infringers. Normally, registration of a mark for the protection of computer software takes place under one of two categories, Class 9 which covers electrical and scientific equipment and Class 16 which gives protection for paper goods and printed matter.[1] As there is no specific use class provided for software, protection could be found by the use of these two classes of trade mark protection. A trade mark could be used on scientific equipment, paper articles—e g the wrappings in which the discs are inserted, for instance—or on promotional or advertising literature. This means that applications for both classes of protection are always necessary in whatever jurisdiction it is decided to sell or manufacture. It is important to remember that service marks are now available to protect the services which computer software manufacturers provide in addition to the hardware and software itself.

1 Nice Convention 1957.

13.31 In the first part of the book I have used the term 'protection' widely, to include the processes involved in the creation of innovation, the sort of internal protective measures which can be implemented to produce a more secure and controlled environment, and the sort of clauses which should be incorporated into the licensing of copyright works or materials. Are there any further particular problems relating especially to the licensing of computer software?

Much depends upon the nature of the product being licensed, most software being of the kind which is sold in normal retail outlets, the program designed for use on home computers and the range of facilities often of a general kind. This is true of word-processors, where the user often requires only the limited facilities offered by such software as sold over the counter, or provided by the computer manufacturer himself for use on the customer's machine. In such cases the sale of such software also operates as a licence, the creator and owner of the software retaining his intellectual property rights in the software, the user requiring permission to reproduce that software from the copyright owner. Such control of use is often difficult for the owner if it is not made explicit in the licence that no reproduction of the product is permitted. A recent phenomenon from the USA is 'shrink-wrap' licensing by which the software is sold in a plastic film with a notice on the outside. This draws the purchaser's attention to the fact that he is purchasing proprietary software according to the terms of the licence which he will find inside the wrapping. In the UK the legal effect of this is unclear and in the USA its legal effect differs from state to state. Even so, it alerts the user to the nature of the proprietor's rights and thus possibly acts as a deterrent to a would-be infringer.

13.32 The needs of the business of industrial user who requires software in the setting up and running of his business will often be determined by the nature of that business. His requirements might be met by a software package designed to deal with just his kind of business. These can sometimes be bought as such, and do not have to be written especially for him. If he buys such software he usually also wants it to be maintained during the running of the system. He might also need to obtain the latest upgraded software produced by the program producer in order that his business takes advantage of the latest developments in that software. Generally such software is licensed to him with the restriction that he may only use it on either a particular machine or a range of machines, its use being strictly defined. If he wants to use a different machine with that software operating on it, he must either obtain a further licence for this purpose or the original licence must be amended to record the parties' agreement to the changes of use of the software. In this case the licensor and licensee should ensure that provision is made as to what is to happen in the event of the software not operating properly, to the detriment of the user. Here care should be taken in the sort of warranties and indemnities which the licensor should be prepared to give in respect of the software and a separate document used to sort out the type of maintenance that the licensor is prepared to provide in the event of problems arising with the software's operation.

13.33 In the case of software which is created specifically at the request of one party to perform a special function—called 'customised' or 'bespoke' software—the question of who owns the intellectual property rights in the product must be sorted out at the beginning of negotiations between the parties. As he is normally paying for its creation, the commissioner of the software would usually like to own all the rights to the software. On the other hand, rights will be demanded by the software house which provides the bespoke software employing its own know-how, knowledge of subroutines, etc, and which probably incorporates aspects of its own proprietary software within the bespoke package. It clearly wants to avoid placing itself in any position where it cannot use that proprietary software, or indeed any of the novel features of the bespoke software, which it has developed and might wish to use in the creation and production of software for other clients. As neither party wishes to place itself in a position whereby its enjoyment of the use of the software is prejudiced, and neither is prepared to allow the other exclusive rights over the ownership of the software, they must reach some form of compromise. Difficulties with intellectual property rights in bespoke software would increase if the software is subsequently improved or enhanced by either party. If it is the licensor, he can offer this to the licensee thereby updating and upgrading his original software package. If it is the licensee who has made the improvements, the licensor can ensure that he has reserved his rights to the benefit of these improvements in the licence so that he is able to employ them without having to seek the licence or permission of the licensee. He can oblige the licensee to grant him a non-exclusive licence of all improvements, upgrades or enhancements for use either by himself or by others whom he may wish to license.

13.34 Such matters are crucial to consider in order to effect satisfactory arrangements in the licensing of computer software, to ensure that the owner's intellectual property rights are protected. It should be a rule that all licences contain a clear and definite statement as to the ownership of the software, a requirement that the licensee does not reproduce or adapt the software, and a requirement that the licensee holds the software under an obligation of confidentiality. The licence must clearly state the restrictions which the licensor imposes upon its use and such other issues as transfer, assignment and sub-licensing.

Often the licensing of computer software is complex. It is hoped that this chapter goes some way towards alerting those involved with this valuable commodity of the main problems likely to be encountered.

CHAPTER 14

Broadcasting, cable and satellite

Introduction

14.1 Developments which take place within a particular information technology are often such that the law is incapable of responding quickly enough to protect those who create innovative works used by it. Is this true of broadcasting, cable and satellite? In this chapter I attempt to answer this question. I look briefly at what might be called the distribution side of information technology and I explore the technologies of broadcasting, cable and satellite as these are becoming increasingly the means of conveying information. The law relating to broadcasting and communications is extensive and complex. This chapter is intended to give a thumb-nail sketch of developments in this area and their legal ramifications. Thus I hope to show how the law of copyright has been developed to protect investment in the products of traditional broadcasting industries such as the BBC and the IBA and how this protection has been and could be extended and developed to cover the products developed by new types of transmission and communication such as cable. Therefore I look at the way in which the law of copyright has been developed to break new ground in its attempts to establish a legal regime to protect the products of new industries where the technology is not yet in place, as is the case with satellites. Technological advances in satellite transmission, together with the deregulation of the airways, have created new forms of communications industries providing the consumer with a choice of information or entertainment. If these industries are to become commercially viable they need some form of legal protection for the products of their investment. Although the technology to be implemented is not traditionally associated with broadcasting, the same copyright protection enjoyed by the broadcasting industry for their products is considered to be appropriate because their content and function is broadly analogous. The government's 1986 White Paper proposed to put in place a copyright regime to protect the products of these new industries, extending the traditional notions associated with the concept of broadcasting. We shall see whether this has been provided by the new Copyright, Designs and Patents Act 1988.

We will see how these proposals analogously extend copyright principles to the new communications techniques and the sort of legal problems which this raises. I will also show how the rights and interests of the various copyright owners interact.

Traditional broadcasting

14.2 Broadcasting has seen major technological advances in the last few years which have posed new problems for the protection of copyright. These advances have meant that there has been a major shift in the concept of broadcasting unimaginable just a few years ago. The role of broadcasting, its structure and funding, have all undergone scrutiny and the original notion of public sector broadcasting has undergone change. Originally the British Broadcasting Corporation enjoyed a monopoly of broadcasting on the air-waves, first for radio and then for television, provided for through a statutory licence fee. This monopoly has been gradually eroded and it now competes with the Independent Broadcasting Association television stations, operating through various methods of private funding. There are further plans proposed to radically re-structure the industry. It is a time of de-regulation, though there still exist restrictions and regulations both nationally and internationally.

14.3 Originally, the impetus behind the development of television, cable and satellite was to advance technologies to further the aims and objectives of the existing radio and television services in order to increase their effectiveness in distributing their services. Paradoxically, it is just these advances which have had the effect of opening up the airways to unprecedented numbers of new services, only some of which aptly fit the concept of traditional broadcasting. Some new services such as information, data transmission, etc, though transmitted and distributed in the same way as traditional broadcasting, are entirely new types of business. Further, this opening up of the airways has meant that, instead of there being only one main procurer and producer of programmes and programme materials, there are now a host of generators of innovative material in, for instance, the arts, news coverage, information, etc.

They themselves are fed by a further underlying sub-structure of industries where literary, artistic, musical and dramatic works are created. Copyright works in the graphic and visual arts for example are created for programme content and advertising—the main source of revenue for most of the independent broadcasting companies. There are thus two basic levels of creation and innovation at work here. The broadcasting organisations provide services such as entertainment, instruction and information and there are individuals and industries serving them with works to be incorporated in their programme content.

The costs of the technology and labour involved in the production of the programme content in these industries are high. Constantly providing innovative material requires enormous capital resources and the generation of revenues. This means that there are considerable financial vested interests in sustaining and maintaining a high level of creative and innovative output. Profits are needed for survival and to enable reinvestment in further innovation. How are the necessary revenues achieved?

The BBC is currently funded by the imposition of a statutory licence fee on those members of the public who have receiving sets for the reception of television broadcasting transmitted by it. The other broadcasting corporation, the IBA, representing the independent broadcasting companies, is funded largely by advertising revenues. In addition, both concerns sell and license their broadcast programmes to foreign broadcasting companies and other organisations. They need to generate revenues which accrue to them alone. The literary and artistic content of their programmes varies in degrees of quality and sophistication, but such quality considerations are immaterial as all programmes so produced have had sufficient labour, skill, etc expended upon them to qualify legally as copyright works and so be protected under the 1956 Copyright Act when broadcast.[1] Further, copyright protection underpins the innovations generated by those industries feeding the programme creators. Such industries depend on copyright to protect their valuable industrial assets; it underpins their investment in their creative and innovative endeavours.

Obviously it is important for the owner of intellectual property rights to control his interests in order to legitimately recoup his expenditure and make profits through the generation of revenue via the payment of royalties. It is as true of the creator of works in these industries as elsewhere that he needs to ensure that he is properly, fairly and adequately recompensed for the expenditure of his time, labour, skill and investment in the creation of his work.

1 Copyright Act 1956, s 14.

The development of cable

14.4 Prior to the advent of cable television as we now know it, cabling was the technology used to carry programmes and broadcasts originated by the BBC or one of the independent IBA companies and diffuse them to receivers, particularly if it was difficult or impossible to obtain broadcast signals in poor reception areas.

At the time of the 1977 Whitford report[1] it was considered that the larger diffusion companies might develop the capacity to 'originate'—make—their own programmes, providing more channels than was possible by traditional broadcasting 'through the ether'. Because of this the Cable Television Association, representing the diffusing companies, argued that the law should provide a separate copyright in the diffusion itself, and not just in the literary or artistic works embodied in the diffused programme, because the same sort of abuses possible with traditional broadcasting were now possible with diffusions. If they originated their own programmes they too could be recorded, broadcast or rediffused. In favour of such copyright protection, it was further argued that a diffusion company wishing to diffuse certain programmes, such as a sporting event, could face difficulties in obtaining permission from the promoters or sponsors unless it could guarantee that its transmission or diffusion was protected against signal piracy, a similar argument to that given to an earlier committee on the law of copyright by traditional broadcasters to justify the protection of their broadcasts.[2]

In recognition of these possibilities Whitford saw that, though there was as yet little in the way of programme origination by diffusion companies, this could grow. For this reason any new copyright Act should grant a copyright in originated diffusions just as broadcasters are granted copyright in their broadcasts. This anticipated the creation and development of separate cable companies capable of generating their own programmes for transmission to the general public.

1 Chapter 8, 'Diffusion', para 423, p 111.
2 The Gregory Committee, 1952.

14.5 In 1981, the Green Paper[1] endorsed Whitford's recommendations to provide diffusion companies with a separate copyright in programmes which they originate, such as broadcasters have, and the 1984 Cable and Broadcasting Act duly amended the Copyright Act of 1956 to now provide that copyright subsists in every cable programme which is included in a cable programme service.[2] Those acts which were restricted under the protection of broadcasting would now apply equally to cable programmes.

1 Chapter 7 'Diffusion', para 22, p 31.
2 Cable and Broadcasting Act 1984, s 22.

14.6 Cable continued to develop. In 1982 the Hunt Report[1] on cable expansion and broadcasting policy recommended building cable networks in the UK, in order to encourage wide-band cable systems as a method of broadcasting. The band width relates to the technical capability of carrying electronic signals containing a wide variety of information in sound, voice, text or visual images on the one cable. This could also provide the foundations for new interactive communications in the UK, eg, between the home and providers of business and information services, etc. Optimistically, Hunt saw no incompatibility between cable expansion and the new technology on the horizon, Direct Broadcasting by Satellite—DBS. And indeed he thought them complementary as cable systems should increase the number of viewers to whom DBS services could become available and so make the service cheaper.

1 'Report of the Inquiry into Cable Expansion and Broadcasting Policy' (1982) Cmnd 8679.

14.7 Even so cable was not to develop without constraints. As cable television had always been regarded as supplementary to, and not an alternative to, public sector broadcasting, its expansion for entertainment and other services had to be accompanied by appropriate safeguards for public sector broadcasting. Therefore, in order to safeguard public sector broadcasting, the Hunt committee insisted that the new multi-channel systems envisaged should carry all BBC and independent television and radio services in the area serviced by them, in addition to their own programmes. Its report set out in detail such considerations as the supervisory framework of proposed cable operations, the key figures in the setting up and running of the new cable systems, the financing of the ventures, and their relationship with the traditional broadcasting companies.

The advent of satellite

14.8 Satellite technology is the next important development in the field of broadcasting, communications and the transmission of data.

Initially it was generally assumed that broadcasting authorities would only use satellite as extra-terrestrial arms or extensions of their traditional terrestrial activities. They would embrace this technology by broadcasting their programmes by it directly to the public by DBS. This would mean that the signal would no longer, as now, be transmitted from a broadcasting station direct to the public who would pick up the signal on their individual receivers. Instead, it would be transmitted to a satellite set in geo-stationary orbit above the earth which would be designed to boost and re-transmit it to the public, who would then pick it up on their individual receivers or through a connection to a cable diffusion service.

14.9 Another type of satellite system envisaged was point-to-point or fixed satellite services (FSS) where the transmission, whether the content was entertainment, information or data, etc, was directed to only those television or radio sets technically capable of receiving it. The system was to be operated by the independent broadcasting stations and other proposed new networks, such as the British Satellite Consortium which is an amalgam of private investors. Unlike the BBC or IBA, the function of an independent station is not to transmit programmes to the general public, but only to those who have paid their subscriptions to the programme provider, and who have specially designed sets for that signal to be received. Let us consider the two positions separately as the problems of their copyright protection sometimes differ.

14.10 The 1981 Green Paper[1] committee considered the DBS method of transmission to be the same in principle as broadcasting by terrestrial transmission. Therefore the protection which was enjoyed by the owners of those works constituting the broadcast and the broadcast itself should be given distinct copyright protection if transmitted by DBS. It did not decide on whether or not FSS transmissions were or were not 'broadcasts'.

1 Chapter 7, para 11 p 28.

14.11 It was not until the White Paper of 1986 that proposals were made to clarify the legal position of transmissions from FSS. Up until then any programme services transmitted by this method were not regarded as 'broadcasts' because (*a*) they had not been intended for direct reception by the public and (*b*) they were not legally permitted to be received under wireless telegraphy law. It recommended that the transmissions of FSS should enjoy the same sort of protection as traditional terrestrial broadcasts and DBS. These proposals, soon to be considered, go some way to providing a system of protective rights to those who have, or are about to invest in, new and (if properly protected by copyright) profitable industries. Although the new technologies are not yet in place, the law already has a framework worked out to protect the rights of those who invest their time, skill, labour and capital in them. Thus they already enjoy some reassurance that their time and money will not be wasted because of legal uncertainties which would operate as a disincentive to their investing in significant advances in the technology itself and in those who feed and operate that technology.

It is time to look, more particularly, at some of the legal problems thrown up by these technologies to see whether the proposals for legislative change in the White Paper and the actual changes effected by the new Copyright Act operate to protect the creators and producers of copyrights.

The legal position

TRADITIONAL BROADCASTING

14.12 In the earlier part of this book I examined the copyright position of the innovator of Part I original works under the old 1956 Act, now known as 'copyright works' under the new Act.[1] Let us now turn to the rights of the creator and producer of broadcast material under Part II of that Act, also known as 'copyright works' under the new Act.[2]

Section 14 of the 1956 Copyright Act provided that copyright protection extended to:

(*a*) every television broadcast made by the British Broadcasting Corporation or by the Independent Television Authority from a place in the UK or in any other country to which this section extends, and
(*b*) every sound broadcast made by the Corporation or the Authority from such place.

Copyright subsisted until the end of the period of 50 years from the end of the calendar year in which the broadcast was made. The new Act ends the distinction between Part I and Part II copyrights, and provides that copyright subsists in (inter alia):

(*a*) the original literary, dramatic, musical or artistic works, and
(*b*) sound recordings, films, broadcasts and cable programmes.

With the new Act, broadcast is defined as 'a transmission by wireless telegraphy of visual images, sounds or other information which,

(*a*) is broadcast for general reception, or
(*b*) is transmitted for presentation to members of the public.'[3]

The old 1956 Act made elaborate provisions for the acts restricted to the exclusive use of the copyright owner, these of course being limited to the BBC and the IBA. Now the restricted acts in respect of broadcasting are copying the work under section 16. They include, under section 17(4), the making of a photograph of the whole or part of an image forming part of the broadcast. Section 9 states that the 'author' (in relation to a copyright work) means the person who creates it. In the case of a broadcast this will be the person who makes that broadcast.

Under the old Act the creator of a copyright work included as a part of a broadcast or 'programme content' enjoyed copyright in his work under Part I of the Act (literary, dramatic, musical or artistic works) or Part II (film, sound recording etc) and the broadcaster had a separate and distinct copyright in his broadcast under section 14. With the new Act the creators of original works included in the broadcast will have copyright in their works under section 1(*a*) and the person who makes the broadcast will have a copyright in his work under section 1(*b*)—in the broadcast itself.

1 Copyright, Designs and Patents Act 1988 s 1(1)(*a*).
2 Ibid, s 1(*b*).
3 Ibid, s 6(1).

The programme or broadcast content and its copyright protection

14.13 Let us now see how works are generated and acquired for the purposes of transmission. Copyright works such as a script, text (a literary work), a piece of music (a musical work), a design, painting, etc (artistic work), if generated by an employee of a programme producer, belong to his employer, subject to any agreement to the contrary.[1] This is retained under the new Act.[2] The copyright in a piece of work produced outside the organisation belongs to the commissioned author and must be secured in order that the programme producer is able to use it.[3] This is retained under the new Act.[4] If the work is already in existence the programme producer must obtain rights clearance from the copyright owner, normally subject to the grant of a licence to use it for a particular purpose. Thus we see that there are a variety of possible copyright interests. The broadcasting organisation could own the original copyright in the work as employer, contractually assure this in a commissioning contract, have the work assigned to it, or negotiate a licence from the work's owner for inclusion in the programme. Negotiation for the use of the work with the rights holder may be direct or the right to use the work granted under a blanket licence issued by a collecting society, such as the Performing Rights Society (PRS), operating on the copyright owner's behalf. So far as the PRS is concerned, this normally entitles the programme owner to use the work as many times as he wishes upon payment of an established standard royalty.

The risk inherent in the creation of the programme, and the expenditure of an often considerable amount of investment in the actual production of the finished work to be transmitted, needs protection. This was provided for by the 1956 Act under section 14 and now under section 1(*b*) of the new Act. Copyright subsists in the various constituent parts of the programme and also in the broadcast itself. Thus in any broadcast work there probably subsist several copyrights, such as in the script, design, music, film, video, sound recording and the broadcast itself. These rights are concurrent and the copyright of the broadcast does not affect the other copyrights subsisting in the original work.

1 Copyright Act 1956, s 4(4).
2 Copyright, Designs and Patents Act 1988, s 11(2).
3 Copyright Act 1956, s 4(1).
4 Copyright, Designs and Patents Act 1988, s 11(1).

CABLE

14.14 The Cable and Broadcasting Act of 1984, section 22 provided that:

> 'Copyright shall subsist, . . . in every cable programme which is included in a cable programme service provided by a qualified person in the United Kingdom or in any country to which this section extends.'
>
> '. . . a person providing a cable programme service shall be entitled to any copyright subsisting in a cable programme included in that service and any such copyright shall continue to subsist until the end of the period of fifty years from the end of the calendar year in which the cable programme is so included, and shall then expire.'

The new Act repeals this section and provides that a cable programme is a copyright work under section 1(*b*). A cable programme is now described as 'any item included in a cable programme service' and 'cable programme service' means a service which consists wholly or mainly in sending visual images, sounds or other information by means of a telecommunications system, otherwise than by wireless telegraphy, for reception

(*a*) at two or more places (whether for simultaneous reception or at different times in response to requests by different users), or
(*b*) for presentation to members of the public.[1]

The author or owner of the copyright work—the cable programme—is the person providing the cable programme service in which the programme is included.[2] The Act goes on to exclude certain activities from being cable programme services and these relate in the main to communications systems which are used essentially for personal or business services.

These restricted acts (the doing of which by any other person would constitute an infringement) are substantially the same as the restricted acts appropriate for broadcasts.

Here then is the legislative framework to protect the interests of those who have invested or who intend investing in the setting up and running of cable programme stations or networks. The same legal considerations apply to cable programmes as in terrestrial broadcasting for copyright owners—they enjoy separate copyrights in the programme content and in the broadcast.

1 Copyright, Designs and Patents Act 1988, s 7(1).
2 Ibid, s 9(2)(*c*).

SATELLITE

Let us consider the legal position of DBS and FSS, taking first DBS.

The legal position of DBS—Direct Broadcasting by Satellite

14.15 DBS is to count as an extension of the normal technique of broadcasting. Section 14 of the old 1956 Act was amended to include direct broadcasting by satellite under the Cable and Broadcasting Act 1984. The new Copyright Act confirms the position of satellite transmissions as constituting 'broadcasts'.[1] The decision to protect was only taken after pertinent discussion on the status of DBS transmissions as broadcasts. As the reasons for the decision will continue to guide legal thinking in this area, they are worth noting. A problem raised by the Green Paper committee of 1981[2] was whether the act of transmission by satellite would be protected under the existing legislation to protect 'broadcasting' if beamed from the earth station transmitter to a satellite and then beamed down to the individual receivers of the general public. The committee suggested that the government look at the precise nature of the novel technique and at the definition of broadcasting itself in order to determine whether the technique of the new technology was protected by the existing laws of copyright as they applied to 'broadcasting'. For if not, there was no protection and new laws might be required. There is no definition of broadcasting in the 1956 Act but there is a general definition of it by the International Telecommunications Union Radio Regulations which partly reads: 'a communications service in which the transmissions are intended for direct reception by the public'. But this raised the further question: what is meant by 'direct reception'? Taken literally it could argue against satellite transmissions being broadcasts. It could be said that the act of an earth station beaming its signal to a satellite was not a broadcast as it was not then communicating a transmission for direct reception of the public. And if it is necessary to bounce the signal off a satellite before it is received by the public, then it is indirect, and so still should not be described as 'broadcasting', as it does not fit the definition. Would the second leg of the signal—ie, the 'down-leg' signal to the earth station from the satellite—satisfy the definition? This signal is boosted by the satellite for earth reception by the use of a 'transponder', a form of re-transmission of the signal designed to be transmitted at such a frequency as to be picked up by the individual receivers of the public. Because it is 'to the public' it might now be considered sufficient to satisfy one criterion of the definition of 'broadcasting' of 'being a communication to the public' and so be a form of broadcasting. This conceptual debate could have been of practical importance. Depending on which transmissions were said to be or not be broadcasts a Part I copyright owner under the old Act whose work was transmitted by DBS might or might not have been able to control what happened to his work, and the broadcaster might or might not have been able to rely upon the law to protect his work.

As I indicated earlier, fortunately the problem was resolved by including such transmissions under 'broadcasting' by an inclusion in the Cable and Broadcasting Act of 1984 amending section 14 of the 1956 Act as follows: 'in the case of a television broadcast or sound broadcast made by the technique known as direct broadcasting by satellite, the visual images or sounds in question, or both as the case may be, are transmitted to the satellite transponder'. The position is further confirmed by the new Act which provides that the place from which a broadcast is made in the case of a satellite transmission is the place from which the signals carrying the broadcast are transmitted to the satellite.[3]

1 Copyright, Designs and Patents Act 1988, s 6(1) and (4).
2 Chapter 7, p 27.
3 Copyright, Designs and Patents Act 1988, s 6(4).

The legal position of FSS—Fixed Satellite Services transmissions

14.16 If DBS transmission signals satisfied the requirements of being 'broadcasts', was this also true of FSS—fixed satellite service transmissions—which are, significantly, different? If not, they were not protected while DBS transmissions were. Obviously, the consequences of such a legal difference would be momentous to the industries concerned, and make the development of FSS practically impossible. The government's White Paper of 1986 has proposed that both sorts of transmission count as 'broadcasts'. The problem was that unless there was a change in the law of copyright the provisions of the old 1956 Act would only cover those programme services transmitted or to be transmitted by the BBC and IBA. Further, programme transmissions by the organisations using FSS techniques could not be protected because they did not fulfil the criterion for being a 'broadcast', that is, they were not intended to be directly transmitted 'to the public generally', as they were to be received only by those who had specifically subscribed to the programme service.

14.17 The White Paper concluded that transmissions by FSS were analogous to 'state of the art' broadcasting techniques and should be given protection as 'broadcasts'.[1] The provisions if made law would remove uncertainty as to the rights of programme producers and providers under this sort of transmission and those who supply the programme content, and pave the way to investment in these new and potentially valuable industries. The new Copyright Act provides that such satellite transmissions are deemed to be 'broadcasts' even though they may not be for general reception by the public provided the transmission 'is capable of being lawfully received' by any member of the public with the appropriate equipment and the appropriate equipment for reception is made available.

The Act states as follows:

> 'An encrypted transmission shall be regarded as capable of being lawfully received by members of the public only if decoding equipment has been made available to members of the public by or with the authority of the person making the transmission or the person providing the contents of the transmission.'[2]

In other words even though the transmission is technically encrypted in some way and not generally available to the public it will constitute a broadcast. But if the transmission is encrypted and there is no decryption equipment made generally available to the public then it will not be deemed to be a broadcast. As FSS techniques are analogous to broadcasting the appropriate copyright protections for broadcasts will apply, allowing the government consistency in its general broadcasting policy.

The amendments to the 1956 Act concerning the legal status of the up-leg and down-leg operation of the broadcasting function will apply equally to the FSS transmissions.

1 White Paper, para 10.11.
2 Copyright, Designs and Patents Act 1988, s 6(2).

Some problems of the owner of copyright in original works

DIFFUSION

14.18 Looking back at the old 1956 Copyright Act we can say that certain of its provisions derogate or detract from the copyright owner's rights to control the use of his work, and may indeed be a negation of these rights. For instance, one of the restricted acts was for a BBC or IBA programme to be re-broadcast. However, under that Act, if a broadcast was re-diffused (by cable or wire) this was not deemed to be re-broadcasting for infringement purposes, for it was not deemed to be a transmission to the public according to the given definition of broadcasting. Traditionally the original re-diffusion would have taken place in poor reception areas, or where there was no reception at all, the broadcast signal being diffused by wire to the subscribers to that system. In these cases why should the owners of the copyright in the broadcast have a right to prevent a diffusion of the original broadcast? After all the diffusion simply provides the same service to people who would be unable to obtain it; it is not competing with the broadcaster. If the answer is that they should not have such a right, then the question arises whether there should be any right to prevent the diffusion of any original works included in the broadcast. Section 40(3) of the 1956 Act specifically provided that anyone diffusing the broadcast would be deemed to have a licence granted to him for the use of a work which is a 'literary, dramatic or musical work, or adaptation of such a work, or an artistic work, or a cinematograph film' which is used in such a diffusion service, ie the owner of the copyright in an original work—included in the programme as broadcast—had no claim against the party supplying the diffusion service for having used his work. So far as the diffusion of the broadcast was concerned, he thus lost control of his intellectual property rights in his work as soon as he allowed them to be used in a broadcast. He could only restrict the use of his work in a broadcast for use other than for a diffusion service. He could not prevent its further use in a diffusion service.

14.19 The diffusion right of a cable operator to diffuse without hindrance, was reviewed by Whitford in 1977.[1] More fully, the argument in favour of retaining the diffuser's right to use the original copyright owner's work without further payment was this: as the diffuser was not extending the use of the copyright owner's work to any audience over and above that which it could obtain by normal means, it does not result in him losing revenue. Anyway, as such an author or creator of an original work has granted a licence to the BBC or the IBA for his work to be included in its broadcasting schedule, he is deemed to have granted that the work be transmitted in any form or medium to those of the British public who have paid their licence fees to the broadcasting authorities. In other words, as in this context the broadcasting and diffusion are one and the same act, diffusion cannot be said to be the provision of a different service; it is merely an alternative method of providing the same service.

However, not everyone agreed with this analysis, and it is important to consider why. In the view of some members of the committee, though it was left to national legislators to decide how it is exercised, the copyright owner's right is enshrined in the Berne Convention to which the UK is a signatory.[2] This allows that the author must have exclusive rights to the use of his work in any communication to the public by wire or broadcasts of such works and get an equitable remuneration for the use of his works. But diffusion rights detract from the law relating to the author's copyright. This argument could have failed to carry the conviction required to become a proposal because the copyright owner could then have negotiated the best possible deal initially with broadcasting organisations using his work, in the knowledge that they might be diffused. That is, he could have adopted a 'one bite at the cherry' principle in his negotiations with the broadcasting organisations which would have obviated the need for such a proposal.

From the point of view of the broadcasting authorities themselves, though they liked to retain as much control over their broadcasts as possible, they usually did not object to the diffusion of their broadcasts provided that it was simultaneous and in an area which would normally receive them, so fulfilling the condition that re-diffusion was simply an alternative method of reception, a means of providing the same rather than being in competition with the services provided by such authorities.

Such views have been reinforced by members of the Green Paper Committee of 1981[3] who recommended that the section 40(3) exceptions of the 1956 Act remain in force if any diffusion was by cable or wire of the whole broadcast, simultaneous to the original broadcast and within an area where the broadcast was normally received.

1 Chapter 8, p 111.
2 Convention of the International Union for the Protection of Literary and Artistic Works 1886 as modified by later conventions.
3 Chapter 7, para 19, p 30.

THE 1986 WHITE PAPER AND DIFFUSION RIGHTS

14.20 Ten years after Whitford, five years or so after the Green Paper, telecommunications had moved on apace, and the problem of diffusion rights needed examining in the light of such developments as DBS and FSS—the latest telecommunications technologies soon to be implemented. The White Paper of 1986, anxious to establish legal consistency in its discussion of DBS with earlier reports, proposed that the same rules relating to the rediffusion of the transmission of broadcasts for those using traditional techniques should now apply to those using new FSS technology. The Cable and Broadcasting Act 1984 had already provided that all DBS transmissions, and copyright works contained in their programme content, would enjoy the protection of copyright but that they would be freely diffusable by cable operators. Thus, a cable operator would not need to obtain the consent of the copyright owners of the contents of the programme if diffusing the broadcast programme, providing the following conditions were satisfied:

(*a*) the whole and not a part of the broadcast was diffused, and it was simultaneous with the transmission of the broadcast with the BBC or IBA transmissions or DBS transmissions;

(*b*) the diffusion took place within the intended reception area of the broadcast and it was 'in-area', that is, within that area where the cable programme service is provided.[1]

The rationale remains the same. Such re-diffusion does not constitute a new or separate communication justifying extra remuneration to the owner of copyright works in the programme content.

What happens when the new satellite technology for FSS is employed by the proposed new independent companies which could produce and transmit programmes for those people who specifically subscribed to their service? How would their interests fare under the re-diffusion provisions? Would the argument for the retention of the section 40(3) provisions—that cable rediffusion is an alternative to 'off air' broadcasts and so not a separate communication justifying extra remuneration to the copyright owner—apply to their proposed use of the original owner's work? We must first consider that the programmes originated by these new independent broadcasting satellite companies are not designed for general reception by the public, but are to be received only by those who have paid a subscription to the station or broadcasting network providing the services. Thus such broadcasts cannot be said to be offering the same service as the normal broadcasts by the traditional broadcasting institutions, with just a different method. It would seem unjust to the satellite broadcaster to allow free re-diffusion of the broadcast or the programme contents in a diffusion system because it would be to a different audience. This would seem to allow the cable re-diffuser to have a free ride on the back of another's investment, which is why it has been argued that FSS satellite broadcasters would need the right to control any re-diffusion of their programmes, and to charge their subscribers for the right of reception and any cable operators who wished to diffuse their programme materials in a cable system. They need to protect their investments to generate revenues. They can only do so by being able to control the use of their intellectual property rights in the copyright of their transmissions.

Further, many have considered that the rights of original creators who are copyright owners providing the contents of cable programmes are in a different situation with the introduction of FSS satellite from that under DBS satellite transmissions. Therefore they should be able to charge for any re-diffusion use of their copyright work contained in programme contents. Though the argument was strong, eventually it was not accepted in the White Paper. To accept it would have allowed the copyright owner of original works to charge twice for the use of his material—first charging the independent satellite programme producer and then the cable re-diffuser. This would disadvantage the subscriber to a cable system who would have to pay more for the programme re-diffused by cable than if the same programme was transmitted to him direct by satellite. He would be paying the equivalent of the satellite service, which included costs of payment to the original copyright owner, and paying the cable programme service owner as well. It is because of this that the White Paper recommended extending the section 40(3) exceptions of the 1956 Act to the cable re-transmission of independent fixed satellite broadcasts for the UK.[2]

The new Copyright Act therefore provides the following:

Where a broadcast made in the UK is received and immediately re-transmitted by inclusion in a cable programme service, copyright is not infringed if it is included in pursuance of the requirements of the Cable and Broadcasting Act 1984 which makes it obligatory for cable services to carry certain programmes ('must carry' provisions), or if the broadcast is made for reception in the area in which the cable programme service is provided and it is not a satellite transmission or an encrypted transmission.[3] So, cable operators will need to obtain the consent of the fixed satellite programme providers.

The Act goes on to provide that the copyright in any work included in the broadcast is not infringed if it has to be included in any 'must carry' provisions or if the broadcast is made for reception in an area where the cable programme service is provided. Thus cable operators re-transmitting fixed satellite broadcasts originating in the UK will be under the same copyright regime as cable operators re-transmitting DBS broadcasts. Therefore cable operators, who re-transmit the above described broadcasts or programme services only within the intended reception area of those services, will be exempted from the need to pay or to seek consent from the owners of original works included in the programme contents of fixed satellite transmissions.

1 Cable and Broadcasting Act 1984, s 23.
2 White Paper, chapter 10, para 10.19, pp 55–56.
3 Copyright, Designs and Patents Act 1988, s 73.

Other matters

14.21 (i) *Signal piracy*. So far we have been discussing the various rights and interests which can subsist under the general heading of broadcasting, how those interests are balanced and inter-act between the various parties, and how the law of copyright can be invoked in the protection of those many and varied interests. What is the position where a broadcast signal, be this from a conventional terrestrial broadcast, from a DBS satellite, or from an FSS point-to-point satellite signal, is picked up, not by the general public who have paid their licence fees, nor by the subscriber to an FSS service with his specially adapted receiving set, but by someone who is not authorised to do so? The Cable and Broadcasting Act of 1984[1] provided that a person who dishonestly received a programme included in a service with intent to avoid any charge applicable to the reception of that programme, shall be liable on the basis of dishonest reception. This criminal provision embraces all the traditional broadcasting organisations' transmissions including cable programme providers. The White Paper proposed that in order to ensure a consistency of rights in the whole field of broadcasting, these protective provisions should extend to the new FSS programme providers.[2] Thus the new Copyright Act provides that a person who dishonestly receives a programme included in a broadcast or cable programme service with the intention of avoiding payment of any charge applicable to the reception of that programme commits an offence and is liable on summary conviction to a fine.[3]

(ii) Section 35 of the Act provides that a copy of a broadcast or cable programme may be made by an educational establishment for educational purposes without infringing the copyright in the broadcast or cable programme or in any work included in it. This is one of the fair dealing exceptions under the Act which allows copying to take place without infringement. It only applies however where there is no certified licensing scheme in operation under section 143.

(iii) The making for private and domestic purpose only of a broadcast or cable programme solely for the purpose of enabling it to be viewed or listened to at a more convenient time does not infringe any copyright in the broadcast or cable programme or in any work included in it.[4]

(iv) Making a photograph of part of an image forming a part of a television broadcast does not infringe the copyright in the broadcast or cable programme provided that this is for private or domestic purposes.[5]

1 Cable and Broadcasting Act 1984, s 53.
2 White Paper, para 10.14.
3 Copyright, Designs and Patents Act 1988, s 297.
4 Ibid, s 70.
5 Ibid, s 71.

CHAPTER 15

Audio/video

Introduction

15.1 The law has a role to play in creating a society where innovative endeavour is justly rewarded for the effort and investment needed for the production of good quality and inexpensive goods which go some way towards the satisfaction of consumer expectations. A legal system which sets out the clearly defined intellectual property rights of such innovators, and which is consistent and just in the sense that it enables enforcement of those rights, seems to be an admirable aim of that system.

However, to achieve this requires that the matter of recompense can be assured, given the certainty of identification of those rights, and necessitates a system which enables the proprietor of those rights to assert his claim. It is presupposed that with a perfect system of identity and enforcement the owner of copyright interests can rely upon the strict rights accorded to him under the law of copyright, and that in pursuing those, he can achieve a proper and effective recompense for any infringement of those rights thus encouraging him to continue to create innovative works.

But when we turn to industries which exemplify the new problems faced by copyright owners in the face of two of the latest technologies—the audio and video industries—we find that they call into question the efficacy of part of the law of copyright, and so this very presupposition. For in these new industries it is possible for a copyright owner to point with certainty to his readily identifiable rights, to there being a remedy of enforcement of those rights in the face of infringement, but he is often powerless to carry out their enforcement. He is unable to enforce his strict copyright interests because of the nature of the mediums in which his work exists.

15.2 So far, how has the law responded to his problems? Is it now adequate to protect his interests? It was thought that the proposals of the 1986 White Paper, if made law, would go some way towards solving these problems and correct many of the injustices he now faces in the attempt to enforce his rights under the law of copyright. Sadly, the government appears to have abandoned its far-reaching proposals for reform in this area but it is important to understand what they were and how they proposed to rectify the problems faced by copyright owners in this field, as it could well be that they might form the basis of future legislation if the position of the copyright owner worsens. In order to understand why, we need to place these proposals in the context of both the law and recent technological developments. For the purposes of the law, video is film, and audio tape recordings are sound recordings.[1] Thus the legal situation for each begins with the law as it was created for the purposes of protecting copyright in the film and record industries. That is where the trouble began, because these industries did not anticipate the copyright enforcement problems soon to confront the new technologies of video and audio materials; as we will see, this is especially true of audio tape recordings.

1 Copyright Act 1956, s 13; Copyright, Designs and Patents Act 1988, s 1(1)(b).

Developments in video technology

15.3 With video, there is an asymmetry between video and films. Both may be duplicated, but the techniques and ability to create and produce traditional films are complex, whereas video reproduction is simple. Section 13 of the old 1956 Copyright Act allowed the maker of a cinematograph film to enjoy the exclusive right to reproduce his film, defining him as 'the person by whom the arrangements necessary for the making of the film are undertaken.' This definition remains virtually unaltered under section 9(2) of the new Act. The cinematograph film itself is defined in the old Act as 'any sequence of visual images recorded on material of any description which is capable of being shown as a moving picture'[1] and a copy of the film means any print, negative, tape or other article on which the film or part of it is recorded. The new Act amends this slightly by defining film as 'a recording of visual images, on any medium, from which a moving picture may by any means be produced'.[2] At the time of the old Act, as only large scale industrial enterprises had the capacity or indeed the facilities to manufacture films, reproduction of these was largely limited to those with the money to invest in such costly ventures. This provided conditions upon which the industry could rely for the exercise of its intellectual property rights, as it was easily able to identify and enforce them against infringers. As with books and their publication, copyright in the film existed in a controllable medium. Only with a like technical capacity could any organisation duplicate the works of another and with an established range of outlets available to the film market, this would be quickly detected and the infringer brought to justice. The usual civil damages would then be imposed by the court in favour of the owner of the copyright in the film, based upon the intensity of reproduction. The technological infrastructure and the medium were therefore largely controlled by the owner of the copyright interests. As far as its interests in its innovative products were concerned, the cinematograph industry was on safe enough ground as it could rely upon the rights accorded it under the laws of copyright, underpinned as it was by the law which had responded to its commercial needs.

How has the situation altered today? With the advances made in the field of information technology, especially in the field of video reproduction, it is now possible for an ordinary member of the public to purchase a video reproduction machine at low cost which is capable of cheaply reproducing a film shown, for example, on television, the reproduction usually being of very high quality. As the reproduction is usually made in the privacy of someone's home, the chances of detecting this activity are slight and the means of preventing him from doing so impossible.

1 Copyright Act 1956, s 13(10).
2 Copyright, Designs and Patents Act 1988, s 5(1).

Developments in audio technology

15.4 So much for the position of developments in video technology. Let us now look at the position of audio technology. Today, for a number of reasons soon to be considered, audio tapes are an even worse threat to copyright owners than is video. Returning to the 1956 Copyright Act, this satisfactorily provided laws against copyright infringement for both the traditional film and record industries, and so covered the new technologies on their introduction. It allowed the owner of the copyright in a musical, dramatic, literary or artistic work exclusive right to reproduce his work in any material form.[1,2] The material form could be a sound recording. If this were the case, the Act additionally provided him with a further copyright in the production of his recordings, the owner of the copyright counting as the person who made the first record of the work. This provision is amended under the new Act to be 'the person by whom the arrangements necessary for the making of the recording are undertaken' which is consistent with the provisions for the ownership of a film.[3] As defined by the old Act, a sound recording was an 'aggregate of sounds embodied in, and capable of being reproduced by means of a record of any description . . .' Under the new Act this is defined as

'(a) a recording of sounds, from which the sounds may be reproduced, or

(b) a recording of the whole or part of a literary, dramatic or musical work, from which sounds reproducing the work may be produced, regardless of the medium on which the recording is made or the method by which the sounds are produced or reproduced.'[4]

The expression 'a record of any description' includes tapes, not only those traditional vinyl discs usually known as 'records'. The new Act covers, as we have seen, sound recordings regardless of the medium or method by which the sounds are reproduced.[5]

1 Copyright Act 1956, s 2(5)(a).
2 Ibid, s 3(5)(a).
3 Ibid, s 12(8); Copyright, Designs and Patents Act 1988, s 9(2).
4 Copyright Act 1956, s 12(9); Copyright, Designs and Patents Act 1988, s 5(1).
5 Copyright Act 1956, s 48(1); Copyright, Designs and Patents Act 1988, s 5(1).

Distinction between audio and video

15.5 Although it is true of both video and audio materials that they make possible the reproduction of copyright works at a fraction of the original price—the only cost being the initial outlay for the purchase of the machine and the materials upon which the work is recorded—at present audio recordings cause an even greater abuse of copyright than do video recordings. Audio tape is normally used to copy records either from broadcast radio or television programmes, or from musical works recorded either on disc or audio tape without the need to buy the original. Video machines, on the other hand, are normally used in order to reproduce and view copyright works recorded from television broadcasts at a different time of day, allowing the person greater convenience of viewing. Even so, as video is a new technology, as yet all its potential uses are not explored; so though its actual use has been less infringing than has the use of audio tapes, its potential uses could be seriously infringing. For that reason I discuss them both.

In the case of audio tapes the present situation is uncontrollable, and the situation can only worsen because of the increasing ability of the owners of audio recording machines to achieve near perfect quality of sound reproduction at ever lower costs. The practical ability of owners of copyright in such works to exercise their exclusive rights of reproduction has all but disappeared. Because of the advances in technology they are no longer in control of the medium in which their copyright work subsists.

Main areas of unauthorised copying and infringement

15.6 As records and films respectively, audio and video recordings on a magnetic tape medium satisfy the requirements of the new Act for the subsistence of copyright. The difficulties are with the copyright owners' enforcement of their strict rights in such materials. As we know, there has been wholesale commercial illegal copying of works in these mediums.

(1) 'BOOT-LEGGING', PIRACY

One of the main areas of copyright infringement comes from the activity termed 'boot-legging', that is, where a record of a live performance is made without the authority of the performer at a concert and without the permission of the record company who may have arranged for the exclusive rights to record that performance. The performance is illicitly recorded, duplicated and sold on the market often long before those with legitimate rights have been able to do so.

(2) UNAUTHORISED COMMERCIAL REPRODUCTION

The next main source of infringement comes from the illegal commercial reproduction of existing copyright audio or video works. In this case the infringers obtain a copy of an already recorded work, be this in audio or video form, and reproduce and sell it on the market at an attractively lower price than the legitimate original, undermining the rights of the copyright owners, with both the original artist and the recording company suffering reduced revenues. It is not only the owner of copyright in the original work who suffers, it is also the maker of the audio or video work who has invested in its creation and production. Thus the composer of the music, the author of the lyrics, and the performer under his agreement with the maker of the work whose remuneration is often related to the number of records actually sold, suffer as a result. The only parties to benefit are the infringers, using the latest reproduction technologies and the people who purchase their cheaper goods. After campaigning by those most seriously affected, the law was changed by amending the 1956 Act to increase the criminal penalties for such infringement.[1] While not eradicating the problem entirely, it has helped alleviate the situation.

(3) PRIVATE RECORDING OF COPYRIGHT WORKS

The third area we shall concentrate on involves a more pervasive erosion of the copyright owner's rights, and is perhaps more serious. This involves the use of these new reproductive techniques and technologies by the individual for—as he sees it—perfectly reasonable purposes. It has become a popular hobby to use the new inexpensive recording equipment to record privately audio or video works, either off air from the radio or television, or from an already pre-recorded work such as a record or a film, all without the difficulty and cost of purchasing the original.

1 Copyright (Amendment) Act 1983.

The phenomenon of 'home taping'

15.7 So let us then examine the legal and commercial problems surrounding the phenomenon of 'home taping', as it is popularly called.

We have now briefly reviewed the copyright interests involved. Under Part II of the 1956 Copyright Act, the protection of entrepreneurial interests was provided for—i e the interests of those whose function it is to commercially exploit the author's or artist's work on his behalf, as he is seldom able to do this himself. Although this distinction between author's and entrepreneur's copyright will be merged under the new provisions, both being referred to as 'works' under section 1 of the new Act, it is important to note that though the author or creator of an original work usually assigns his copyright over to someone else to exploit it in the video medium and grants a non-exclusive licence for audio reproduction, copyright in the original work is not thereby destroyed through the record or film maker gaining his own copyright. This additional right is retained under the new provisions, the original literary, dramatic, musical or artistic works having their own copyright under section 1(a), and the old Part II materials (films and records, broadcasts, etc) all now described as 'copyright works' under section 1(b). Thus there are often a number of copyrights in an audio or video work running concurrently with the entrepreneurial copyrights, each right being separate and distinct. The situation becomes more complicated where there is a broadcast of the recorded work, for as we have seen the old 1956 Act provided that there is no restriction upon someone recording a broadcast provided that this is for private purposes only. Thus there could be copyrights in the original work together with separate copyrights in the audio or video work, and a further copyright in the broadcast. The owner of the original work could have licensed or assigned his rights to the audio or video producer, who in turn could have assigned or licensed the use of his rights to the broadcaster to use the work for a specific purpose. There is no further implied licence for anyone to copy the individual elements constituting a broadcast with total impunity. The creator of the original copyright could have imposed restrictions on the use of his rights in his agreement with the producer of the audio or video work, but normally this does not imply any licence for the reproduction of that work by any individual to record it privately at home, or indeed anywhere. The position under the old Act was that the copyright which subsists in a record or film was infringed if it was recorded privately, and the copyright in any original works were also infringed. The new Act provides that a copy of a broadcast or cable programme may be made provided that this is solely for the purpose of viewing or listening to it at a more convenient time. Further, this sort of copying does not infringe any original works contained in the broadcast. So it will still be an infringement of the copyright in films or records and the original works which they contain, to reproduce these without the permission of the owner but not if this is a reproduction of a broadcast and it is only for the specific purpose of enjoying this at a later time.[1]

1 Copyright, Designs and Patents Act 1988, s 70.

Some proposals for reform: Whitford 1977

15.8 Let us now look at what has been said about the phenomenon of home taping and at the various proposals for reform of the law of copyright to counteract the effects upon the legitimate rights of the copyright owners described above. The committee which drew up the Whitford Report in 1977[1] concluded that the law had to come to terms with the fact that home taping was on the increase due to the widespread use and development of audio and visual recording techniques and machines designed to be used with the ordinary home television set. Audio and video copyrights in the works recorded were being infringed by such action, as were the rights of those who had contributed in the creation of the original literary, artistic, dramatic or musical works which were a constituent element of the audio recording or film. By then most families in the UK had purchased or hired television sets and the video recorder was becoming a commonplace adjunct to it. Ownership of tape recorders was common and the technology was such that the machines for recording works direct from disc onto tape were cheap and improving in quality.

As the phenomenon was not confined to the UK the committee considered it legitimate to look elsewhere, as well as at home, for a remedy. It was impressed by the West German experience. As home taping was here to stay, West Germany's approach was to regard the sale of the actual recording machine as embodying a licence allowing the purchaser to record copyright material. This is known as a 'blanket licence'. It is a general licence deemed to be granted to all who purchase the recording machine to record copyright protected works and therefore does not allow the selection of licensees by the copyright owner. The suggestion was to impose a levy upon the actual recording machine itself, deemed to be the licence fee, for the right granted to record either an audio or video work. This was considered to be a realistic solution to the deleterious commercial effects which the new technology was having on the rights of copyright owners. After all, the machine could be used for only one purpose, to reproduce works which would normally be copyright-protected works. Up to now their commercial manufacture and sale was only operating to the benefit of the manufacturers and purchasers of the machines. The latter, by being able to record copyright works, were in the happy position of enjoying these works whenever they wanted without going to the expense of purchasing either the record or the film. As this had been to the detriment of the owner of the copyright in the original work, who depended upon sales of the records for his return on his efforts, and to the producer or maker of the audio or video work whose industry depended upon the ability to make a profit from the sales of its copyright recordings, Whitford considered the solution was to make the profiting manufacturer pay.

In fact, as we will see, this concept of placing the levy on the equipment itself was not accepted as a solution by more recent review bodies on the law of copyright. But as there is always the chance that such levies might be charged with the ever-changing laws to cover ever-changing new technologies, it is worth remembering how Whitford worked out his proposed scheme for a levy on equipment. The levy was to be imposed on the manufacture of each item of recording equipment, as a percentage of the value of the machine, the levy monies being paid into the account of a specially constituted collecting society whose sole function it would be to administer the fund and distribute the money to the owners of the copyright materials. In order for the collecting society to be able to act on the copyright owners' behalf and legally demand payment from the manufacturers, the copyright owners would have had to assign their rights to the society. In return for a lump sum annual payment by the manufacturers, the user of such recording machines would have been authorised to record, i e make reproductions of as many works as he wanted to, but only for his own consumption.

Obviously impressed by the West German experience, Whitford was in favour of introducing some such levy scheme for the coverage of private use, possibly also for the educational and business use of copyright materials. Whitford himself dismissed a suggestion, later proposed by the 1986 White Paper, that levies should be imposed on the sale of the blank tapes, the actual medium used to record the works, rather than on the machines themselves. It is interesting to note why. In the committee's view, though a levy on tapes might be fairer, its collection would be more difficult than with a levy on equipment. Presumably then, if he could have envisaged a reasonable method of administering levies on blank tapes, he would have looked more favourably upon such a proposal.

While dealing with the problem of compensating the copyright owner for illicit or illegal home taping, Whitford also reviewed the educational use of audio and video works, and we shall look at this briefly. In Whitford's view the wholesale recording and use of copyright materials in educational institutions without the consent of copyright owners should be dealt with by establishing a permanent body to represent the interests of the copyright owners who could then negotiate the materials to be used by such institutions. In its proceedings, the Whitford Committee made it clear that its aim was to amend the law in order to redress the imbalance now existing between the copyright owner, the general public and educational institutions resulting from illicit taping procedures, an aim which later review bodies have shared. But in all its reviews and suggestions for the reform of the law of copyright, both for private and educational recording, it made it perfectly clear that, in its view, the law should remain as it was for the strictly commercial use of copyright material which should be negotiated in the usual way, that is, by commercial negotiation for use of the material on payment for a licence. The ambit of reform was to extend only to the effects of home taping and thus to the private and personal use of the copyright materials recorded by the individual in his home i e in a non-commercial or non-industrial context.

1 Chapter 5, p 75–85.

Further proposals for reform

THE GREEN PAPER 1981

(1) Audio

15.9 We can now learn something from the 1981 Green Paper, a consultative document designed to elicit responses from interested parties in its proposals for the reform of the law based upon the findings of Whitford, but discussed in the ever worsening context of growing high technology and its use to infringe copyright.[1] Members of the committee which drew up this Green paper also saw that the traditional solution of granting an exclusive right of reproduction of the work to the record maker and leaving it to him to ensure that those who infringe are brought to book was now hopelessly inadequate. Even so, no more than had Whitford, it could not recognise as a solution to the copyright owners' problems blanket licensing by placing levies on blank tapes and collecting them by means of collecting agencies. But neither did it agree with Whitford's chosen solution of having levies placed on the equipment itself, making the manufacturer pay. It also discounted another suggestion, to prevent infringement by means of a 'spoiler'. This is a possible technical device which might be affixed to a recording machine to allow only some recordings and not others to take place, in allowed circumstances. It felt the problem with such a device is that it would simply present a new technical challenge to potential infringers to invent yet another device to cancel its effects. Apart from remaining sceptical about Whitford's option of a levy on equipment, the Commission itself offered no definite solutions to these ever-growing problems, but threw the discussion open for further contributions at the public level, hoping that some as yet unfound solution might yet present itself.

Of course, this did not mean that the Commission dismissed the problems. It recognised that although it was difficult to establish with any degree of certainty the precise losses occasioned to the copyright owners through home taping, losses there were.

1 'Reform of the Law relating to Copyright, Design and Performers' Protection' (1981, HMSO) Cmnd 8302.

(2) Video

15.10 Video was different. The Green Paper agreed with the conclusion of Whitford, that enforcement of the rights of the copyright owner in the privacy of the home would be impossible.

Furthermore, video was not, as yet, as great a threat to copyright owners as was tape recording because its normal users were more concerned about changing their time of viewing than producing reproductions of the work which would themselves be substitutes for the work, obviating the need for some to purchase it. In other words, the Commission distinguished between the two types of recording, audio and video, concluding that they were not analogous today as far as the law was concerned. After all, an audio work is generally taped in order to repeatedly play a recording, as is usually the case with a disc or tape. But since home video taping is used for 'time-shifting', it usually does not deprive the copyright owner of his rights, as probably the same tape is to be used on other materials rather than operating to keep a permanent record of the work, as is done with audio.

THE GREEN PAPER 1985

15.11 Real progress on the basis of these papers seemed to be made by a second Green Paper in 1985 which the government produced under the title 'The Recording and Rental of Audio and Video Copyright Material'[1] which, for the first time, came down strongly in favour of the imposition of a levy on the sale of blank tapes, a recommendation which was put forward by the White Paper.

If the problem of collecting the levies could be overcome, the committee, which prepared the paper, believed such a levy offered a balanced and equitable solution which remunerated the copyright owner for the copying of his work. At the same time it could solve the problem of educational establishments which need unlimited access to the recording of works for educational purposes. Now convinced of the gravity of the problem, the government opted for this radical solution, keeping in mind however the distinction between audio and video recordings and the differences in the problems posed by them to copyright owners, a distinction already made by the 1981 Green Paper. In the case of audio taping, only sweeping legislative changes would secure to the copyright owner the benefits, profits and return on his labour which he deserved. Before deciding on levies on blank tapes, the Committee had discussed the possibility of some form of levy upon the manufacturers of the new technological medium either on the blank tape or on the equipment designed for the use of that tape or possibly both. It pointed out that as future technological advances in the field are not likely to abate, any new legislation should be made to cover 'any recording medium', not just present ones, so that any new inventions which could serve the same infringing purposes should also be covered by the law. Though it hoped that levies on blank tapes would suffice to remunerate copyright owners, if experience proved it wrong, it left open the possibility of raising levies also on the equipment, as Whitford, following the West Germany pattern, had suggested. In any case, levies on either would be in accord with present EEC proposals for levies on blank tape and equipment, as set out in the 1977 report 'Community Action in the Cultural Sector' which suggests means for harmonising European copyright. As copyright problems often face copyright owners with international problems of infringement, clearly the more harmony between national copyright law, the better.

1 'The Recording and Rental of Audio and Video Copyright Material' (1985, HMSO) Cmnd 9445.

(1) Audio

15.12 How would such a scheme operate under UK law? In view of the fact that, by and large, this is an important type of scheme, it is worth outlining the 1985 Green Paper proposal. In return for the payment of a levy by the manufacturer on the tapes, the purchaser would be free to copy any broadcast material from TV or radio on to these tapes and use them, if for private use. As a blank tape is only a medium upon which there is a potential ability to record copyright protectable material the levy could not relate to any actual, but only to a supposed, intended use. The Committee welcomed the fact that there were already organisations, such as the Performing Rights Society, with sufficient experience in such matters. At present, owners of musical works negotiate for the potential or intended use of their copyright materials through such a collecting agency rather than enter, as individuals, into licensing negotiations each time there is a potential requirement for use of their copyright material. The Performing Rights Society, for instance, negotiates general licences on behalf of the owners of musical copyright to organisations such as the BBC who use a lot of musical copyright material in their broadcasts. The advantage to the user is that it does not have to enter into separate licensing negotiations each time it wants to use a particular piece of music in one of its programmes. The copyright owner would assign his copyright interests over to the society to negotiate reasonable terms of use of those rights on behalf of its member, collecting levies on his behalf and administering and distributing returns in a fair and reasonable way, reflecting as closely as possible the potential use of the work. Assignment of rights to the society would be restricted only to use of copyright materials or works for home taping. This means that the copyright owner could still retain his right to negotiate commercial licences with licensees in the usual way upon payment for use of that work and to take proceedings against someone who is engaged in the infringement of his rights by commercially exploiting these without his consent or permission.

This means that under the proposed scheme an owner of a copyright work or material would enjoy two separate types of right: firstly, those strict copyright rights in which he retains his control, allowing him to freely exploit especially commercially, and secondly, those quite different rights which he assigns over to a collecting society. In this latter case he relinquishes the exercise of his strict rights against the illicit activity of the home taping of his copyright work or material and is compensated by receiving a proportion of a levy as a potential royalty to which he has legitimate claim, but which, in practice, he had not the slightest chance of receiving, given the nature of the medium upon which his work would have been reproduced. Obviously, in the first case he is in control of his intellectual property rights, in the latter case he is not. He has lost something, but not, as at present, nearly every hope of revenue. In other words, he eschews control in favour of the possibility of some form of fair return otherwise denied him.

With the experience of present collecting societies to draw upon it was thought that audio tape levies should be possible. Their know-how could operate to the benefit of the copyright owners in collecting levies on the first sale of the tape, and if the manufacturer or importer did not comply with such impositions, then, on behalf of its members, the society would have the right to take the required legal action.

Two problems about the imposition of such levies were raised: first, what should be the position of those who would not be using the tape for the recording of copyright materials? After all, they would not be profiting from the owners of copyright works or materials in any way. A rebate scheme was suggested for such bona fide non-infringing uses. The problem was how to work out such a scheme by knowing the identity of such users; yet, neglecting to introduce such a scheme would mete out 'rough justice'.

Second, a proportion of the collected monies for the levy scheme could be distributed to foreign individuals or companies with no reciprocal arrangement for the distribution of levy on blank tape used abroad in respect of UK copyright. Fortunately, evidence has shown an increase in the use of levy systems in Europe, so the new UK scheme could dovetail with these other schemes. In fact the UK was moving in accord with a European consensus on the way in which the problem should be solved.

(2) Video

15.13 What about the position with video? Concurring with previous opinion, the committee did not propose to introduce a blank tape levy on video tapes for the reasons given. It might have approved doing so if the situation became more exacerbated with further technological developments, though, as it pointed out, there were serious difficulties in collecting such levies of this nature as no-one had any experience of doing so, the experience of the collecting societies having been confined largely to the operations on behalf of the owners of musical copyright.

Again the question of recording for educational purposes was discussed. The law should operate for the benefit of the educationalist as well as the copyright owner. Even so, if copyright owners are not sufficiently rewarded by being legally protected, then eventually the interests of both are foregone, as creators cease to create copyright works. The position was that the law operated more in favour of educational institutions than in the interests of copyright owners. In order to protect the interests of both, the committee decided that taping in educational institutions, whether audio or video, should be included within the provisions of home taping.

THE 1986 WHITE PAPER

15.14 Let us now turn to the 1986 White Paper which marks the culmination of ten or so years of debate on what should be done to alleviate the worsening position of the owner of copyright in audio and video works.

The recommendations of this Paper may yet form the basis of future legislation in this field even though the proposals have not been effected under the new Act.

Through its 1986 White Paper[1] the government came to the following view:

(1) Intellectual property rights of copyright owners are certain, copyright subsisting in both audio and video works giving the owner exclusive rights to reproduce his works. Taping of his works is an infringement of the copyright in the work, as much as any commercial or piratical taping is illegal.

The new technologies have given rise to widespread and uncontrollable home taping, the rights granted being unenforceable under the system of individual rights ownership. This has created an imbalance between the creator, the manufacturer and the consumer with only the manufacturer and the consumer benefiting. If this situation is allowed to continue, the law of copyright, designed to underpin industrial investment in innovation and creativity, will have failed. The failure of such industries, for lack of viable protection, would mean less incentive for creative innovation, and the livelihoods of a number of people would be seriously jeopardised.

(2) As the exclusive rights accorded to the owners of copyright works were clearly being eroded, the mechanism which had operated to benefit the copyright owner needed adjusting in order to shift the balance once more in his favour without unduly restricting the rights of the individual to make use of the new technologies and any future technologies. This argument, in the context of the above, led to these conclusions:

(a) copyright owners must be rewarded or recompensed for the use of their material by those who tape it at home to the prejudice of their interests in the work or material;
(b) there is no realistic alternative to a compulsory levy on blank recording tape as a means of effecting such remuneration;
(c) any levy scheme should give the public an entitlement to record for private purposes.[2]

As far as home taping was concerned the mechanism would change from one of self-help and the assertion of individual rights, to one where the certainty and value of those rights could only be maintained by:

(1) the creation of a new system of rights;
(2) the enforceability of existing rights put in the hands of an organisation capable of, and empowered to carry out, such functions;
(3) the ability to ensure that the scheme establishing the system of remuneration was fair and just and capable of responding to any future or potential advance in technology which may have the effect of once more creating an imbalance.

1 Chapter 6, p 37.
2 White Paper, para 6.6, p 38.

(1) Audio

15.15 How would this be achieved under any new legislation? There would be primary legislation empowering the Secretary of State to create new orders to put the provisions of the Act into effect, these orders to provide the following:

(1) Initially a levy would be imposed on blank audio compact cassettes of 35 minutes or more playing time, the restriction to this duration to cover the main medium on which most home taping of audio materials takes place.
(2) The rate of such a levy would be set at 10% of the retail sales value of the blank tape. This would be the maximum levy and not be subject to any review or negotiations and be a fair and just remuneration to the copyright owners.
(3) The Secretary of State would be empowered to provide by order a levy on any blank recording medium. In the event of technology advancing at such a rate that the present medium becomes obsolete, the law still to be applicable to all new media on which the copyright work may be reproduced.
(4) The levy would be payable by the manufacturers and importers who are the first traders in the UK in that particular recording medium as specified by the Secretary.
(5) The levy payable by the manufacturers or importers who are the first traders in the UK to be collected, not by the state as a tax, but by a collecting society set up to represent the beneficiaries of the proceeds of the levy, the society producing a detailed scheme first to be approved by the Secretary of State.
(6) The Secretary to specify the various categories of copyright owners entitled to benefit from the levy proceeds of any such scheme.
(7) The collecting society would be entitled to demand further information necessary for the computation of the levy payment, with power, if necessary, to go to court to obtain an order of disclosure or inspection. Any manufacturer trading in 'leviable' tapes without notifying them would have committed an offence carrying a penalty of £5,000. Disputes between the manufacturers and the society to be referred to the new Copyright Tribunal. A collecting society would be required to maintain and provide annual reports of its activities, the sums collected and paid out to the beneficiaries in its administration of the scheme.

15.16 The proposed structure sought to solve a current problem presented by the new technology of audio recording tape of a particular kind—those audio cassettes of 35 minutes' or more playing time, the usual length of tapes. Manufacturers or importers of tapes would be immediately liable to pay such a levy, and if the Secretary of State so decided, levies could be charged on any other types of tape, and taping in any other medium. In other words, manufacturers of the specified tape would have an immediate liability on the passing of the Act, with a potential liability in the face of any amendment to the leviable medium. When would the Secretary of State decide whether a new medium becomes leviable?

The trigger mechanisms for the levy to apply to a new or additional medium would be:

(a) if the medium were being used to such a scale and intensity in the making of private recordings of copyright works, that
(b) this use were to unreasonably prejudice the legitimate interests of the copyright owners.

In this way the law could adjust to any new technological medium capable of reproducing works faster, cheaper or in greater density or intensity, which could undermine the interests of the copyright owners by only operating for the benefit of the user or the manufacturers. This could, for example, apply to the latest phenomenon of audio digital tape (or DAT) which is capable of reproducing perfect copies of pre-recorded works on compact discs. Recently it has been argued, however, that such is the scale and intensity of their potential impact, that even the imposition of a levy on such recording techniques would not adequately compensate the copyright owner, and that only legislation requiring the manufacturers of such equipment to build in a copyguard or copycode anti-copying device would protect the legitimate rights of the copyright owners.

(2) Video

15.17 Proposals did not include video tape as a leviable item because, as we have seen, the government did not intend introducing it. The same sort of wholesale taping of copyright works would have to take place first, other than for the time-shifting function. Therefore video tape owners would still enjoy an exclusive right to the reproduction of their works. Although remaining a restricted act under the law of copyright for the user of recording equipment to make video recordings of copyright material direct from television broadcasts even for time-shifting purposes, domestic users would be free to do this for private purposes.

The copyright owner's rights and his recompense

15.18 Provided that he was the owner of copyright in a category provided for in such a collecting society scheme, the copyright owner would be able to claim a proportion of the levy collected on his behalf from the manufacturers of the blank tape. Confirming the 1985 Green Paper, the White Paper proposed that the collecting society would be empowered to collect 10% of the retail selling price of these 35 minute or more tapes from the manufacturers and to distribute a proportion of this to the copyright owner. Otherwise the law would remain the same and the copyright owner could enforce his strict copyright against any commercial infringer of his copyright, or, if possible, enforce copyright against any party taping his work on a medium to which the levy did not yet apply. In the case of home taping, he would receive just a percentage of the generally collected proceeds which would represent or constitute a royalty payment for the use of his work under normal circumstances were he in a position to enforce his strict rights under the law of copyright.

In conclusion then, if made law, the White Paper's proposals would have at last recompensed copyright owners threatened by audio taping. The copyright owners' revenues, up until now often nil, would have increased as a proportion of the total amount collected by a collecting society acting on his behalf, which it collected from the manufacturers or importers on what are deemed to be leviable tapes. Furthermore, if his works were reproduced intensively on any other medium—yet to be invented—if this acted to his detriment in the home taping context, then provided it satisfied the criterion established by the Secretary of State, he would have been able to claim a proportion of this leviable medium.

Rights of the user

15.19 So far as audio is concerned, once a member of the public had purchased a leviable tape at a point of sale, he would have been entitled to record and use any copyright material either from a broadcast or from a pre-recorded work, if for his private use. He need not have concerned himself as to whether the levy had been paid or not, as it would have been a matter between the collecting society and the manufacturers. But this does not mean that he would be entitled to record copyright works on any non-leviable medium. However, in the event of a medium becoming leviable for the reasons above, he would have become entitled to record on it for private purposes only, the copyright owner being compensated by the corresponding increase in the tape levy collected from the manufacturers or importers of that medium.

It must be said that the White Paper had taken into its calculations the fact that not all leviable tapes would be used for home taping purposes, in which case there should be a rebate scheme where there was sufficient proof that the tape was not being used in this way. It would be up to those who used such tape for non-infringing purposes to negotiate the rebate with the appropriate collecting society, to obtain the necessary reliefs.

The government decided to drop the idea of a levy on blank audio tapes because it felt that the financial benefit to the copyright owners would be outweighed by the adverse effects on the consumer. Thus despite many years of discussion about the need to protect the copyright owner by the imposition of such a levy, together with detailed recommendations as to how it could be effected, the whole scheme has been dropped. It might well be the case however that should the position of the copyright owner deteriorate further it might become necessary for the government to consider implementing a scheme to protect the interests of the copyright owner. If so it will have ample working materials at its disposal to decide just how such a scheme should operate.

The 1988 Act

15.20 With the abandonment of the blank tape levy the government introduced an alternative remedy, the new rental right. This creates a new restricted act under copyright law. Generally, the Act provides that the issue to the public of copies of a copyright work is an act restricted by the copyright which subsists in every description of copyright work.[1] This restricted act of issuing copies of the work to the public now includes any rental to the public of sound recordings, films and computer programs. 'Rental' is defined in the Act as meaning

> 'any arrangement under which a copy of a work is made available—
> (a) for payment (in money or money's worth) or
> (b) in the case of a business, as part of services or amenities for which payment is made on terms that it will or may be returned'.[2]

The original idea was to grant a rental right exercisable by the copyright owner for one year only after the copies had been issued to the public. After that, he would not be able to control their rental and anyone could rent out the works subject only to the copyright owner receiving a royalty on each rental. This was abandoned and the right to control is now a full rental right, that is, the copyright owner has an absolute right to prevent the rental of his works. However, under the Act there is power for the Secretary of State to make orders to the effect that in certain cases the rental to the public of sound recordings, films or computer programs will be treated as licensed by the copyright owner subject only to the payment of a reasonable fee.[3] However no orders would be made if there is a certified licensing scheme in operation under section 143 of the Act providing for the grant of licences.

Why have these provisions been made in this form? For the following reasons: the grant of a rental right as a restricted act gives the copyright owner the opportunity of preventing unauthorised rental of his copyright works. This only applies to the owners of records, films and computer programs and not to any other copyright works. Therefore anyone wishing to rent out copies of those works to the public will need a licence to do so under commercial terms to be agreed between the parties. If however a sufficient number of copyright owners of recordings or films refused to allow rental to take place the consequences of this could be to depress the rental market for such products. If the rental market stagnated because the rights owners refused to allow rental of their products and insisted that their products may only be purchased, then this would be considered an abuse of the rental right. The Secretary of State would then be justified in making an order for specific rental provisions to apply. Such copyright works would then be treated as licensed by their owners subject only to the payment of a royalty. However, such an order would not be made if the copyright owners themselves had already established a licensing scheme making their works generally available for licensing. It remains to be seen how these provisions will operate in practice.

The Act strengthens the audio/video copyright owner's rights to control the commercial exploitation of his products and gives him a return on his investment. This is some recompense for the loss of potential earnings which he would have gained under a blank tape levy scheme. It also seeks to balance the rights of the copyright owner with those of the consumer who expects to be able to legitimately rent products without having to purchase them. In addition it prevents some possible abuse of rights by the copyright owner by allowing the Secretary of State powers to order the compulsory rental of such products. He will not order compulsory rental however if the copyright owners have decided to set up their own scheme to make their products available for rental.

1 Copyright, Designs and Patents Act 1988, s 18(1).
2 Ibid, s 178.
3 Ibid, s 66(1).

CHAPTER 16

Photocopying/reprography

Introduction

16.1 In the last chapter we found that sweeping changes were needed for the economic survival of owners of the copyright works in the media of audio and video, both for the creators of original works and for the industries engaged in exploiting them, who depend on being able to protect their interests through the enforcement of copyright. Unfortunately, as we have seen, these changes are not forthcoming under the new Act but other measures have been effected in their stead. The modern law of copyright needs to ensure the following: first, that those individuals and organisations which invest in innovative industries are able to benefit commercially from the products of their innovation, despite the virtually uncontrollable medium in which their works subsist, and second, that the consuming public generally, and educational institutions in particular, are able to take full advantage of the new technologies which make it possible for them to have greater access than ever before to a fuller range of information by being able to reproduce these works. The present amendments to the law reflect these aims.

16.2 We tend to believe that the creation and dissemination of information is a good of society itself, and that any technology which predisposes towards this should be made available to the public as cheaply and in as unfettered a manner as possible. Unfortunately, as modern technology advances in the field of reproduction, the pattern favours the manufacturers and users of technology at the expense of the owners of copyright. Though they feed that technology, they themselves are often left in the position where they have to seek the protection of the law to prevent the negation of their rights; if not, they are left virtually unprotected. Thus an imbalance of interests arises at their expense.

It is clear from the intellectual property rights dealt with so far, that the rights of the copyright owner are under attack in two main ways: first, when the work or material is reproduced wholesale by an infringer who uses the works for commercial gain without the permission of, or payment to, the copyright owner; second, and more pervasively, where an individual allowed access to a new piece of technologically advanced equipment, such as a reprographic, photocopying or recording machine, employs it to reproduce and so infringe copyright works, often for his own personal consumption and use.

16.3 With some success, at least in the case of computer and audio/visual material, the law has responded to this first activity by increasing criminal penalties attached to the act of unauthorised reproduction of copyright works for commercial gain.[1] But such success is lacking in deterring the second kind of reproducer. This is because there is no way in which to prevent such reproduction once someone has access to these machines, so in practice the copyright holder's interests are simply unenforceable. Whatever his legal rights, the practical problem is how to ensure they are enforced, at least to the extent that he is recompensed by those who benefit from the use of his work. Just as multiple copying through the widespread use of audio and video machines, often in the privacy of our own homes, is part of our daily lives, so too is this type of reprographic reproduction or photocopying, where it is possible to infringe with impunity the copyright owner's work, either in our homes, or in libraries or other organisations. As we will see, there are problems peculiar to photocopying and reprographic reproduction. Reproduction by use of the photocopier of copyright works takes place on a massive scale. It is possible to reproduce a work quickly, efficiently, cleanly and cheaply by the use of a modern photocopier. If a machine is available to the wholesale infringer of copyright works, he could produce multiple copies of a work at a fraction of the cost expended to publish it without payment to the copyright owner. As photocopiers are used extensively for legitimate purposes, that is, for the reproduction of non-copyright works or for copyright works belonging to the owner of the reprographic machine, in all manner of institutions, they cannot be banned without dire effects on modern industry and life. But if a copyright work is reproduced in multiple copies for dissemination throughout an institution, then it is the institution which enjoys the maximum benefit of the work at the least cost, and with no payment to the original creator of the work. Today this abuse of the copyright owner's rights is commonplace in commerce and industry, in national and local government and in libraries and educational institutions, as they all possess reprographic machines of some kind, which they can, and do, use with impunity.

1 Copyright Act 1956, ss 13, 21; Criminal Justice Act 1982.

16.4 Often depending financially on the licensing of rights for the reproduction of his work, the copyright owner today finds himself without a legitimate proportion of his income; not so the manufacturers of the reprographic equipment, the producers of the medium on which the reproduction takes place, or the user, who all find themselves at a profit with the new technologies at hand. As copyright owners today are themselves often large industrial concerns, some industries are profiting at the expense of others, and those that are losing are those which depend largely for their revenue on the exploitation of their copyright works by the means of licensing, the revenue being directly related to the intensity of reproduction which has taken place. Obviously, it should be the case that any party wishing to reproduce a copyright protected work should have to get the permission of the owner of that work and pay a royalty according to the number of times it is reproduced. Unhappily, frequently this is not happening. Commercial, institutional and individual photocopying of copyright works is widespread; payment of royalties for them is not.

With the advent of ever faster, cleaner and cheaper machines, using different reprographic technologies, the position of the copyright owner was likely to deteriorate without legal help in the form of new legislative measures to combat such abuses.

The present position on the photocopying of copyright works

16.5 In order to understand the new legislation designed to solve the problem of unfettered reprography, as proposed by the 1986 White Paper, we must go back to the 1956 Copyright Act. Under the Act, the paradigm case of a copyright owner is where a creator of an original work expends labour, skill and capital sufficient to claim an exclusive copyright for a specified period of time. He is not obliged to do anything with that work but he can exploit it himself or assign it, or license another party to exploit it on his behalf. Does such a creator of copyright work have the right to prevent any photocopying of his work, even if he depends upon the legitimate successful exploitation of his work in the market for that type of innovation and argues that he should be justly recompensed as a reward for his labour in the creation of the work? After all, if he were granted a right to restrict totally the reproduction of his work, might this not interfere with the legitimate interests of others to enjoy an unfettered free flow of information which they may wish to use in ways which are not only profitable to themselves, but indeed to our present society which relies upon such information?

16.6 So we must ask when is it, and when is it not, an abuse to photocopy and reproduce the copyright owner's works? The problem is to reconcile the need for a free use of information in society with the need to reward those who create it in the first place. No recompense, then no generation of new and valuable information. Under the law of copyright there is no restriction on the free flow of information, as it is a desirable state of affairs to be encouraged. For example, the basis of someone using the facilities of a library is that use of the information contained in its books or magazines is free. Is that person free to reproduce it? Not without the permission of the copyright owner.[1] But who is to stop him when he has, placed at his disposal, machines such as the photocopying machine? Anyway, if he were prevented, would this not negate his rights to use the material, resulting in a decrease in the flow of the dissemination of information and ideas? A dilemma was posed: allowing the user to reproduce encourages the free use of information but discourages the creators of such information from further creation. Prohibiting the user from reproducing encourages the copyright owners to create, but discourages the dissemination of their work. What is the solution to such a dilemma, most acute in the case of libraries and educational institutions, especially as the library's function is to provide information services to the public as cheaply and as effectively as possible, and the function of educational institutions is to do likewise for their students?

At the time of the 1956 Copyright Act the solution decided upon was to temper the law by providing it with exceptions so that the copyright owner could not prevent all reproduction of his work. To a measurable extent, he could not prevent some of its reproduction and use for criticism or review and for private and personal purposes. Newspapers need to be able to include portions of copyright works for review purposes, as do learned and other magazines for criticism and review, otherwise the flow and stimulus of information would be effectively stemmed, to the detriment of society. For this reason the 1956 Copyright Act provided for exceptions to the strict enforcement of the copyright owner's rights under specific conditions, hoping at the same time that these would not detract from his rights and thus discourage his creative work or his rights to derive his sources of revenue or royalty income from his works through the usual commercial exploitation channels at his disposal. Unfortunately, some of these hopes were to founder. At the time these exceptions were named the 'fair dealing' provisions (not actually defined anywhere in the Act) and it was mistakenly believed that the relaxation of the strict rights of the copyright owner, which they represented, would not harm him.

1 Copyright Act 1956, ss 2(5) and 3(5).

THE 1956 ACT PROVISIONS—THE EXCEPTIONS

16.7 Let us first examine these provisions of the 1956 Act which apply to any literary, dramatic, artistic or musical work in order to understand, in general, what went wrong with them.

First, there are a series of general exceptions from the protection of literary, dramatic, musical or artistic copyright works; second, special exceptions in respect of their use in libraries and archives; and third, provisions for the use of copyright material for educational purposes. Let us look at these in turn.

(A) First, general exceptions under sections 6 (literary, dramatic or musical works) and 9 (artistic works) of the Act. There may be fair dealing with a literary, dramatic or musical work for the purpose of

(1) research or private study;
(2) criticism or review (provided accompanied by a sufficient acknowledgement of title and author);
(3) reporting of current events in
 (*a*) a newspaper, magazine or similar periodical (with an acknowledgement as above), or
 (*b*) by means of broadcasting, or in a cinematograph film
(4) reproducing for purpose of a judicial proceeding or reproducing for purposes of a report of a judicial proceeding;
(5) reading or recitation in public by one person of any reasonable extract from a published literary or dramatic work (together with an acknowledgement);
(6) including a short passage of a published literary or dramatic work in a collection intended for the use of schools;
(7) reproducing the work where a broadcasting company has taken an assignment or a licence of a work for broadcasting purposes, provided it is in the course of the broadcasting

function and that the reproduction of it is destroyed within 28 days.

(B) Second, special exceptions for use in libraries and archives under section 7 of the Act (the first part of the section deals with articles contained in periodicals and the second part with literary, dramatic and musical works in general).

(1) The copyright in an article contained in a periodical is not infringed by the making and supplying of a copy of the article by a librarian provided that the person requesting the copy wishes to use it for private study or research, that it is limited to one copy and the library charges for the costs it incurs.

(2) The copyright in a published literary, dramatic or musical work is not infringed if the librarian provides no more than a reasonable proportion of the work in question, but only if the librarian does not have or could not ascertain the name and address of the person entitled to authorise the making of the copy. Again, the provisions as to private study, research and review etc, apply. The librarian is empowered to make a copy of the whole or a part of a published work for another library provided he does not have the name and address of the person entitled to authorise the making of the copy.

(C) Third, educational provisions under section 41 of the Act. When copyright subsists in a literary, dramatic, musical or artistic work, copyright shall not be taken to have been infringed by reason only that the work is reproduced or an adaptation of the work is made

(*a*) in the course of instruction (whether at a school or elsewhere) where the reproduction or adaptation is made by a teacher or pupil (otherwise than by use of a duplicating machine), or

(*b*) as part of the questions to be answered in an examination or in an answer to such a question;

(*c*) a literary, dramatic or musical work if performed in class in pursuance of the activities of the school and the audience is essentially a school audience.

'Duplicating process' means 'any process involving the use of an application for producing multiple copies'. Thus the reproduction of a work under (*a*) above means for example that the work may be written on the blackboard for all to copy but there must be no actual multiple copying of the work on a reprographic machine of any kind.

16.8 The aims of the Act are clear enough: to ensure a balance is maintained between the control which an individual has to prevent the reproduction of his works and to allow its fair use for the purposes of information. It could not have been foreseen that those in-built checks, balances and safeguards sufficient to resolve past conflicts of interest would not suffice in the light of technological developments yet to come. One of the weaknesses of that Act was not to define the scope of 'fair dealing' under section 6. This has meant that each case which has come before the court has had to be dealt with on its own merits as to what does or does not constitute 'fair dealing'. In order to resolve the problems this has created for users, and more particularly for creators of copyright works, the Society of Authors and the Publishers' Association in 1965 agreed to give some guidance to the users of copyright material as to just how much they could reproduce individual works without fearing prosecution by copyright owners for infringing their rights. This was to achieve some certainty for users and copyright owners, taking some cognisance of the real situation where infringement of copyright by reproduction was increasing. In order to retain some control of their rights, copyright owners agreed to forego their strict enforcement by not suing for infringement in the event that only the agreed amount would be reproduced, and if and only if the material was used for the purposes of study or research for an individual in these following cases of the reproduction of:

(*a*) a single copy of an article from a periodical, provided that there is a declaration signed and an undertaking to the effect that it is for private research or study; normally this will not be regarded as unfair, if a single copy is made.

(*b*) a single copy of limited abstracts of a copyright work for the purpose of research or private study, not normally to be regarded as unfair if a single copy is made from a copyright work of a single extract not exceeding 4,000 words, or a series of extracts (of which none exceeds 3,000 words) to a total of 8,000 words, provided that in no case the total amount copied exceeds 10% of the whole work. Poems, essays and other short literary works must be regarded as whole works in themselves and not as 'parts' of the volumes in which they appear.[1]

The above is not a legal position. It is only a statement of a position taken by those in the field of the creation and exploitation of essentially literary works; and as such it is but an interim solution made in desperation because of the inability of the law to satisfactorily cope with an increasingly serious threat to the rights of copyright owners. As such it is a compromise due to the limitations of the fair dealings provisions of the 1956 Act in a changing situation. This can be seen by the new attempts of the law to come to terms with what is happening.

1 *Photocopying and the Law* (1965).

Some recommendations for reform

16.9 Let us begin with the Whitford Report 1977[1] which looked at the growing practice of reprographic reproduction with some misgivings. It tried to gain guidance as to what it might recommend, in order that it might be seen to be fair and reasonable in respect of our commitment to our international copyright obligations, by studying what was happening in other countries. But this was to little avail. There were too many cultural differences which made impossible an international solution to the growing practice of reproducing copyright works; so it was forced back on the necessity of finding a national solution to the problems faced in the UK. Individual nation states, it concluded, would simply have to create those sorts of laws which they needed to satisfy their own educational, cultural, social and economic requirements. Therefore, the more important evidence submitted to the committee was from those in UK educational institutions, libraries, publishing houses and by authors, which showed that, nationally at least, the problems were common and should be dealt with on a common practical basis in order to control the phenomenon of photocopying. It was now widespread and copyright protected works were being freely and uncontrollably reproduced throughout the UK especially in educational institutions and libraries.

1 Paras 204–290.

EDUCATIONAL COPYING

16.10 The difficulties which such widespread use were creating, especially for copyright owners, were now crucial as the 1956 Act had made little provision for the needs of educational institutions vis-à-vis the rights of copyright owners, having been promulgated in an era when there was as yet little need to reproduce copyright works. Then, the educational structure was based upon fairly strict and rigid learning patterns, students being expected to make full use of libraries or purchase the required books in question. In this situation it was easy to control the rights of copyright owners as any reproduction required usually got, with payment, the consent of the copyright owner. In thus limiting any reproductive use of the copyright material the creators of the 1956 Act did not envisage, of course, that this might result in a widespread detraction from the owners' rights of the copyright material.

Such was the scene then, but with the new technology and indeed with widespread reprographic reproduction, the pattern of learning in educational institutions was radically changed, and there has come about what Whitford referred to as 'resource-based learning'. Resource-based learning, enabled by the new technology, is learning away from the library, facilitated by the availability of audio/visual material, reproduced texts being taken from published works and arranged by tutors into courses. It is here, and in Whitford's opinion, here to stay, now that it is possible for an individual to copy cheaply, cleanly and quickly, and suitably reproducible materials. With the reduction of the more traditional structured approach to learning and teaching has come a more flexible and adaptable method of trying to achieve the same or similar ends by encouraging and allowing students access to as wide a range of educational materials as possible on a wide range of media. The new technologies include reprographic reproduction, audio/video material, computers and information technology generally, allowing the student to access, manipulate and reproduce material simply, cheaply and in quantity. From the new technologies have resulted new teaching methods, and, in turn, new teaching methods become more dependent upon the new technologies. It is not surprising then that Whitford concluded that it is the application of resource-based learning applied to independent or class activity which has encouraged the need for, and the availability of, a great diversity of material extracted from many sources. These new developments, not unnaturally, have coincided with a development of educational theory and philosophy, itself stimulated by the availability of a range of technical devices capable of increasing the amount and variety of resource materials, embraced by both teacher and pupil alike. Nor was it surprising that Whitford was able to gauge that, though section 41 of the Act expressly precluded the making of multiple copies of copyright works, infringing reproduction of copyright works was taking place on a vast scale. The law had to accept that the new technologies were making available to those engaged in the educational process vast new areas of information hitherto inaccessible, benefiting the educational function, and that this process, now begun, would continue its use of such technology to its widest possible use and advantage. Free and unfettered use of the new technologies was now a feature of the educational system and would continue to be so. Furthermore, the system would doubtless want to incorporate into the teaching function any further evolution of those technologies. The law should not stand in its way if it could devise a fair means of recompense to copyright owners, in any case essential to the continuance of this enjoyment of the new technology. Before we come to proposed compromises in this direction, we need to survey Whitford's review of the use of copyright materials in libraries.

LIBRARIES

16.11 Currently libraries are required to bring the law of copyright to the attention of individuals who wish to photocopy single copies of an article from a publication or an agreed quantity of a work.[1] In either case the copyright owner agreed to forgo the exercise of his strict rights of enforcement of his copyright in that work. The user of the copyright work is required to make a declaration and undertake only to use the material for private use. But evidence given by libraries to the committee clearly showed that this system is abused. The Act only provides for the use of such material for private study and does not refer to private research.[2] Thus, on a strict interpretation of the Act, the use of materials for research purposes is not restricted to private research and may thus be used for commercial research purposes. It is common practice for individuals to obtain copies of articles from libraries which are often then not used only by those individuals but by large research institutions which are part of commercial enterprises. What is to stop them? It is impossible for libraries always to check whether someone is using an article for bona fide purposes. As there is no practical sanction, the rights of copyright owners are unenforceable against the profitable use of their works by large industrial commercial research concerns. This is particularly serious in the case of industrial use of publications such as specialist scientific or technical magazines containing scientific or technical information. Publishers have been losing large revenues because concerns avoid paying subscriptions for a magazine by obtaining relevant photocopies of it from libraries, etc, thus gaining vitally important information for their industrial development, which certainly is not used for private study. Whereas others welcomed the arrival of the new technologies, publishers, authors and composers found their rights being eroded by such uncontrolled use of them.

1 *Photocopying and the Law* (1985).
2 Copyright Act 1956, s 7(2)(b).

16.12 Effective dissemination of information has always been considered a vital element in the progress of the development of any field of technological innovation. But as we have seen, publishers of scientific and other technical and learned journals are finding that library copying is seriously affecting subscriptions to their journals, putting in jeopardy their very publication. To help solve the problem they suggested to the Whitford Committee the exclusion of any multiple copying under section 6 (that is, for commercial rather than private research) and that commercial libraries should not have any rights under section 7 (that is, no rights to make copies of articles or periodicals for either research or private study). The Publishers' Association recommended the establishment of a blanket licensing scheme to replace the present provisions so that recompense of some sort could be assured to their members who were copyright owners, by having libraries pay for a licence for the owners' rights in works to be reproduced. Libraries did not welcome this suggestion. Though at present they are under a statutory duty to charge for the cost of the copying, they made clear in their submissions to the committee that they did not want the onerous burden of collecting and administering any such blanket licensing scheme. Once again, conflicting interests were evident. Were copyright owners again to miss out, this time due to the administrative difficulties facing libraries, or would a compromise solution to their problems at least allow them some security of recompense?

Whitford was faced with a law, now unenforceable, which if it continued would lead to damaging consequences for everyone concerned—for copyright owners certainly, but also for those employed by the new technologies and the users of such technologies for the reproduction of the works, if such owners gave up creating new works. Publishing scientific and technological materials without sufficient subscriptions would become impossible, and this in turn would lead to a reduction in the dissemination of just that information so vital to the UK's commercial and industrial research, which the law is meant to encourage and facilitate. As industry needs the stimulus of new ideas, the law must provide sufficient security to enable their continued replenishment by protecting those many industries today engaged in their creation and effective dissemination.

Unpopular though it was with libraries, Whitford concluded that a blanket licence would secure the needs of all interested parties to some extent, because it would provide financial recompense to copyright owners while allowing the continued use of reprographic facilities everywhere where such licences had been paid.[1] Even though Whitford's recommendation has been overturned by the committee which drew up the 1986 White Paper, and indeed it is not included in the present legislation, it is interesting to pursue it, because it developed into a different but related solution.

Whitford envisaged the following scheme: the copyright owner would forgo his individual rights—which he was unable to enforce in any event—vesting his interests in a collecting society. This society would represent his interests in the negotiating of licences to interested parties and potential users, who would then distribute a proportion of the collected revenues to the various copyright owners. The revenues would be based upon the expected or anticipated intensity of reproduction of any particular work. An experienced collecting society could operate a sampling system to ensure a fair, just and equitable distribution of such negotiated revenues. Initially, any scheme would need approval by the Secretary of State, any disputes arising as to its operation being referred to a new Copyright Tribunal proposed to be established under new copyright legislation. The essence of the scheme was that it was to be statutory, that is, obligatory.

Having a care for the continuing erosion of the rights of copyright owners, two points made by Whitford were as follows. First, the imbalance operating to the benefit of the user of the new technology and to the copyright owners' detriment had come about because technology today moved too swiftly in advance of the law's ability to react or respond to the copyright owners' rights. He therefore proposed that a blanket licensing scheme should generally apply automatically to any new technological developments in the reprographic process in order to prevent yet further erosion of the copyright owners' rights. Second, the individual rights of the copyright owner to enforce his rights would only extend to the reprographic and facsimile copies for library, governmental, industrial and professional copying. Thus the copyright owner's rights to negotiate individual licences for the normal commercial exploitation of his copyright work would remain unchanged.

1 Para 274.

Further proposals for reform

THE 1981 GREEN PAPER

16.13 While the Commission responsible for the 1981 Green Paper agreed with much of what Whitford had to say about the problems which had arisen in the field of reprography due to the advent of the new technologies, it did not agree to his proposal that a statutory, that is to say, obligatory, blanket licensing scheme should be introduced, and in that form this proposal has been dropped.[1] The reason blanket licensing was unacceptable, apart from its unpopularity with libraries, was because of its suppression of the idea of the continuing right to use copyright works even for private research and study. This seems unreasonable and eventually counter-productive. Instead, it was judged that what was needed was an amendment to the relevant sections of the 1956 Copyright Act so as to ensure against abuse. In its view this meant:

(1) multiple copying of the same material should be expressly excluded from the provisions;
(2) the exceptions of the Act should not be used for the purposes of research carried out for the business ends of commercial organisations;
(3) contrary to Whitford's advice, the provisions of sections 6 and 7 should remain, allowing the reproduction of single copies of copyright works providing there was fair dealing.

Whereas Whitford had suggested a compulsory blanket licensing scheme, and the removal of sections 6 and 7, the Commission responsible for the Green Paper was suggesting a non-statutory blanket licence. This was different, as in this case the owners of copyright works would themselves collectively negotiate licences with those parties engaged in producing reprographic services. The fair dealing provisions would remain, restated to prevent abuse—ie to stipulate that what is reproduced is used for private, not commercial purposes.

1 'Reform of the Law relating to Copyright, Designs and Performers' Protection' (1981) Cmnd 8302.

THE 1986 WHITE PAPER

16.14 The government took into account the new technological industrial scene in the UK, much of which had arisen since the Green Paper was published in 1981, and during which copyright owners have seen their rights increasingly abused. It also took account of recent successful interim efforts to stop these abuses by the representatives of authors and publishers themselves who have been attempting measures to secure an equitable return for their members' works. Indeed, the Copyright Licensing Agency Ltd was formed by them in 1983 specifically to collect and make effective their rights. They did this by approaching educational and other institutions to establish fair and reasonable voluntary licensing schemes. Under these schemes permission is granted by them for schools, colleges and other institutions to take a licence upon payment to the agency to copy from books belonging to their members. The licence is usually for a period of one to three years and it allows the licensee to copy the CLA's repertoire of members' works provided that this takes place on specified premises, and the licensee keeps records of the photocopying which has taken place and allows sampling to take place, this being the method whereby the Agency is able to remunerate its members.

The Agency has also concluded a series of licences with a number of local authorities and has entered into an experimental scheme with the representatives of British universities. It intends entering into reciprocal arrangements with European and other similar licensing agencies. As these voluntary licensing schemes operate well, the government was convinced that there was no real need for a statutory or obligatory licensing scheme such as Whitford recommended but rather there should be active encouragement for the development of voluntary schemes.

THE 1988 ACT—A SOLUTION TO THE PROBLEM?

16.15 The Act seeks to remedy the abuses taking place of copyright owners' rights, to make the law relating to fair dealing more certain, to encourage copyright owners to set up voluntary licensing schemes and generally to create a fair balance between those who create copyright works and those who need to use them. Has the government found a solution to the conflicting interests between users and copyright owners? Probably, yes. In the light of the above it decided that its role was to help these presently existing and ever-growing voluntary schemes to work properly by encouraging an increase in their membership. This is necessary if they are to work and thus provide a framework to ensure generally a fair, equitable and workable scheme, where disputes between interested parties can be satisfactorily resolved. The voluntary licensing schemes are to be limited to the context of non-statutory blanket licensing in terms of the reprographic reproduction of the copyright owners' works. The new provisions do not interfere with the individual copyright owner's rights to exploit his work commercially. He can continue to do so by using the normal commercial mechanisms available to him under the general law of copyright. The provisions of the Act are intended to help him by providing a framework within which his rights are recognised so that he can gain an equitable recompense for his labour and efforts in creating his work, while allowing those who need to use his work to do so if recompensing him. He is thus given a greater degree of certainty over the subsistence of his rights in the work than with its uncontrolled use, exercising a degree of control over the use of his works through an established copyright licensing scheme.

16.16 What will the legal, economic and commercial ramifications of the new provisions be on the owners of copyright works, on the providers of photocopying equipment, and on the users of such works?

The legislation is facilitating, that is, it is designed to encourage owners of copyright works to subscribe to a licensing scheme. Instead of the present ambiguities in the law due to the new technologies, the copyright owners will have a degree of certainty in respect of their interests which are now often unexploitable and unenforceable. Under such voluntary schemes the individual forgoes some of his rights only to have them better assured by a collecting agency negotiating on his behalf. We saw that the main area of use where multiple copying took place was in the educational field and in libraries. Let us look at the new situation.

Education

Teachers need the use of the new technologies as these are part of resource-based learning. Necessarily, for this kind of learning, the teacher needs access to reprographic equipment for the multiple copying of copyright works for group instruction in the classroom. Without this access it would not be 'resource-based learning'. Usually the teacher uses portions of a text for instruction, not the whole work.

The new Act provides that educational institutions will be freely licensed to copy (reproduce reprographically) up to 1% of any individual work in any quarter year, provided, that is, that the institution has not already been offered a licence to reproduce that particular work.[1] Thus an institution will be allowed to reproduce a part of an individual copyright owner's work in this intensity without any payment to the copyright owner, but this right of free copying ceases as soon as the institution is offered a licence. Then it has to pay for the right to copy the work in accordance with the agreed royalties under the licence. Any licence which is granted must not be for less than 1% per quarter year. Here is an incentive for individual copyright owners to offer licences to institutions to reproduce their works as they are not in a position to exercise their rights individually in such situations. It should become clear to them that, in order to benefit from their works, they should assign their individual rights in their copyrights to appropriate licensing agencies, if only for the purpose of negotiating their reprographic reproduction rights. With time and accumulated experience, such agencies can be expected to become increasingly better able to handle such negotiations on behalf of their members, and so assure the protection of their members' rights and economic benefit by collecting and distributing their monies. If these incentives do appeal sufficiently to convince copyright owners that their interests are best served in the collective assertion of their individual rights, then this could well solve the difficulties of today's often inconsistent, ambiguous and virtually unenforceable laws in the area of reprography. But if these incentives are not a sufficient inducement to the copyright owners to individually or collectively license institutions, then the government has in reserve other measures it would probably take to give effect to the same aims. Under the Act the Secretary of State has powers to make a specific order stating that the owner of a particular copyright should be treated as if he were a member of a licensing scheme by providing that the scheme or licence shall extend to those works. This would be the case where works of a description similar to those covered by the scheme or licence are unreasonably excluded from it, and making them subject to the scheme or licence would not conflict with the normal exploitation of the works or unreasonably prejudice the legitimate interests of the copyright owners. Thus, if the individual rights owner refuses to join such a scheme or he makes an appeal to the Copyright Tribunal, he could find the Secretary of State making an order compulsorily licensing his particular class of work.[2]

Unless the individual rights owner either licenses his work individually to educational institutions or assigns his rights for their collective licensing, any educational institution will be deemed to be freely licensed to copy up to 1% of the work for the period described. It will not have to make any payment to the copyright owner until such time as it is either offered a licence from the individual himself or from a collecting agency negotiating a licence on the owner's behalf for a work which may be used in that particular agency's repertoire of collected works.

To complete the picture of the legislative changes, the provisions of section 41(1)(a) of the 1956 Act are re-stated to make it absolutely clear that the exception relating to reproducing of a part of a copyright work does not permit use of a photocopier or any other process for making facsimile copies.[3]

Libraries and archives

The new legislation on library reproduction does not include any definition as to fair dealing, but the library exception under section 7 which allows single copies of works for research or private study is re-stated to ensure that the original intention of the old Act is preserved and the related production of multiple copies of the same material explicitly excluded from the library exception.[4]

1 White Paper 1986, para 8.8; Copyright, Designs and Patents Act 1988, s 36(1) and (2).
2 White Paper 1986, para 8.9(a) and (b); Copyright, Designs and Patents Act 1988, s 137(2).
3 White Paper 1986, para 8.19; Copyright, Designs and Patents Act 1988, s 32(1)(b).
4 White Paper 1986, para 8.10; Copyright, Designs and Patents Act 1988, ss 38, 39 and 40.

CHAPTER 17

The future

Introduction

17.1 In Part 2 of the book we have examined the legal problems which beset copyright owners due to the developments which have taken place in information technology. We saw that owners' interests have been constantly under threat due to the convergence of the new technologies relating to the creation, manipulation, accessing and distribution of information and because of the new, less controllable medium in which such works either originate or into which they can be readily converted. The law has had to respond by ensuring that works in these new media are recognised and given legal protection. I have argued that if works are less protectable because the copyright owner is unable to enforce his strict rights of copyright against unauthorised users, the law should provide mechanisms to ensure that the owner of the work is adequately compensated for the labour, time and effort expended in its creation. Otherwise the incentive to invest in the creation of new works is lost and the cultural and industrial world is poorer. I have discussed the problems of a number of industries whose livelihoods and investments depend upon, and in some cases are underpinned by the law of copyright, and I have appraised the adequacy of the law to protect those investments. We have also seen instances where the law has failed to provide adequate measures for enforcement and where compensatory legal mechanisms have been designed and proposed to ensure continued innovation. I put forward the view that the UK will rely increasingly upon information technology products for its new industrial base as the old traditional industries continue to decline, and that therefore it is necessary to have a system of intellectual property laws which are up to date and which offer proper protection for these new industrial assets. I discussed some of the inadequacies of the present system and the proposals for change in the fields of copyright and patents, the impetus for change being related to the inability of the system as it stands to respond to the needs of those who rely heavily upon the protection of their intellectual property. I concluded that generally there was a concern and a growing awareness for the need to protect what are, increasingly, our new industrial assets. The legislative changes proposed by the government in the 1986 White Paper and the provisions of the new Copyright Act reflect this concern.

17.2 What has become clear is that the protection of intellectual property rights, especially copyright, depends upon the strong industrial presence of those interested parties who are able to plead that their particular industry is one which conveniently comes within the scope of the laws of copyright. We saw this with the computer software industry. The old 1956 Act did not specifically include by name computer software, because at that time there was little computer software industry as we know it today. Thirty years on, this industry is widespread and thriving. Lobbying by it brought a response from the government which realised that it needed protection because it was vital to the general overall economy in the generation of revenues and jobs, and likely to have a profound industrial, commercial and social impact. Thus we saw that after the software industry had sought protection in the courts by presenting its case, software came within the protection of the present law of copyright as a 'literary work'. It was eventually with the support of a Private Member's Bill that the Copyright (Computer Software) Amendment Act was brought into being in 1985.

I have said all along that while copyright serves to protect the expression of the intellectual endeavours of the author or artist it is essentially an entrepreneurial copyright. Its primary function is to protect the creators of copyright works and those who invest in their exploitation. In many cases an industry itself has been granted a copyright to protect its products whether these were based upon the work of a sole author or whether it was essentially the result of a team effort. Thus the old 1956 Copyright Act, in addition to the grant of individual copyrights to the creators of those whose works constituted the actual content of films, recordings or broadcasts, granted separate copyrights to their makers.

Future challenges to copyright

ARTIFICIAL INTELLIGENCE (AI)

17.3 In this chapter I look briefly at a field of technology which presents copyright law with a considerable challenge. I give a thumb-nail sketch of the make up of the technology and discuss some of the potential legal problems which are likely to occur. It is hoped that this general discussion will outline how developments in information technology could continue to challenge copyright and how it might be capable of responding to these challenges. As the information technology revolution proceeds virtually unabated, we are likely to see the creation of new works in as yet unheard of media. With the technologies of computer science, telecommunications, opto-electronics and micro-electronics developing and converging, what are the foreseeable legal problems of the future?

One major area which is likely to challenge the ingenuity of those engaged in intellectual property matters in the protection of copyright interests is the new technological development known as artificial intelligence (AI).

Before looking at the technical make up of this development and its commercial and legal ramifications, it will be useful to set the technology within the framework of the matters already discussed. When we speak of artificial intelligence we are still in the realm of computers, how they can be developed and what they are capable of. Therefore the problems which we faced in the chapter on computers are obviously related to those of AI. AI is largely to be based upon, and concerned with, a new generation of computers, commonly referred to as 'fifth generation' computers, where the computer's functions and capabilities are considerably enhanced. We saw that the original role of the computer was to relieve human beings of the drudgery associated with many types of mental activity. Clearly, this current role of the computer is of enormous benefit. Its ability to process vast amounts of material in an organised and rapid way will continue to be a considerable asset to those in industry and commerce. This role is largely non-creative in that the machine mimics certain mundane or repetitive functions of the human brain at far faster speed and more effectively and efficiently than human beings themselves ever could. As such it is essentially a machine which has human agents instructing it as to what it is required to do.

To get a better understanding of AI, which attempts to simulate the more creative aspects of human intelligence, it will be helpful to look at the structure of the technology.

17.4 AI represents the next stage in the development of computer science and technology, where the computer is required to simulate some of what might be considered to be the higher functions of the brain, that is, where it might be said to behave in such a way as to exhibit some form of human 'intelligence'. There are considerable conceptual and practical problems still to be overcome in the development of a machine which might be said to be 'intelligent'. Little is known about the functions of the human brain, so what is meant by 'simulate' is itself in question.

Even when these conceptual problems have been resolved for the purposes of research, the simulation by computers of mental processes possessed by humans has only begun. The objective is to create a machine which will carry out certain tasks analogous to some of those carried out in the human brain (which might be traditionally considered to exhibit the exercise of intelligence) so that what is meant by 'computing' is enlarged. Projects for the development of AI are attracting great interest and there is a race to see who will be the first to succeed in creating such a machine. The principal contenders to date are the Americans and the Japanese.

17.5 One idea behind some AI research is to build a computer with a structure of 'architecture' different in many respects from traditional computer architecture and in doing so to eliminate some of the limitations to which traditional computers were subject.

The first generation of computers, largely designed and built in the 1950s, used the vacuum tube as a method of controlling the flow of electrical currents. The second generation of computers took advantage of the development of transistors which were wired together as controllers of the electrical impulses and replaced the old vacuum tube system. In the 1960s the third generation of computers was developed in which electrical circuits were integrated and replaced the individually wired transistors. The latest, fourth generation computers, created in the 1970s, use large scale integrated circuitry, which is a combination of interconnected circuit elements connected to or set within a continuous substrate. It is essentially 'chip' technology. So developments in the first four generations of computers have depended largely upon the development of hardware and circuitry. The fifth generation computer will be different in that it will be the result of the convergence of separate technologies. It will have the following elements or features:

(1) it will be a knowledge-based expert system; that is, something like a database, only the contents will be the accumulated knowledge of an expert in a particular field of practical endeavour, such as medical, financial or legal;
(2) it will use very high level programming languages;
(3) it will be decentralised computing;
(4) it will use VLSI, that is, very large scale integrated circuitry.

The idea of bringing these together is to produce a new form of computer which will be able to offer a powerful problem-solving function by the use of intelligent input and output.

Let us look briefly at the component parts of this architecture. The knowledge-based systems will be in the form of a large database, together with a representation of some of the accumulated knowledge of an expert or experts operating in a particular field of endeavour, for example, medical diagnosis or financial analysis. The purpose of the high level programming of the computer system is to allow the user of the system to set out what the user wants the computer to do, rather than have to tell it how to perform a particular task, i e 'what is to be performed' rather than 'how to perform it' as is now the case with computers.

Instead of having all the processing unit set out in one machine, the various elements making up the system may be distributed. It is the aim of the developers of the new computer to produce a machine with a problem solving capability, with what they call 'intelligent' input and output facilities. The possibility of creating such a system, enhanced by recent developments in superconductivity, will enable the transmission of electronic pulses to travel at incredibly fast speeds, a necessary feature of the new system. Although the processing of data takes place at phenomenally fast speeds already, this is limited by resistance which takes place in the present conducting medium. It is likely that this problem, and thus one of the problems of building such a computer, will be resolved by very recent scientific advances.

It must be said that AI is not only about the building of a super-computer. Considerable research is taking place in such diverse fields as robotics, speech synthesis, voice recognition and in many other areas of man/machine interface, all of which can be considered to be AI oriented. However, it is pertinent to our interests in the law of copyright to restrict the dicussion on AI products to that of expert systems, because it is here that potential copyright problems are likely.

Expert systems

17.6 Before appraising the commercial significance of expert systems and AI and pointing to some of the legal problems which they are likely to raise, let us look at some expert systems which, far from being in the realms of science fiction, are in operation.

[i] What are expert systems?

They are essentially computer-based systems designed to emulate or reflect the decision-making processes of the human expert or specialist. They are designed to operate within a clearly defined field such as medical diagnosis, tax planning for businesses, and even legal decisions. In other words, where there are difficult practical problems to solve that require expert assistance, an appropriately designed system can sometimes operate in giving the advice that an expert normally gives.

[ii] How are they structured?

They contain a large database of facts pertaining to the relevant field. However, they are not simply a database, as they are constructed in such a way that the data is used in conjunction with an inbuilt set of rules which are applied when the user operates the system. These rules are regarded as 'rules of thumb'; that is, they are based on the experience or practice of real experts. The system is based on 'if' 'then' types of inference rules, so that the user of the system is able to state a condition ('if') which can be matched with an appropriate action response of what to do if that condition prevails ('then'). The result is like that of the rational inference response of a human being or expert. The answer, or conclusion, is couched in terms of what could happen, ie it is probabalistic. For example, with a medical diagnostic expert system, if the symptoms of the patient are stated and these correspond to or closely resemble a number of stated conditions or data in the system, then the conclusion or diagnosis shows the disease which probably corresponds with the symptoms. The machine infers that such a disease probably exists from the data available to it. Even if unable to reach a conclusion on the information fed to it, the machine may request further information from the user.

What is their commercial and legal significance?

17.7 As AI and expert systems will have increasing significance in their application to problem solving in many fields of endeavour they will continue to raise legal problems not only as to ownership of their 'output' but as to where responsibility lies for the advice given. This latter problem is however outside our present brief. There are already in existence many expert systems, mainly in the USA, but they are gradually appearing in the UK. The commercial significance of AI is reflected in the prominence given to, and the funding for, the development of such systems. Ambitious projects are taking place, in the USA and Japan in particular, and there is an increasing European interest in this field. The UK interest is reflected in the money made available by the government under its

Alvey Programme. Developments in AI and expert systems are both funded by the government and private sources. It is clear that the commercial application of such systems will have a significant economic impact, not only in terms of their application in the creation of more effective industries, but in the actual revenue which can be generated by the manufacture and application of the systems themselves. Similar economic arguments apply for the investment in expert systems as for investment in computers and software generally. To maintain a presence in an increasingly technologically developed and developing world, it is essential to keep pace with these developments, or else be left behind. This is as true of the legal system which must protect these developments as it is of these developments themselves. It is as true in the application of computer systems as it is in their actual development. If such systems are not applied to traditional industries, then these industries lose their ability to compete with those which have implemented them. Such is the case with expert systems. If there is insufficient funding, interest, or research into the new technologies at a fundamental level, then the ability to understand the nature of the technology is lost. Expert systems are now fact and their significance and range of applications are having an impact upon a whole range of activities including the law. The benefit of their application lies in the ability of the user to apply the accumulated expertise of a specialist to a specific problem in a particular field of endeavour. Let us now look at some of the applications of already developed expert systems. We shall see what is their present range of applications, who they are designed to be used by, and how valuable they are, in order later to examine the legal problems which may arise. This will give us some indication of the potential legal problems which may be encountered when fully developed AI products come on-stream in the market.

Some expert systems

17.8 In their current state of development those expert systems which are already operating are usually not used by the uninitiated or naive computer user. They are currently used as aids by experts themselves. For example, a doctor who specialises in one particular field of medicine finds that his expertise does not extend to all aspects of that field of practice in a given situation, and he needs assistance, or detailed expertise; to help him in seeking a solution to a particular medical problem he might use an expert system. Thus a human expert might find himself in a position where his competence is limited and he needs further expert advice. In this way such systems augment the already existing skills of experts in a variety of practical fields of application.

Indeed, one area where they have achieved such success is in medicine. In the USA and elsewhere there are a number of systems used in the diagnosis of disease and illness. As I have said, such systems function by the operator of the system feeding in the patient's symptoms and the computer system making a judgement as to the identity and treatment of the disease from the information in its data bank. The rate of success of such systems is sometimes comparable to the competence of experts in diagnosing disease, and in some cases they have been even more successful.

Other areas to benefit from the use of expert systems are the scientific, mathematical and engineering fields. Expert systems are used extensively by industry, research laboratories, universities and a host of other institutions, largely for data interpretation as an intelligent aid to experts. One system used to assist geologists, when given the same field study data as that of mining experts, successfully concluded that there existed a particular metallic substance, molybdenum, in a geological region, though previously it was surveyed and studied by expert geologists who, incorrectly, had concluded that there were no such deposits.

Expert systems are also of significant benefit to industrial design. They are particularly useful for the computer industry in the design of microcircuit structures, developments in this field being vital to the VLSI, already referred to (see p 278). Another application for them is in the field of fault diagnosis, where the system is designed to diagnose faults in either the hardware or software of computer systems. Business uses of expert systems are increasingly available. There are systems which give financial advice, analyse investment opportunities and which can assist in tax planning.

Though currently usually used by experts to augment their present levels of competence in a particular field of practical endeavour, AI products will increasingly be of use to the non-expert, aiding him in solving problems in an unlimited number of fields of activity.

The legal problems

17.9 Let us advance our arguments already touched upon in the chapter on computers.

The usual way of looking at the role and function of a computer has been to see it as a tool in the hands of a human agent. The machine is equipped with a program which controls the sort of functions the machine is capable of, such as information processing. It has an applications program which establishes precisely what the human operator wants the machine to do. In this role it poses few legal problems. The authorship and ownership of programs reside in their creator or creators and they may be used under licence by the owner of the computer who pays for this use by an arrangement with the creator, the licensor. In the simplest cases, the ownership of the output of the information or product belongs to the party who has put in the raw data to be processed by the machine. For example, the computer system may be used to process a company's payroll, where the system is required to process the input of data from human sources. This removes the mental drudgery of having to calculate each item individually. Again where the computer is used for word processing, its software is really a tool in the hands of its human user. As this software is a substitute for the sort of medium in which a human agent would otherwise work, authorship and ownership will be the same, residing in the human user, or in those who employ him. In these cases there are few difficulties in terms of the traditional copyright requirements for authorship and ownership.

The legal situation becomes less than clear where the computer becomes creative, inferring solutions to problems. It is less clear because it is more difficult to describe the role of both the computer and those dealing with it. Rather we are looking at a situation where the computer, loaded with a particular piece of software, is so used that the output or outcome of the human sourced data is not always predictable, and we must ask: what has the computer contributed to the output? With information processing, the outcome or result of the human input is predictable, so we would say that it was due to that input. The human operator was its author. The computer is given tasks which are fairly pedestrian, such as might be given by the payroll processing package. The output of the computer sometimes becomes less predictable if its software behaves in an inter-active way as a sophisticated aid in solving a particular problem. It stretches the analogy to regard the computer, loaded with its software, as being like a tool in the hands of the user. For if the user is only using it as a tool, he is expected to be effectively in control of the medium, as he would be of a pencil, pen or paint on paper or canvas, where the human agent directs the outcome of what he is doing. Where the computer is being used as an aid, for example in computer-aided design, the computer is programmed to engage in a very sophisticated range of functions. With the design of a component part, the result or outcome of the use of the computer, questioned as to what it is or is not possible to use for a particular design in particular circumstances, will be an amalgam of the sophisticated ability of the computer software and the skills of the human user. In this case the computer takes on an inter-active role, and sometimes the outcome is not predictable. Now the computer, loaded with its software, behaves interactively with the human agent, with the software contributing most to the finished outcome or output, the output being 'computer-aided'.

It is a puzzling situation for the law, however, where the computer, loaded with its software, takes on a role where the input by the human agent is not only greatly reduced but indeed, in many cases, absent. The computer's output in such cases is said to be 'computer-generated'. What happens is that computer software is developed to operate on a computer which is further loaded with other software. The two pieces of software then interact in such a way as to produce an output of some kind. The total input by the human agent has been merely to load the two sets or pieces of software on to the computer. There is thus little or no human skill, judgement or effort involved in the creation of the completed output. Examples of computer generated works are: weather maps produced by communication from satellite to computer, or computer data used to generate maps indicating likely areas for oil exploration.

Another illustration: developments are taking place in software for the creation of designs to be used in the manufacture of silicon chips and also where software is being used to upgrade, enhance and develop software itself. Here the human agent is restricted to the creation of the original software and the outcome of the interaction becomes highly unpredictable because of the 'creative' role of the software. Certainly, there would appear to be 'a material expression' of something which could have qualified as a copyright work but this creative interaction with the machine calls into question whether any person can claim copyright protection for this output, much of which might be of considerable value eg the weather maps referred to, or the enhanced software. If there is no copyright protection then this output could be taken, reproduced and used by anyone with impunity. The underlying legal argument for the recognition of copyright here is similar to that put forward by the computer lobby to obtain protection for software in the first place: the industrial significance of computers generally, and of software in particular, is so great that to neglect to protect it would result in piracy and uncontrolled wholesale copying by others, resulting in a downturn in investment. Just as the English language had to be developed in order to convince the courts that software was analogous to a 'literary work expressed in a material form', so then it had to look to see how it could be made to cover future cases of IT development. One argument advanced for the protection of computer-generated output was as follows. By its very nature, the product created by the software acting in concert, though not analogous to a Part I 1956 Act type copyright, is analogous to a Part II type copyright under the Act. It is the result or product of a concerted or team effort and therefore should qualify as an entrepreneurial copyright. We have seen that there is normally no single individual author in the creation of a film, record or broadcast, but that a copyright is granted to these. In particular some believed that a useful precedent was established by the provisions for copyright in films which stated that the ownership of such copyright be accorded to 'the person by whom the arrangements necessary for the making of the film are undertaken'.[1] In the same way, they argued, copyright should be granted to the person by whom the arrangements necessary for the making of the output (e g for telephone directories etc) are undertaken. Commercial arguments for such protection were obviously strong. Computer-generated output, so valuable to industry, could not be ignored. Such products needed protecting in order to advance further investments in them.

1 Copyright Act 1956, s 13.

17.10 Many of the new legal problems relate principally to the protection of output. I have already mentioned the problems relating to computer output, either where the computer is engaged as an aid, as in computer-aided design, or where the computer generates the work, as in the creation of maps from satellite data. In these cases we see a decreasing amount of input in terms of the skill, labour or judgement of the human agent or operator, and an increasing dependence upon the exhibition of these qualities by the machine. In the case of the expert system there is even less input by the human user, virtually all the work being carried out by the machine, though there is an initial input of large quantities of skill, labour, judgement, etc by those who are engaged in its development and who have invested large amounts of money in its creation. The system may have been developed by a company for its own use, and be geared specifically to increase the efficiency of the concern in maintaining, for instance, a market lead or additional competitive edge in a particular commercial, manufacturing or industrial field. Clearly this type of user would not wish the valuable product or output of its system to be used by others, such as market competitors or rivals, and will therefore seek to protect it. In the absence of any readily identifiable or recognised property right such as copyright in that output, the creator of valuable output from an expert system would have to rely upon the law of trade secrets and confidentiality for protection. We have already discussed confidentiality and the limitations it imposes when it is relied upon to protect industrial assets. Sometimes the creator of an expert system produces a system which he makes available generally for use in industry, i e like a piece of software. He requires assurance that he is able to engage in the industrial exploitation by licensing his systems and that his database or knowledge base is a protectable asset of his business. Without legal protection in either of the above situations there would be wholesale copying by unauthorised users who could seriously undermine the financial viability of those who have invested in such valuable industries.

It is for this reason that the government departed from its conclusions in its White Paper of 1986, when dealing with the problem of authorship of computer-generated works, that 'no specific provisions should be made to determine this question' (i e the question of authorship).[1] Under the new Copyright Act the following provisions apply:

> 'In the case of a literary, dramatic, musical or artistic work which is computer-generated, the author shall be taken to be the person by whom the arrangements necessary for the creation of the work are undertaken.'[2]

Confirmation of the protection of databases was provided for by the specific reference to a compilation as a literary work.[3] This is essential for the protection of the database systems used in AI products. Further, protection was assured for the creator of computer software who as we have seen now enjoys additional control over and thus protection of his products.

It remains to be seen whether copyright will be able to meet the challenge of as yet unknown technologies, but it is hoped that the foregoing has demonstrated how flexible and adaptable it could be in the protection of the industrial innovator. As John Locke wrote:

> 'Thus the Grass my Horse has bit; the Turfs my servant has cut; and the Ore I have digg'd in any place where I have a right to them in common with others, become my Property, without the assignation or consent of any body. The labour that was mine, removing them out of that common state they were in, hath fixed my Property in them.'[4]

In this telling statement we see how the concept of property was established and developed to cover ownership not only in the products of the efforts of the individual, but also in products resulting from the efforts of that individual's 'servants'. This is seen in the law's assertion and presumption of ownership of intellectual property rights in the context of the workplace—the servant's or employee's efforts often being seen as a product of the owner's labour. It could be argued that the underlying basis for ownership also extends to the efforts of the individual's chattels, such as to his horse. The expert systems of today and other AI systems of the future will be used by people who might want to claim that the output of these is their own—just as Locke claimed the horse's output was due to the labour of its owner—though there is no human agent directly involved.

1 'Intellectual Property and Innovation' (1986, HMSO) Cmnd 9712.
2 Copyright, Designs and Patents Act 1988, s 9(3).
3 Copyright, Designs and Patents Act 1988, s 3(1).
4 John Locke, Two Treatises of Government, Second Treatise, chapter 5, 'Of Property', para 28.

Part 3
Patents revisited

CHAPTER 18

A patent system for the future?

Introduction

18.1 No system of laws is perfect. In the last few chapters we have investigated the problems of copyright owners in the face of new technology. Despite the fact that there exists an armoury of intellectual property rights both at common law and under already existing legislation these have not proved particularly effective in protecting the owners of such interests and those industries which are underpinned by such laws. The new Act certainly improves the situation for some but not all copyright owners. My first chapter on patents was designed to examine the already existing law on patents, showing how it worked and the advantages which could be gained by patenting. Now I turn to considering whether the patent system is capable of responding to the pressure created by new and innovative industries, particularly small to medium-sized enterprises, to protect their investment and thus encourage further investment in new industrial technical information. The patent system should be able to respond to their need for easy access to inexpensive protection of their innovation.

18.2 It is useful to recap briefly on what patents are and how they are exploited and protected. They exist to help reward invention in technology generally, in order to keep the nation's stock of industrial assets constantly maintained and replenished. Safeguards are built into the system to prevent abuses by the holder of the monopoly rights granted. Thus, if a patent is not, or is insufficiently, worked the owner of the patent may lose control over its exploitation and may be forced to license it under terms established by the Comptroller of the Patent Office.[1]

After all, the grant of patent rights is made on the basis that the invention, embodying a new technological concept, is disclosed to the public and is actually used. It is not in the nation's interest to suppress invention, which is why the system is designed to discourage the development of trade secrets—though the inventor can sometimes rely upon these when the idea underlying an invention cannot satisfy the formal criteria for a patent. Patenting is meant to encourage the disclosure of inventions to the world, thus providing a continuous flow and dissemination of new technological ideas by laying the basis for the transfer of technologically significant inventions to others either through use, assignment or licensing. To provide incentives to investment in innovation, a patent offers protection for the fruits of industrial research and development programmes for a period of 20 years so that the owner has a monopoly for that period of the right to prevent others from using or working the invention, the subject of the patent. Any other party aware of the invention who wishes to use it must obtain the owner's permission. If he uses it without such permission, he is infringing the patent and the owner can force him to desist.[2] Enshrined in a public register, these patent rights operate as a source of technological information for potential licensees and as a warning to potential infringers.

1 Patents Act 1977, s 48.
2 Patents Act 1977, s 60.

Who uses the system?

18.3 Patents are frequently relied upon for the protection of intellectual and industrial property rights by large industrial concerns. The benefits of patenting are easily reaped by them. They can invest in good advice in intellectual property law and practice and often have teams of 'in-house' patent and trade mark agents, lawyers and licensing personnel, capable of recognising, isolating, identifying, exploiting, protecting and maintaining their industries' intellectual property. Such industries generate substantial patentable material, industrial copyright, designs etc. Among them is an ever-growing awareness of the subsistence and value of intellectual property rights, matched by a careful appraisal of research and development in innovation, and the ability and resources needed to maximise their potential. At the earliest possible moment they ascertain their rights in innovation, implement appropriate policies for its protection, recoup the costs of its creation and generate revenue from its proper exploitation, taking maximum advantage of the total armoury of rights available to them. This revenue is ploughed back into still further innovation, either in the form of pure scientific research, or into specific product research and development programmes.

Though this is true of large-scale concerns it is not normally so of small to medium-sized concerns. Patent protection is not cheap. Here the small concern faces a dilemma. Although it often may not be able to afford the sums required for patent protection, neither can it afford to be without it. Often its inventions are valuable, but a prey to predators and potential infringers. If its rights look vulnerable because insufficiently protected, they are dangerously exposed.

Today, obtaining and maintaining intellectual property rights such as patents can be complicated and expensive. As we have seen, even if a patent is obtained and it is valuable, the owner has to make as much a commercial as a legal decision as to whether to proceed against an infringer or not. If he decides to proceed, the infringer could be deterred by the threat of legal proceedings and the prospect of engaging in long and often costly patent litigation, with the result that he desists from illicit use of the invention, perhaps settling with the owner by taking a licence to use the invention. But sometimes he does not. If the infringer decides to fight this will be of less concern to the big industrial conglomerate than to the small to medium-sized concern. Prolonged litigation could mean considerable commercial anxiety and result in ruin. Such a concern may either decide not to proceed against the infringer and thus lose the revenue legitimately owing to it, or commit the necessarily substantial resources of personnel and finances and suffer the uncertainties of litigation. In other words, in the field of patents, although rights are sufficiently defined, their enforcement can be a problem for many. Yet it is just these smaller concerns which provide more and more of the nation's innovative technology, and many would say our industrial future lies with them. If so, we must have adequate laws to effectively protect their rights.

18.4 It would seem to be true that a growing sector of our economy depends on small to medium-sized concerns, especially in high technology and particularly in information technology. These have flourished first in the USA, and are now having a considerable impact on the industry and the economy of the UK. What has been the cause of this phenomenon? One of its causes, both here and in the USA, is the diminishing ability to compete with countries having lower labour costs and high industrial potential in large heavy-duty manufacturing industries. We have failed to remain competitive in the face of newer industrial nations, such as Taiwan. These are capable of producing goods, such as ships, for a world-wide market at a fraction of the cost of anything comparable in the UK. Further, where once we had operated overseas with little or no competition, now many national industries are protected, as for example are textiles in India, making the sale of our goods there more difficult. This shrinking of traditional markets accelerates the decline in our traditional industrial base. Looking back, we can see that we have moved from an agrarian to an industrial society, then rapidly to a post-industrial phase. We have shed many traditional industries, unable to compete because of competitors' cheaper costs of production, or because the goods have become obsolete and thus no longer needed. In this context it is not surprising that today we welcome the emergence of a new and rapidly expanding industrial base which does, and increasingly will, rely on smaller, less labour-intensive industries, concerned with scientific and technological advance and the development and creation of new products. That is why today these highly innovative industries are encouraged financially by a variety of institutions both public and private. The UK is world-renowned for its inventive skills; it has had, and will have, an influence on the world's scientific and technological advance. Today we look to the new technological industries to continue this tradition, depending as they largely do on the creation of new ideas applied to the technological world. In this context the UK contributes many technological innovations, sometimes to the remaining traditional industries, making them more effective and thus more competitive, and sometimes (and increasingly) in the service of the new technological industries themselves. Often their innovators must turn to the patent system for the proper protection of their property rights, and often the difficulties of enforcement of these rights are overwhelming.

Yet the patent system, which operates well to protect the rights of large concerns, operates sparingly for the benefit of these smaller concerns. And given their importance, this has been of growing concern. It is a moral responsibility of the law to furnish these new elements of our industrial structure with a legal system capable of providing the kind of protection they look for in obtaining patents.

Needs of the user

18.5 But what are their needs and what is the best way in which to meet them? The government posed that question in its Green Paper of 1983. This was produced by a committee headed by the Chief Scientific Adviser to the Cabinet Office, in order to determine whether the national system of intellectual property rights was well suited to encouraging innovation. In the area of patents the committee was of the opinion that urgent measures were needed to reform the patent system if such innovation was to be encouraged among small to medium-sized concerns. In order to carry these out it recommended that a new Intellectual Property and Innovation Bill should be introduced '. . . to bring together the new measures proposed in this report and to form the core of a major statement of policy'.[1] One of the aims was to provide a less expensive patent system which small to medium-sized innovative concerns of a modern consumer-oriented industrial society would find less prohibitive and more accessible. Even so, despite this broad agreement in aim there were interesting differences in the solutions offered by both the Green Paper and White Paper committees which reveal themselves when their proposals are considered and the possible impact their acceptance might have on the rights of existing and potential patent holders is worked out.

1 Green Paper 1983, p 3.

(A) STRUCTURAL CHANGES

18.6 In order to reform the patent system, the 1983 Green Paper proposed the entire transformation of the Patent Office itself, making it more entrepreneurial, freeing it of civil servant constraints, and making it self-financing and fee-charging; it would become a non-departmental and non-Crown public body.[1] Still under the auspices of the Comptroller, it would promote the level of awareness of the value of intellectual property rights, encouraging the spread of the use of patents.[2] Furthermore, the Office could provide small to medium-sized enterprises with services such as search facilities on an on-line patent database, currently offered only by private organisations.[3] Added to this was a proposal for a Whitehall liaison group to be set up to disseminate an awareness of intellectual property law in government circles, and to ensure that the Department of Trade and Industry provided more cash grants to industry for the protection of intellectual property rights.[4]

As patents have an international, and not simply a national context, clearly the patent owner would be better served by being able to secure a single European patent. This would be valid throughout the member states of the European Community under a common community system of patent law, an improvement on the present system which requires the owner to make separate applications in each state in which he requires patent protection or, where he can, to obtain what is called a European patent—in effect a bundle of individual national patents. A common community patent would mean simpler and cheaper processing of patent applications and would give a more certain and uniform level of protection throughout the entire Community. Partly for this reason the committee believed it was an urgent matter to support and bring such a patent system into existence.

The committee which drew up the Green Paper suggested crucial changes in the substantive law to help the future growth of small to medium-sized concerns. At present, if he cannot depend upon the provision of a monopoly grant in the form of a patent, the inventor has no alternative but to rely upon the law of trade secrets and confidentiality. Indeed, if an inventor cannot afford the patent pathway he is often forced to rely upon the latter. But this law is unsatisfactory. The overall advantages of patenting are that the innovator is rewarded and so encouraged to invest in further innovation, and valuable information is disclosed to the benefit of industry generally. But with the law of trade secrets and confidentiality the contrary is true, suppression of information being encouraged instead. Not only is this law uncertain as to what can be considered confidential, but also the protection which it offers is uncertain; worse, reliance on the law means that useful technical information embodied in the invention needs to be suppressed to the detriment of industry. An inadequate patent system therefore abandons the innovator to an alternative resort, but one which operates as a disincentive to invest in innovation. By not responding to the challenge of today's innovators, the patent system forces them to rely on laws likely to restrict access to the use of innovation. This is the threat of an outdated and thus ineffective patent system.

1 Para 3.17.
2 Para 3.18.
3 Paras 3.26–3.29.
4 Para 3.36.

(B) SOME PROPOSED CHANGES IN THE SUBSTANTIVE LAW OF PATENTS

18.7 Modernising the Patent Office would have been one step in the right direction. It is not among the provisions of the new Copyright, Designs and Patents Act 1988. What else could be done? The Green Paper committee discussed:

(1) the introduction of a new property right known as the registered invention right;
(2) validity;
(3) compulsory licensing;
(4) employee inventions.

Let us look at each of these in turn.

(1) The registered invention right[1]

18.8 In countries such as Germany, France and Spain, a form of intellectual property right operates, sometimes called a registered invention right or a 'petty patent'. Though it has now been decided not to introduce it here, some members of the committee for the Green Paper believed it should be because it might help remedy the deficiency in the present patent system which tends to discourage application from small to medium-sized concerns. In their view the patent system acts as a disincentive to such concerns because it is too cumbersome, slow, lengthy and expensive. Why is it like this? In their view, largely due to the rigorous search and examination procedure which every application has to undergo. The applicant can obtain a strong patent, but such a thorough system is geared to, and operates in favour of, the large industrial organisation with the resources, means, time and managerial capacity to devote to prosecuting its patents. The registered invention right suggests itself as a cheaper, faster and less expensive route, reflecting more adequately and sensibly the requirements of the smaller organisation which need not require such an extensive protective property right. It would be a more appropriate sort of protection for it would be one which lasted only as long as it would take for it to gain a lead time in a particular technology market. Furthermore, if an invention is, in any case, likely to be obsolete in a short time, a full 20 years' protection would seem to be excessive and the inventor may well rely upon the law of trade secrets instead. As such lesser rights exist in other European countries and are considered by some to be incentives to invention, some members of the committee believed that such a system may be of equal value in the UK. The smaller business might be prepared to accept these lesser rights, rather than a full-blown patent which it may not be able to afford, and so gain some, rather than no, protection.

The attractions of the petty patent are that the inventor can register his invention simply and cheaply under a registered invention scheme. There would be no examination of the invention, until a challenge to his rights is claimed, when the validity of the claim is then tested. The inventor would enjoy as it were, only an 'inchoate' or undeveloped right in his invention—he cannot know if it is valid or not until that point of challenge. However, the introduction of such petty patents in the UK was rejected by the Government White Paper because:[2]

(a) a scheme which allowed the registration of a number of inchoate and so uncertain rights, would defeat the objectives of the patent system which is to ensure certainty of ownership and dealings in inventions by establishing a register of clearly identified rights;

(b) subsidising a separate system of registered rights was unreasonable. The government remained unconvinced that such a system would be cheaper than obtaining full patent rights; indeed with two registered lists it could turn out to be more expensive;

(c) unlike many other jurisdictions, the U K was fortunate enough to already have a system which granted some protection against the copying of functional articles through the law of copyright thus, to some extent, assisting small to medium-sized enterprises. Certainly more needed to be done to help them, but the petty patent, if introduced, would probably fail to do so. In any case, in its White Paper the government decided it is not so much the actual cost of patenting which discourages these concerns as their inability to protect their patent rights in any subsequent litigation. The mechanism fails them at this point, because they cannot afford to defend themselves against infringers. Any solution to this problem must begin with the next issue: the validity of the patent.

1 Paras 4.7–4.13.
2 Paras 3.4–3.16.

(2) Validity

18.9 It is not necessarily only the petty patent whose validity is in doubt. This is true of the patent itself. Though examination takes place prior to awarding a patent, making of it a strong right, even then it could be invalid. The Patent Office examiner could always have overlooked material which might have been relevant to the validity of the invention. And if this turns up later at the time of litigation against an infringer, the patent owner could find that he holds something of less value than he had anticipated, which is invalid. The costs, delays and concerns of the litigation could perhaps lead to ruin. In the view of many it is this threat which naturally deters the small to medium-sized concern from patenting its inventions. The Patent Office cannot guarantee the absolute validity of the patent, and thus the right of the registered proprietor of the patent is always limited, as the patent is only a claim subject to defeasibility. Furthermore, even if the patent is believed valid, the alleged infringer can still argue, as a second line of defence, that he has not infringed the patent. It is small wonder, then, that in the case of small to medium-sized concerns, most patent disputes are

settled out of court. In order to help these concerns, members of the Green Paper committee decided it must be made cheaper and easier to determine the patent's validity.[1] Would this be achieved by dealing with the question of validity separately from that of infringement, as is done in the USA? Would this help prevent some litigation by allowing the question of validity to be disposed of before the question of infringement needed to be tackled? Unfortunately, evidence about the USA system was discouraging; it showed this provision was rarely used, and when used, often abused.

Furthermore, in rejecting the suggestion, the White Paper committee pointed out another disadvantage.[2] The parties could reopen the issue by appealing to the court, making the matter once more litigious. Instead, in its view, if small to medium-sized firms are to find encouragement to use the patent system, there must be the following radical change in the whole structure and mechanism of determining patent rights:

(1) All future patent proceedings, such as infringement, declaration and revocation proceedings, should proceed before the Comptroller at the Patent Office and not, as now, in the Patent Court.[3]

(2) Such proceedings should be transferred to the court however, if either both or all the parties ask the Comptroller, or if he were to decide that this was a more appropriate forum because, for instance, difficult and complex areas of law were in question.

(3) The Comptroller should be given additional powers:
   (a) to grant any relief, including injunctions, which may be presently granted by the court;
   (b) to grant an exclusive jurisdiction to hear applications for interlocutory injunctions where the owner immediately sought to restrain the acts of the alleged infringer in order to limit further damage to his economic rights. Usually, this would effectively stop an alleged infringer from continuing his activities, or do so at least until the issue was heard at a full trial.

(4) The above would effectively replace the present adversarial system with an inquisitorial system in proceedings before the Comptroller. At present, to the disadvantage of patent owners particularly in small to medium-sized concerns, patent litigation is like any other form of commercial litigation. Proceedings take place in an atmosphere of dispute and contention, where the protagonists or their representatives verbally argue

the legal merits of the case. By contrast, in the proposed inquisitorial system, already much used in Europe, proceedings would rely more upon the presenting of written argument and evidence given prior to the hearing. This would limit verbal argument to issues judged to be relevant in the written submissions, thus saving time and money.

(5) The automatic right of appeal to the court from the decisions of the Comptroller would become only discretionary.

In conclusion then, the proposal would have meant that patent litigation would take place before an independent body endowed with the powers to make orders in respect of the rights of the parties, as would a normal court, the full range and gamut of reliefs being dispensed by the Comptroller. Thus, besides having an entrepreneurial function thrust upon it, the Patent Office would also have a judicial function, though not the actual power to enforce any of the orders which it might grant. Thus if an injunction were broken, the party in whose favour it was granted would have to return to the court to have it enforced.

These bold proposals would have seen the end of the Patent Office as we have known it. Many believe now it does not respond adequately to the needs of the small entrepreneur, an increasingly important user of the system who plays an increasingly important part in the UK economy. They believe that these wholesale changes would have helped make process of determining patent validity, and the prospect of litigation with infringers, a less expensive and hazardous matter for the smaller enterprise patent holder, and thus have added another measure to the modernisation of the UK patent system.

The advantages of a system that would have offered a cheaper, less legalistic and less formal service, which was more responsive to the needs of inventors generally and to those in small to medium-sized concerns in particular, need not be spelled out. But one question which arose was this: is the Patent Office properly equipped to deal with the whole range of issues, often of a legal nature, which typically arise in patent disputes, and which have little bearing on the technical construction of the patent itself? Making the Patent Office respond better to the needs of a modern technologically based industrial society would mean more than making it provide a cheaper, more effective technical service: it would mean making it capable of meeting the legal requirements thrust upon it. As we shall see shortly, the new Act has made other provisions.

1 Paras 5.4–5.10.
2 Paras 4.1–4.13.
3 Paras 4.7–4.13.

(3) Compulsory licensing

18.10 We have examined some of the main issues of patent reform. In my first chapter on patents it became clear that the rationale behind the granting of patents was that the nation should reward its inventors for the disclosure of new and valuable technical information. On disclosure the inventor was granted a monopoly to work his invention, with the proviso that the invention was actually worked and not suppressed. If the patent was not, or insufficiently worked, then after a period of three years from the date of grant, any party interested in working it could apply to the Comptroller for a compulsory licence, the terms of which were to be set by him.[1] The arbitrary figure of three years was considered a sufficient period of time for the owner of the patent to have commenced use of the patent himself or to have made arrangements for others to work it. The non-working of the patent or the refusal to license it on reasonable terms is considered to constitute an abuse of the patent monopoly right.

It was thought that a solution to this abuse might be to make an unwilling patent owner grant a licence to a potential licensee, through the licensee proceeding to the Patent Office for a compulsory licence. But members of the Green Paper committee found little use had been made of the provision because it was difficult for a potential licensee to prove that insufficient use was being made of the invention by the owner, and, even if he were able to prove this and so obtain a compulsory grant, the information disclosed was often insufficient, without the patent holder's know-how, to work, or work effectively, the patent.[2] This raises the question: could the patent holder's know-how also be transferred with the grant of the compulsory licence? Some believed it could, and that this would prevent the patent holder abusing his patent right and also stimulate the licensing of virtually unused patents.

But The White Paper committee dissented.[3] In any case, it found little support for the view that patent owners were abusing their monopoly as pre-supposed by the above argument. If instead they were mostly engaged in the exploitation of their rights, the above recommendation was superfluous to requirements and hardly offered an incentive to innovation. But most important, how could it be decided just what did and did not constitute that part of the patent owner's know-how which had to be transferred with the licence? To this there were no satisfactory answers.

1 Patents Act 1977, s 48.
2 Paras 5.11–5.22.
3 Paras 4.14–4.20.

(4) *Employee inventors*

18.11 In their analysis of the workings of the system of intellectual property rights in the UK, as it serves the needs of innovative concerns, especially those of small to medium-sized enterprises, the Green Paper committee reviewed the position of the innovative employee within the context of his industrial concern, and made recommendations for changes in the law with regard to his rights in inventions.[1] In my first chapter on patents I have already noted that an invention, created by an employee in the course of his employment, normally belongs to his employer, his title to any personal inventions only extending to those which he created outside the scope of his employment. Within his employment the most he could hope for from his contribution to the creation of a patentable invention would be some kind of reward from his employer. Sometimes this seems unfair to the employee, and so acts as a disincentive to his future contribution, especially if his work has made a substantial contribution to the profits of his employer's patent. Other European systems reward the inventor employee more, and thus encourage him to continue his good work. Under West German law, if he invents something in the course of his employment he stands a better chance of profiting from his invention. True, the employer must take action in respect of it, perhaps claiming title to the invention and exploiting it. But then he has to reward the employee, at the same time taking action to protect the patent, for otherwise, if he leaves it unprotected, he must pay compensation to the employee. Furthermore, if the employer does not take up the rights in the invention, then the employee can exploit it himself.

The committee for the White Paper limited its concern to those inventions generated by an industrial concern which are not being exploited by anyone, as can sometimes happen under the present UK system.[2] The employer is under no obligation or compulsion to do anything about inventions produced by his employees, and they have no right to do anything about them either. The committee recommended employee inventors be given rights to take title to their inventions which are not being exploited by their employers in the belief that the possibility and the experience of ownership should act as a stimulus to both further invention and exploitation. This aim might also be furthered, in the committee's view, by implementing some form of employee ownership scheme as carried out in some concerns in West Germany. But before recommending such measures in the UK the committee decided to commission an independent study of the West German experience, to assess whether it contributed significantly to the West German system and whether, even if it did, it would be relevant to the very different legal and industrial environment of the UK.

1 Paras 5.29–5.31.
2 Paras 4.21–4.32.

What are the provisions of the new Act?

18.12 The new Copyright, Designs and Patents Act[1] jettisons the recommendations of both the Green Paper and the government's own proposals under the White Paper. The structure of the Patent Office will remain the same and the proposal for it to operate an extended judicial function has been abandoned. Instead, disputes relating to patents and other intellectual property matters may be dealt with by county courts which have been specifically designated by the Lord Chancellor as patent county courts and which will be empowered to operate a 'special jurisdiction' in such matters. The jurisdiction will be to hear and determine 'matters (a) relating to patents or designs or (b) ancillary to, or arising out of the same subject matter as, proceedings relating to patents or designs'[2] subject to possible financial limits being imposed. The special jurisdiction can be exercised even if no pecuniary remedy is sought. The financial limits relating to amount or value may be established by Order in Council. There is a power of transfer of cases between the High Court and the patents county courts. Patent agents will be able to appear in the patents county courts and the courts will be empowered to appoint scientific advisors and assessors to assist the court or to order the Patent Office to make enquiries and report on any question of fact or opinion. The government considers that in this way the problems relating to delays and costs in bringing proceedings in intellectual property matters generally, and patents in particular, will be reduced by the new regime, and thus encourage use of the patent system by the small to medium-sized enterprise.

1 Copyright, Designs and Patents Act 1988, Part VI.
2 Copyright, Designs and Patents Act 1988, s 267.

Index